NEW Keystone

STUDENT EDITION
with Digital Resources

Pearson

NEW
Keystone Ⓒ

Smithsonian American Art Museum contributors: Project director and writer: Elizabeth K. Eder, Ph.D.; Writer: Mary Collins; Image research assistants: Laurel Fehrenbach, Katherine G. Stilwill, and Sally Otis; Rights and reproductions: Richard H. Sorensen and Leslie G. Green; Building photograph by Tim Hursley.

Cover credit: Sergii Mostovyi/123RF

Library of Congress Cataloging-in-Publication Data
A catalog record for the print edition is available from the Library of Congress.

The publishers would like to recognize the contributions of our original Series Consultants, Anna Uhl Chamot, John De Mado, and Sharroky Hollie. This edition is published in memory of Dr. Chamot, an extraordinary educator, writer, and scholar.

Printed in the United States of America
ISBN-10: 0-13-523277-5 (with Digital Resources)
ISBN-13: 978-0-13-523277-4 (with Digital Resources)

www.english.com/keystone

5 2020

Welcome to **NEW** Keystone

New Keystone has been specially designed to help you succeed in all areas of your school studies. This program will help you develop the English language skills you need for language arts, social studies, math, and science. You will discover new ways to use and build upon your language skills through your interactions with classmates, friends, teachers, and family members.

New Keystone includes a mix of many subjects. Each unit has three different reading selections that include literary excerpts, poems, and nonfiction articles about science, math, and social studies. These selections will help you understand the vocabulary and organization of different types of texts. They will also give you the tools you need to approach the content of the different subjects you take in school.

As you use this program, you will discover new words, use your background knowledge of the subjects presented, relate your knowledge to the new information, and take part in creative activities. You will learn strategies to help you understand readings better. You will work on activities that help you improve your English skills in grammar, word study, and spelling. Finally, you will be asked to demonstrate the listening, speaking, and writing skills you have learned through fun projects that are incorporated throughout the program.

Learning a language takes time, but just like learning to skateboard or learning to swim, it is fun! Whether you are learning English for the first time, or increasing your knowledge of English by adding academic or literary language to your vocabulary, you are giving yourself new choices for the future, and a better chance of succeeding in both your studies and in everyday life.

We hope you enjoy *New Keystone*, and we wish you success on every step of your learning journey.

Consultants and Reviewers

Sharena Adebiyi
Fulton County Schools
Stone City, GA, USA

Hien Chung
YOLA Education
Ho Chi Minh City, Vietnam

Carlos Eduardo Aguilar Cortés
Universidad de la Salle
Bogotá, Colombia

Jose Augusto Lugo
Cerros
Bogotá, Colombia

Jennifer Benavides
Garland ISD
Garland, TX, USA

Tracy Bunker
Shearer Charter School
Napa, CA, USA

Gabriela Cecilia Diaz
Grilli Canning College
Buenos Aires, Argentina

Dan Fichtner
UCLA Ed. Ext. TESOL Program
Redondo Beach, CA, USA

Trudy Freer-Alvarez
Houston ISD
Houston, TX, USA

Helena K. Gandell
Duval County
Jacksonville, FL, USA

Valeria Goluza
Grilli Canning College
Buenos Aires, Argentina

Glenda Harrell
Johnston County School Dist.
Smithfield, NC, USA

Michelle Land
Randolph Middle School
Randolph, NJ, USA

Joseph E. Leaf
Norristown Area High School
Norristown, PA, USA

Le Tue Minh
Wellspring International Bilingual
School
Hanoi, Vietnam

Minh Phuong Nguyen
CIEM-Education
Hanoi, Vietnam

Richard Nickless
Kwong Chow School
Thailand

Ilona Olancin
Collier County Schools
Naples, FL, USA

Patricia Parroquiano
Gimnasio Campestre Reino Britanico
Bogotá, Colombia

Jeanne Perrin
Boston Unified School Dist.
Boston, MA, USA

Cheryl Quadrelli-Jones
Anaheim Union High School Dist.
Fullerton, CA, USA

Sergio Rivera
Liceo Hermano Miguel La Salle
Bogotá, Colombia

Mary Schmidt
Riverwood High School
Atlanta, GA, USA

Kampanart Thammaphati
Wattana Wittaya Academy
Thailand

Daniel Thatcher
Garland ISD
Garland, TX, USA

Denise Tiffany
West High School
Iowa City, IA, USA

Lisa Troute
Palm Beach County School Dist.
West Palm, FL, USA

Smithsonian American Art Museum

Dear Student,

At the end of each unit in this book, you will learn about some artists and artworks that relate to the theme you have just read about. These artworks are all in the Smithsonian American Art Museum in Washington, D.C. That means they belong to you, because the Smithsonian is America's collection. The artworks were created over a period of 300 years by artists who responded to their experiences in personal ways. Their world lives on through their artworks and, as viewers, we can understand them and ourselves in new ways. We discover that many of the things that concerned these artists still engage us today.

Looking at an artwork is different from reading a written history. Artists present few facts or dates. Instead, they offer emotional insights that come from their own lives and experiences. They make their own decisions about what matters, without worrying if others agree or disagree. This is a rare and useful kind of knowledge that we can all learn from. Artists inspire us to respond to our own lives with deeper insight.

There are two ways to approach art. One way is through the mind—studying the artist, learning about the subject, exploring the context in which the artwork was made, and forming a personal view. This way is deeply rewarding and expands your understanding of the world. The second way is through the senses—letting your imagination roam as you look at an artwork, losing yourself in colors and shapes, absorbing the meaning through your eyes. This way is called "aesthetic." The great thing about art is that an artwork may have many different meanings. You can decide what it means to you.

This brief introduction to American art will, I hope, lead to a lifetime of enjoyment and appreciation of art.

> **Elizabeth Broun**
> The Margaret and Terry Stent Director
> Smithsonian American Art Museum

Glossary of Terms

You will find the following words useful when reading, writing, and talking about art.

abstract a style of art that does not represent things, animals, or people realistically

acrylic a type of paint that is made from ground pigments and certain chemicals

background part of the artwork that looks furthest away from the viewer

brushstroke the paint or ink left on the surface of an artwork by the paintbrush

canvas a type of heavy woven fabric used as a support for painting; another word for a painting

composition the way in which the different parts of an artwork are arranged

detail a small part of an artwork

evoke to produce a strong feeling or memory

figure the representation of a person or animal in an artwork

foreground part of the artwork that looks closest to the viewer

geometric a type of pattern that has straight lines or shapes such as squares, circles, etc.

mixed media different kinds of materials such as paint, fabric, objects, etc. that are used in a single artwork

oil a type of paint that is made from ground pigments and linseed oil

paintbrush a special brush used for painting

perception the way you understand something you see

pigment a finely powdered material (natural or man-made) that gives color to paint, ink, or dye

portrait an artwork that shows a specific person, group of people, or animal

print an artwork that has been made from a sheet of metal or a block of wood covered with a wet color and then pressed onto a flat surface like paper. Types of prints include lithographs, etchings, aquatints, etc.

symbol an image, shape, or object in an artwork that represents an idea

texture the way that a surface or material feels and how smooth or rough it looks

tone the shade of a particular color; the effect of light and shade with color

watercolor a type of paint that is made from ground pigments, gum, and glycerin and/or honey; another word for a painting done with this medium

Unit 1

Contents

Unit Preview

Reading 1: Science/Social Studies

Reading 2: Science

Reading 3: Short Story

Unit Wrap-Up

Unit 2 Contents

Unit Preview

Reading 1: Biography/Science

Reading 2: Personal Narrative/Poem

Reading 3: Short Story/Science

Unit Wrap-Up

Unit 3

Contents

Unit Preview

Reading 1: Novel

Reading 2: Social Studies

Reading 3: Legend

Unit Wrap-Up

Unit 4

Contents

Unit Preview

Reading 1: Social Studies

Reading 2: Novel

Reading 3: Poetry

Unit Wrap-Up

Unit 5

Contents

Reading 3: Short Story

Unit Wrap-Up

Unit 6

Contents

Unit Preview

Reading 1: Myth

Reading 2: Poems/Social Studies

Reading 3: Science

Unit Wrap-Up

How can change improve people's lives?

THE BIG QUESTION

This unit is about change. You will read informational texts that describe how inventions can improve people's lives. You will also read about how and why the way we eat is changing and about a girl who discovers a community garden. Reading, writing, and talking about these topics will give you practice using academic language and will help you become a better student.

Reading 1 Science/Social Studies	**Reading 2** Science	**Reading 3** Short Story

"What's for Dinner?"	"Early Inventions"	"Milkweeds from Nevaeh"
Reading Strategy Preview	**Reading Strategy** Recognize sequence	**Reading Strategy** Visualize

Listening and Speaking—Team Presentation

At the end of this unit, you will choose a topic and give a team **presentation** about it.

Writing—Descriptive Essay

At the end of this unit, you will write a **descriptive essay**. To help you do this, you will write one paragraph that describes an event or experience, one that describes an object, and one that describes a place.

Quick Write

In your notebook, write the word *change*. List some words or phrases that you associate with this word. Then share your list with a partner.

View and Respond

Go to your Digital Resources. Watch the video and answer the questions.

Prepare to Read

What You Will Learn

Reading

- Vocabulary building: *Context, dictionary skills, word study*

- Reading strategy: *Preview*

- Text type: *Informational text (science/social studies)*

Grammar

- Sequence words and phrases

- Appositives

Writing

- Describe an event or experience

❓ THE BIG QUESTION

How can change improve people's lives? In many places, people have access to a bigger selection of foods than ever before. Scientific advances, along with global transportation, allow people to enjoy foods all year long that used to be only available in season. And globalization has made many foreign foods available as well. Have you noticed any change in the availability of foods? Are there any other changes in food that you would like to see? Do you think these changes have made life better? Use your prior experience to discuss with a partner.

Build Background

You are going to read an informational text titled "What's for Dinner?" Informational texts often inform the reader about the natural or social world.

This text is about changes in the foods we eat and the way we eat them. Transportation, selective breeding, and hybrid plants have made a greater selection of foods available year-round.

In addition, food production and consumption has been revolutionized with changes such as vertical farming, genetic engineering, new types of foods, and new ways for us to cook.

People can enjoy hybrid watermelons with fewer seeds. ▶

Vocabulary

Listening and Speaking: Key Words

Read aloud and listen to the sentences with a partner. Use the context to figure out the meaning of the highlighted words. Use a dictionary to check your answers. Then write each word and its meaning in your notebook.

Key Words
advantages
developed
disadvantages
produce
shipped
traits

1. A big advantage to globalization is a greater selection of foods available year-round.
2. New foods can be developed through genetic modification.
3. One disadvantage to transporting foods long distances is the impact on the environment.
4. France produces a lot of different kinds of cheese.
5. The farmer's vegetables are shipped to supermarkets in the city.
6. An important trait for a fruit or vegetable that is going to travel long distances is a thick skin.

Practice [W B] 1

Work with a partner to complete each activity.

1. What traits do you look for in a food? Think of three different foods and complete the sentences below.

   _____ are traits that I look for

   in _____.

   _____ is a trait that I look for

   in _____.

   _____ are traits that I look for

   in _____.

2. Think of two advantages and two disadvantages to the globalization of food. Write sentences in your notebook.

3. Write responses to the following questions in your notebook.

   What does your country produce a lot of?

   What is shipped out of your country?

   What new food would you like to see developed?

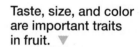

Taste, size, and color are important traits in fruit. ▼

Listening and Speaking: Academic Words

Study the **purple** words and their meanings. You will find these words useful when talking and writing about informational texts. Write each word and its meaning in your notebook, then say the words aloud with a partner. After you read "What's for Dinner?," try to use these words to respond to the text. Ask your peers and teacher for their feedback and support.

Academic Words

achieved
advances
attitudes
illegal

achieved = succeeded in doing something, especially by working hard	➡	Researchers **achieved** a breakthrough against blindness with Golden Rice.
advances = developments or improvements	➡	There have been important **advances** in the food industry in the past decade.
attitudes = thoughts or feelings about something or someone	➡	People have different **attitudes** about eating genetically engineered foods.
illegal = not allowed by law	➡	In some countries, certain genetically engineered foods are **illegal**.

Practice
W B
2

Work with a partner to answer these questions. Try to include the **purple** word in your answer. Write the sentences in your notebook.

1. What goals have you **achieved** in your lifetime?

2. What kinds of **advances** would you like to see in the food industry in the future?

3. What are some of the different **attitudes** people might have about eating genetically engineered foods?

4. Are there any kinds of food that you think should be **illegal**? Explain.

▲ People don't always agree about genetically modified foods.

Word Study: Double Consonants

Adding an ending, such as *-ed* or *-ing*, to a word can change its meaning. When endings are added to a single-syllable word that ends in a vowel + a consonant, the final consonant is doubled. For words with more than one syllable, the consonant doubles only if the stress is on the final syllable of the word.

Base Word	+ Ending	= New Word
ship	-ed	shipped
run	-ing	running
occur	-ed	occurred
begin	-ing	beginning

Practice
3

Work with a partner. Copy the chart above into your notebook. Add four blank rows. Then add *-ed* and *-ing* to the words below and write them on the chart.

clap	rebel	regret	visit

Reading Strategy **Preview**

Previewing a text helps you understand the content. To preview, follow these steps:

- Look at the title and headings.
- Look at the visuals and read the captions or labels.
- Think about your purpose for reading the text.
- Read the first and last sentences of each paragraph.

Before you read "What's for Dinner?," think about what you already know about changes to how and what we eat. What more would you like to know?

4

Set a purpose for reading Read the text to find out how food has changed over time. How have scientific research and farming methods changed the food we eat?

What's for Dinner?

People have always needed to eat. But the foods we eat, and the way we eat them, have changed a great deal since people first started asking, "What's for dinner?"

Food on the Go

Transportation is one of the biggest changes in modern food. Today's **crops** are grown to be shipped long distances so they can be sold in markets far from the farms where they are produced. Fruits and vegetables need to be tough to survive the journey from the farm to your table.

Tomatoes are a perfect example of a food that has changed. Originally, tomatoes had very thin skins. They were perfect for eating right away, but if you put a lot of them in a truck, they would quickly get smashed. In shipping, tomatoes are all piled on top of each other, so they need to be much tougher than the first tomatoes.

One secret to new tomatoes is **selective breeding**. Farmers pay close attention to the crops they grow. Long ago, they began to choose seeds from tomatoes with thicker skins. They also culled, or removed, tomatoes with very thin skins. Over time, tomatoes got tougher.

Then, in the twentieth century, farmers began to produce new plant hybrids. A **hybrid** is created by breeding two different varieties of plants together. A good hybrid has the best traits of each of the parents. For example, a tomato hybrid might be sweet and tasty but also have a thick skin that will stand up to long shipping distances.

> **Reading Skill**
>
> To understand the words in bold type, read the definitions at the bottom of the page. Later, use the words in your own sentences.

---

crops, plants grown on a farm
selective breeding, choosing which plants or animals to grow or reproduce
hybrid, crop grown by choosing parents of different varieties

A tomato truck holds 20,000 kilograms of fruit. That's about 300,000 tomatoes ▼ in one truck!

▲ Modern melons come in different sizes and colors.

Summer Every Day

Because plants can now be shipped around the world, the foods we eat may not always be in season. On a farm, plants have growing seasons. For example, watermelons are planted in the spring and grow bigger and juicier until they are ready to be picked in the summer. But many supermarkets today carry watermelons year-round. These fruits were grown in other regions or countries and then shipped.

Once again, selective breeding and hybridization make it possible for us to eat watermelon any time of year. The first watermelons were grown in Africa around 3,000 B.C. They were just 5 cm wide, very bitter, and hard. By carefully choosing which plants to grow, and later by cross-breeding, farmers now grow much bigger, super-sweet melons. They have skins tough enough to ship safely but are much easier to open than those tiny original watermelons.

In markets around the world, people can choose foods every day that would have been impossible to find a hundred years ago. Almost any food you want, from apples to zucchini, can be found at any time on your supermarket shelves. Now you don't have to wait until summer to snack on your favorite summer foods!

Before You Go On

1. How have tomatoes and watermelons changed over time?

2. How has transportation changed seasonal crops?

On Your Own

What food crops are grown locally in your area?

 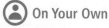

Science on the Farm

How can you make foods even better? Ask a scientist to help!

Scientists and farmers work together to develop new foods. They can create foods that are tastier, easier to transport, faster growing, and more resistant to diseases. They can even create foods that are better for you!

Scientists look at the basic material that makes every food unique. Like any plant or animal, a crop has **genes** that determine its physical traits. Scientists use genetic engineering to introduce a new trait that does not naturally occur in a species. For example, suppose that every year, a farmer's cucumbers are eaten by a kind of insect. Scientists might change the genes of a cucumber to make a variety that tastes good to us but bad to the insect.

Golden Rice, a genetically modified food, shows the promise of this new technology. Millions of people in Africa and Asia don't get enough Vitamin A. With genetic engineering, they don't have to be at a disadvantage. Researchers developed Golden Rice by changing the genes of a variety of white rice. The new yellow rice could help prevent blindness caused by Vitamin A **deficiency**. One bowl of Golden Rice supplies 60 percent of a child's daily Vitamin A requirement.

Scientists are now working on ways to add other genes to rice to create varieties that provide other key **nutrients**, such as iron.

---

genes, parts of living cells that cause a particular trait to be passed on
deficiency, not having enough of something that is needed
nutrients, materials in foods that help people live and grow

The yellow color of Golden Rice is a sign that it provides Vitamin A—a nutrient that's not found in ▼ white rice.

▲ Vertical and hydroponic farms could change the future of food.

New Ways to Grow Food

Scientists aren't just looking at what foods farmers grow—they're also finding new ways to grow them. These new growing methods have some surprising advantages.

Picture a farm. What do you see? Did you picture a large, flat area where crops are growing? That picture may change if vertical farming really takes off.

Vertical farms grow up, not out. Instead of taking up huge plots of land, a vertical farm is a tall tube with many different levels. Each level might include a different crop. Corn on Level 1, pumpkins on Level 2, all the way up to strawberries on Level 10. These farms of the future are tall towers. Inside, the temperature and light conditions are carefully controlled. In fact, they don't even rely on the sun. Plants get the light they need from powerful LED lights.

Vertical farms will use less land and less water than traditional farms. They can also grow crops without using dangerous **pesticides** or **fertilizers**. Because they don't rely on land resources, they can be built in cities and other areas where farming has never been possible.

When you pictured a farm, one of the other key features was probably dirt. But hydroponic farms grow plants without soil. Hydroponic plants grow in a special mixture that provides all of the nutrients the plant needs. The mixture includes water as well as necessary chemicals.

Hydroponic farms offer many advantages. They use 20 times less water than traditional farms, and the water can be reused. The growing mixture is **sterile**, so farmers do not need to use pesticides. They also require less space for growing.

---

pesticides, chemicals used to kill harmful insects
fertilizers, materials added to soil to make it better for growing plants
sterile, without any living germs or bacteria

Before You Go On

1. What determines the physical traits of a crop?

2. What are some of the advantages of vertical farming?

 On Your Own

What is your attitude toward genetically modified foods like Golden Rice?

New Foods to Grow

Researchers aren't just looking for new ways to grow foods—they're also looking for new foods to grow. Foods of the future may help people eat more healthfully, while they also protect our planet.

Would you eat bugs for breakfast? A growing number of people believe that crickets are part of a perfect meal.

People are beginning to develop new foods that will bring health benefits, including crickets and plant-based products. Crickets can be eaten whole or ground into flour that is equally nutritious. This lean and complete **protein** has a subtle flavor that people compare to nuts or popcorn. Crickets are a more efficient food than many other animals because they require less food and water to raise them.

Scientists are also looking for ways to create meat that won't hurt animals. A new technique allows scientists to grow meat in a laboratory using animal cells. The results have been called "test-tube burgers." The meat is chemically similar to animal meat but was never alive.

Scientists are also developing new plant-based products that resemble meat. Plant proteins can be processed to imitate the structure of meat. The result is a vegetable product that has the taste and texture of meat. It can even have "blood," which is another part of this new plant structure.

Crickets and other insects are already popular and healthy snacks in many ▼ countries.

---

protein, a substance found in all living things; protein is a necessary part of the human diet

▲ New appliances make cooking faster and more efficient.

Cooking Changes

Once you bring your food home, there's one more thing you need to do before you finally decide what's for dinner. How will you cook your food?

Home cooking methods have changed greatly since the days when people only used fires to cook. The first home ovens brought the fire inside and made cooking more convenient. Then, in the nineteenth century, people began to use gas and electric ovens. These ovens were easier to turn on and set specific temperatures.

The twentieth century brought a new kind of oven into many homes: the microwave. These ovens cook food using one form of **electromagnetic radiation**. Microwave ovens heat foods quickly, efficiently, and more evenly than other cooking methods.

More recently, many kitchen cooks have been enjoying a new electrical applicance: a modern version of a **pressure** cooker. Like its predecessor, it places foods and liquids under pressure to cook them either slowly or quickly. The tasty results have delighted many users and made the pot a huge success. During one special sale in 2015, more than 215,000 of these appliances were sold in a single day!

So, What's Cooking?

Your food options are far greater than they would have been one hundred or one thousand years ago. New foods, new farming methods, and new cooking techniques have changed the way we eat. Think about all of your choices the next time you ask, "What's for dinner?"

---

electromagnetic radiation, a form of energy that includes radio waves, microwaves, X-rays, and visible light
pressure, a steady force upon a surface

Before You Go On

1. Why do some people believe that crickets make a perfect meal?

2. How are scientists able to grow meat in a laboratory?

👤 On Your Own

Has the text given you any ideas about what you'd like or not like for dinner? Explain.

Review and Practice

Comprehension

Recall

1. What kind of skins did tomatoes used to have?
2. What can Golden Rice help prevent?

Comprehend

3. What are some advantages to vertical farms? Explain.
4. How and why is the food we eat changing?

Analyze

5. What do you think the author's **attitude** toward genetically modified foods is?
6. Why do you think scientists are so interested in finding new foods?

Connect

7. What food goal would you like to see researchers **achieve**?
8. What did you find most interesting about this article? Why?

In Your Own Words

Review the reading. Look at the **advances** listed below. In your notebook, make a chart like the one below. Use the effects provided for you. Then complete the rows by adding an effect that goes with the advance listed to the left. Finally, present your ideas to the class.

Advances in What and How We Eat	Effect
selective breeding and hybrids	easier transport, focus on best traits
improved transport	
genetic engineering	disease resistance, added nutrients, less pesticides
new foods	
new cooking techniques	quicker, more efficient, more even

Speaking Skill

Speak clearly and loudly enough for everyone to hear.

Reading Skill

The answers to some questions can be found directly in the text. These questions often include words such as *who*, *what*, or *where*. For other questions, the text doesn't give the answer directly. It's necessary to infer, or draw conclusions about the answer from other information. These questions often include words such as *why*, or *how*.

Discussion

Discuss with a partner or in a small group.

1. Do you think it's important to keep changing what and how we eat? Why?

2. What is your attitude toward eating high-protein insects, like crickets? Which advances in food do you think are positive ones? Negative? Why?

 How can changes in what and how we eat improve our lives? Explain.

Read for Fluency

It is often easier to read a text if you understand the difficult words and phrases. Work with a partner. Choose a paragraph from the reading. Identify the words and phrases you do not know or have trouble pronouncing. Look up the difficult words in a dictionary.

Take turns pronouncing the words and phrases with your partner. If necessary, ask your teacher to model the correct pronunciation. Then take turns reading the paragraph aloud. Give each other feedback on your reading.

Extension

Work with a partner. Create a menu for a new restaurant that uses the latest in food trends you read about in this article. Include hybrid foods and unusual foods like crickets. Add some details about how the food was grown or where. Do research to include other unusual foods available due to genetic engineering or other details you find interesting. Illustrate your menu. Take turns sharing with the class.

Grammar

Sequence Words and Phrases

When you read an informational text that tells how something has changed over time, it's important to notice sequence words.

> Foods have changed a great deal since people **first** started asking, "What's for dinner?"

Sequence words and phrases help you follow the article about what happened to foods over time. A sequence often begins with *first* and ends with *finally* or *last*. *Then, next, now,* and *after that* can be used in any order within a sequence. Use a comma after sequence words and phrases. Read about the sequence of points made about improvements in food in the article.

> **First,** the article discusses how farmers used selective breeding.
> **Then,** it presents information about new plant hybrids.
> **After that,** the article points out how new methods in farming and ways to cook food have improved what we eat and when we can eat it.
> **Now,** you don't have to wait until summer to snack on your favorite summer foods!

Practice A
6

Put the events in the correct sequence. The first one is done for you.

_____ Then he got dressed.

_____ Now he was ready to go.

__1__ First, Mike took a shower.

_____ After that, he combed his hair.

Practice B

Complete the paragraph with the sequence words in the box. The first one is done for you.

After that	Finally	First	Then

We had the most incredible meal at the restaurant last night. _____First_____, we all had an appetizer. I had a cup of soup. _____ we all shared a beautiful salad with lots of vegetables. _____, we all had a main course. I had delicious fish. _____, it was time for dessert!

Appositives

An appositive is a noun or noun phrase that renames another noun next to it. The appositive can be short or long. A dash may be used before the appositive.

> For the main course, you can choose anything we have—fish, chicken, or pasta.

When a comma is used with an appositive, it gives extra information and is called a *nonrestrictive appositive*. When there is no comma, the information is essential and is called a *restrictive appositive*.

> They served unusual snacks, crickets.

Practice A
7

Underline the appositive in the sentences below. The first one is done for you.

1. The device, <u>the modern version of a pressure cooker</u>, is very popular.
2. The nutrient Vitamin A is critical to good sight.
3. Crickets, common insects, are good sources of protein.
4. Gary Paulsen's book *Hatchet* is about survival.
5. Gary Paulsen, my favorite author, signed this book.

Practice B

Insert commas, when necessary, to create restrictive and nonrestrictive appositives. The first one is done for you.

1. Golden Rice, a genetically modified food, can help prevent blindness.
2. Anna's cat Milo sat in the sun on her porch.
3. The pesticide DDT is now illegal in many countries.
4. Her company an organic food farm has been very successful.
5. The genetically modified foods corn and soy are common around the world.
6. They were unable to achieve their goal a fruit-vegetable hybrid.

Writing

Describe an Event or Experience

At the end of this unit, you will write a descriptive essay. To do this, you will need to learn some of the skills to use in descriptive writing.

> **Writing Prompt**
>
> Write a descriptive paragraph about an exciting event you participated in or attended, for example, a sports event, a party, or a family celebration. Before you write, list the events in chronological order, using a graphic organizer. Be sure to use sequence words correctly in your description.

① **Prewrite** Begin by choosing an event or experience that was exciting for you. W B 8

• Decide on a title for your description.

• List what happened in a sequence-of-events organizer.

• Decide which sequence words you can use.

Here's a sequence-of-events organizer created by a student named Haley. She is describing how she got ready for her first school formal.

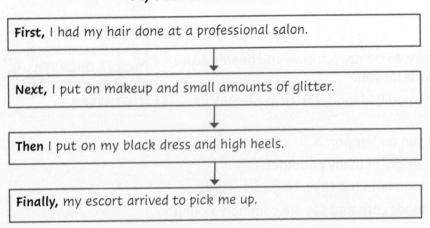

My First School Formal

| **First,** I had my hair done at a professional salon. |

⬇

| **Next,** I put on makeup and small amounts of glitter. |

⬇

| **Then** I put on my black dress and high heels. |

⬇

| **Finally,** my escort arrived to pick me up. |

(2) Draft Use your organizer to help you write a first draft.

- Remember to use chronological order
- Add details to make your description more vivid.
- Make sure to use sequence words correctly.

(3) Revise Read over your draft. Look for places where the writing is unclear or needs improvement. Complete (√) the Writing Checklist to help you identify problems. Then revise your draft, using the editing and proofreading marks listed on page 401.

(4) Edit and Proofread Check your work for errors in grammar, usage, mechanics, and spelling. Trade papers with a partner to obtain feedback. Use the Peer Review Checklist on Workbook page 8. Edit your final draft in response to feedback from your partner and your teacher.

(5) Publish Prepare a clean copy of your final draft. Share your descriptive paragraph with the class. Save your work. You'll need to refer to it in the Writing Workshop at the end of the unit.

> ### Writing Checklist
>
> **Organization:**
> ☐ I used chronological order.
>
> **Word Choice:**
> ☐ I used sequence words to make the order of events clear to the reader.

Here is Haley's description of her first school formal.

Haley Coy

My First School Formal

Getting ready for my first school formal was hectic and exciting. First, I had my hair done at a professional salon. Countless bobby pins and squirts of hairspray were used before the style was complete. The updo gave me an elegant look. Next, I applied gentle brush strokes of makeup and small amounts of glitter on my cheeks. Then it was time to put on my black dress and high heels. The heels gave me enough height so that my dress just grazed the floor. Finally, my escort arrived to pick me up. He looked great in his elegant black tuxedo. As he placed a yellow rose corsage on my wrist, my parents started snapping pictures of us. Now, I'll have plenty of photographs to remember just how incredible we looked on that memorable night.

Prepare to Read

What You Will Learn

Reading

- Vocabulary building: *Context, dictionary skills, word study*

- Reading strategy: *Recognize sequence*

- Text type: *Informational text (science)*

Grammar

- Simple past: regular verbs

- Simple past: irregular verbs

Writing

- Describe an object

❓ THE BIG QUESTION

How can change improve people's lives? What kinds of tools or devices do you use on a daily basis? A toothbrush? Television? Computer? Pen? Copy the chart below into your notebook. List objects that you use every day. Include a brief description of how you use each item. Then share your chart with a small group. Discuss how people's everyday lives have been changed by these items.

Tool or Machine	How I Use It

Build Background

"Early Inventions" is a science article about inventions, or devices that people design to improve their lives. Many of these inventions have made a big difference in how we live.

Inventions are created for various reasons. Some are created so people can do things they couldn't do before. For example, the music cylinder allowed people to record music and listen to it whenever they wanted. Some inventions, like the microwave oven, are designed to make the things we already do easier. And some inventions are made just for fun, like cotton candy.

▲ Paper was invented in China by Tsai Lun in the year 105.

Vocabulary

Listening and Speaking: Key Words

Key Words

device
emergency
idea
identical
invention
patent

Key words are important, topic-related vocabulary. Read aloud and listen to these sentences. Use the context to figure out the meaning of the highlighted words. Use a dictionary to check your answers. Then write each word and its meaning in your notebook.

1. The device opens metal cans.

2. The plane had to turn around due to an emergency. One of its engines was on fire.

3. The architect's home is identical to the small model she had built. Every detail is the same.

4. The invention of the vacuum cleaner made cleaning the house faster and easier.

5. The inventor applied for a patent from the government. He didn't want anyone else to make or sell his invention.

6. She has a good idea for a new device that can open doors remotely.

Practice
9

Use a key word from the box above to complete each sentence. Then take turns reading the sentences aloud with a partner. Ask your peers and teacher for their feedback and support.

1. The medical team was ready to respond to any _____ during a natural disaster.

2. Guillermo Gonzalez Camarena received a(n) _____ for his invention of the color TV in 1942.

3. A microphone is a(n) _____ that allows someone to speak to a large group of people.

4. The twins wore _____ clothing to the party so no one could tell them apart.

5. The _____ of the internet allowed people to find information quickly.

6. I have no _____ how to solve this problem.

▲ The invention of the smartphone changed the world.

Listening and Speaking: Academic Words

Study the **purple** words and their meanings. You will find these words useful when talking and writing about informational texts. Write each word and its meaning in your notebook, then say the words aloud with a partner. After you read "Early Inventions," try to use these words to respond to the text.

created = made or invented	➡	Alexander Graham Bell **created** a new way for people to communicate with each other—the telephone.
function = the purpose of something	➡	The **function** of a washing machine is to clean clothes.
significant = noticeable or important	➡	The invention of the computer had a **significant** impact on society. We will see the effects of this invention for many years to come.
technology = all the knowledge and equipment used in science	➡	As **technology** has improved, scientists have been able to develop many new products.

Practice W B 10

Work with a partner to answer these questions. Try to include the **purple** word in your answer. Write the sentences in your notebook.

1. Have you ever **created** something you were proud of? If so, what?

2. What is the **function** of an airplane?

3. In your opinion, what is one of the most **significant** inventions ever created?

4. What kinds of new **technology** might be invented in the future?

The airplane is one of the most significant inventions of the ▼ 20th century.

Word Study: Nouns That Modify Nouns

A noun is a person, place, or thing. Sometimes, a noun is used to decribe, or modify, another noun. For example, two nouns make up the phrase *bear cub*. However, the first noun acts as an adjective—*bear* gives you more information about the *cub*. Look at the sentences below for examples of other nouns that modify nouns.

He always has a ballpoint pen in his shirt pocket.	➡	*ballpoint* modifies *pen*
I cooked dinner in the microwave oven.	➡	*microwave* modifies *oven*
Instant noodles are popular with university students.	➡	*instant* modifies *noodles*
I poured the juice into a paper cup.	➡	*paper* modifies *cup*

Learning Strategy

Use a concept map to acquire new vocabulary. Adding words or phrases to a chart like the one here will help you see the relationships between words and their meanings.

Practice 11

Work with a partner. Circle each noun modifier and underline the noun being modified.

1. The lie detector said that he wasn't telling the truth.

2. Since the invention of color television, it's hard to imagine watching TV in black and white.

3. Ben spilled juice on his computer keyboard.

4. She snapped her bubble gum loudly.

5. The ice pop melted in the sun.

Reading Strategy Recognize Sequence

Recognizing sequence in a text, such as the one you're going to read about inventions, is important because it helps you better understand the importance of each one. To recognize sequence, follow these steps:

- As you read, look for words used to show time and sequence: for example, *today, every year, at the time, ten years later, soon,* and *at the beginning of the 19th century*.
- Look for dates and periods of times: for example, *in 1804* and *many years*. If possible, make a timeline of events.
- Notice verbs that show what happened earlier or would happen later.

As you read "Early Inventions," note when things were invented.

12

Set a purpose for reading As you read about inventions, consider how our ancestors' lives were different from ours today. What impact did these inventions have on us?

Early Inventions

Inventors Change the World

One good idea can change people's lives in surprising ways. Inventors spend hundreds of hours thinking of large and small inventions. Here are just a few of the thousands of inventions that have changed the way we work, eat, and play.

Who? John Joseph Merlin
What? Roller Skates
When? 1760s

Belgian inventor John Joseph Merlin's big idea was to find a way to try **ice skating** on dry land. He attached some metal wheels to a wooden plate and took a very dramatic ride at a fancy party in London, England. Unfortunately, he could not control his new invention very well. He crashed into an expensive mirror and hurt himself badly. It took many years for people to develop safer roller skates.

---

ice skating, wearing shoes with sharp blades attached to move smoothly on ice

Who? Seishu Hanaoka
What? General Anesthesia
When? 1804

Japanese doctor Seishu Hanaoka developed a way to use traditional ingredients to place his patients in a sleeplike state. Under this **general anesthesia**, the doctor could perform surgery without the patients feeling pain. He performed the first cancer operation, using general anesthesia in 1804. He went on to perform many successful operations and train more than 2,000 students.

---

general anesthesia, placing patients in a sleeplike state during surgery, instead of numbing just a small area of the body

Early roller skates ▶

Who? Philippe de Girard, Bryan Donkin
What? Tin Can
When? 1810

French inventor Philippe de Girard came up with a new way to store food: in metal containers. British **manufacturer** Bryan Donkin bought the rights to the idea. The first canned foods were made for Great Britain's Royal Navy in 1813. Today, more than 40 billion cans of food are produced every year.

Who? Margaret E. Knight
What? Flat-Bottomed Paper Bag
When? 1871

Margaret Knight was working in a factory, making paper bags, when she got her big idea. Wouldn't it be a lot easier to put things into bags if the bags had flat bottoms? Paper bags at the time were more like flat envelopes. Knight got to work and invented a machine that folded and glued paper bags. Many grocery stores today still use paper bags that are almost identical to Knight's first designs.

Who? Maria Beasley
What? Life Raft
When? 1880

Before Maria Beasley's invention, boats didn't carry special life rafts in case of emergency. They just had some wooden boards that were not very safe. Beasley invented a much better life raft that saved many lives. Her raft was **fireproof** and could fold. It also had railings that kept riders from falling off. Some of Beasley's life rafts were on board the *Titanic* in April 1912. When the boat sank, 706 people survived because of Beasley's life-saving invention.

---

manufacturer, someone who makes goods to sell
fireproof, able to withstand fire or great heat

▲ Seishu Hanaoka

Before You Go On

1. In what kind of operation was general anesthesia used for the first time?

2. Who probably ate food from the first tin cans made?

 On Your Own

Why are some inventions so important?

Who? Mary Anderson
What? Windshield Wipers
When? 1903

Early cars didn't have **windshield** wipers. Drivers had to get out to wipe off snow and just drive through rain. Mary Anderson was riding a streetcar in New York City in 1902. It started to snow and she saw the driver get out to clear the windshield. She got the idea for automatic wipers. A year later, she received a patent for her invention—even though she didn't know how to drive herself!

Who? Victor Ochoa
What? Electric Brake
When? 1907

Mexican inventor Victor Ochoa patented the electric brake in 1907. This device uses magnetic attraction to make it easier for trains to slow down and stop. Later the same year, he received another patent for an improved version of the brake, which would soon be used in streetcars traveling through many cities. Ochoa also invented a clip to hold pens and pencils in a pocket and a small airplane with wings that could fold down for easy storage.

---

windshield, a window at the front of a car or other vehicle

Who? Gideon Sundback
What? Modern Zipper
When? 1913

Like many inventors, Gideon Sundback came up with his most famous invention by improving earlier inventions. Earlier inventors, like Elias Howe and Whitcomb Judson, had created zipper-like closures. But they had some big problems. These early devices opened too easily. Sundback added more teeth to create something that looked a lot like the zippers we use today. His first closures were only used in boots and some pouches. But soon, they were used for everything from clothing to luggage. However, Sundback didn't invent the name *zipper*. That word was used ten years later in 1923 by B.F. Goodrich.

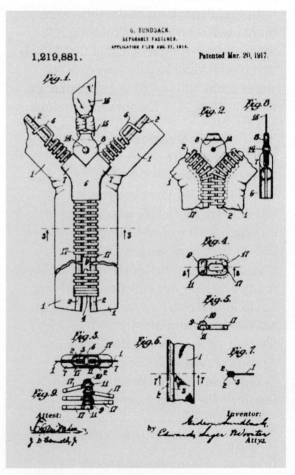

▲ Today, you can zip a lot of zippers thanks to Gideon Sundback.

Who? Guillermo Gonzalez Camarena
What? Color Television
When? 1942

When he was just 17 years old, Guillermo Gonzalez Camarena changed the world by building the first color television, using parts he had found in flea markets. In 1942, he received a patent for his invention. Four years later, he made the first color broadcast from an office building in Mexico City. Soon, this new technology would bring bright colors to screens around the world.

Who? Laszlo Biro
What? Ballpoint Pen
When? 1944

At the beginning of the nineteenth century, people used fountain pens, which had to be filled with wet, messy ink. Laszlo Biro came up with a new design that was much easier to use. He replaced the point of a fountain pen with a tiny ball. His new pen used quick-drying ink and could write for months without being refilled.

Who? Momofuku Ando
What? Instant Noodles
When? 1958

Momofuku Ando realized that food shortages were a serious problem after World War II. He also saw that people in Japan were willing to wait in long lines for fresh noodles. These observations inspired him to invent instant noodles. The tasty noodles and broth are made by just adding hot water to a dry mix.

▲ Momofuku Ando's company has sold more than 20 billion cups of noodles.

Before You Go On

1. Where did Camarena get parts for his first color television?

2. How were ballpoint pens an improvement on earlier writing tools?

On Your Own

If you could be the first to invent something, what would you invent?

Review and Practice

Comprehension
WB 13

Recall

1. Who **created** the electric brake?
2. What was the one big problem with early zippers?

Comprehend

3. Why did Momofuku Ando invent instant noodles?
4. Which inventions that you read about helped people do things they couldn't do before? Which ones just improved an experience or situation?

Analyze

5. Why do you think an article like this one about early inventions is important? Explain.
6. Which inventions do you think are the most important kinds? Explain.

Connect

7. What characteristics do you think an invention must have in order for it to be **significant**? Why?
8. Which invention that you read about has had the biggest impact on you? Explain.

In Your Own Words

Review the reading. Choose the four inventions that you think are the most significant. Look at the date of each invention. In your notebook, make a timeline like the one below. Add the dates to the timeline in chronological order. Then write a sentence describing each of the four inventions. Present your timeline and summaries to the class.

1810

Philippe de Girard created a new way to store food: in metal cans

> **Reading Skill**
>
> Make sure you understand different types of sentences. Questions are used routinely to ask for information. They often include words such as *who, what, where, why, when,* or *how.*

Discussion

Discuss with a partner or in a small group.

1. Which invention did you find most interesting to read about? Why?

2. What type of device or process would you like to invent? Why?

 How can change improve people's lives? Name new **technologies** that have been invented during your lifetime. What was your life like before these inventions existed? How have they changed your life for the better?

Listening Skill

Look at the speaker as he or she speaks.

Read for Fluency

When we read aloud to communicate meaning, we group words into phrases, pause or slow down to make important points, and emphasize important words. As you read aloud, pause for a short time after a comma and for a longer time after a period. Pay attention to rising and falling intonation at the end of sentences.

   Work with a partner. Choose a paragraph from the reading. Discuss which words seem important for communicating meaning. Practice pronouncing difficult words. Take turns reading aloud and giving each other feedback.

Extension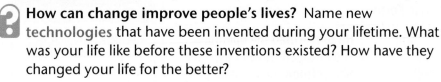

Work with a partner. Choose an object that you use every day. Use the library or the internet to research that object. Describe the **function** of the object and find out who invented it and when and how it was invented. Use the information to complete the chart below. Then, share your results with the class.

Object:
Function:
Inventor:
Year object was invented:
How object was invented:

Learning Strategy

To better acquire and understand new academic language, use and reuse these words in meaningful ways in your writing.

Grammar

Simple Past: Regular Verbs

Use the simple past to talk about actions that happened in the past. There are rules for forming the simple past of regular verbs.

Rule	Base Form	Simple Past
Add -ed if base form ends in two consonants, C-V-C*, or C-V + y.	perform stay refill	He **performed** the operation. Food **stayed** fresh in tin cans. She **refilled** the fountain pen.
If base form ends in -e, just add -d.	change receive	Camarena **changed** the world. He **received** another patent.
For one-syllable C-V-C words, double final consonant and add -ed.	can plan stir	He **canned** the food. She **planned** to get a patent. I **stirred** my soup.
If base form ends in -y, change y to i and add -ed.	try apply	Inventors **tried** to find a way. They **applied** the technology.

*C stands for *consonant* and V stands for *vowel*.

Grammar Skill

The base form of a verb is also called the simple form. There are no endings (-s, -es, -d, -ed) on the base form.

Grammar Check

✔ When do you just need to add -d and not -ed to form the **simple past** of **regular verbs**?

Practice A
14

Work with a partner. Complete the paragraph using the simple past form of the verb in parentheses.

The Hungarian journalist Laszlo Biro (1. invent) ___*invented*___ the ballpoint pen in 1938. Biro (2. notice) _____ that the type of ink used in newspaper printing (3. dry) _____ quickly. As the pen (4. move) _____ along the paper, the ball (5. rotate) _____, picking up ink from the ink cartridge and leaving it on the paper.

Practice B

Work with a partner to answer the questions in your notebook. Use the simple past of the verb in the question in your answer.

1. Did Donkin invent a new way to store food?
   Yes, he invented the tin can

2. Did Hanaoka perform the first operation with general anesthesia?

3. Did Camarena receive a patent in 1917? If not, when?

4. Did Ochoa patent the electric brake?

Apply

In your notebook, write five sentences telling what you did yesterday, using the simple past. Use a dictionary if necessary. Then talk to a partner about what you did last weekend.

Simple Past: Irregular Verbs

Many verbs have an irregular form in the simple past. Their simple past form is not formed by adding *-d* or *-ed*. You will need to memorize them. Form questions with *did* and the base form of the verb. Form the negative with *did not* (*didn't*) and the base form of the verb. For the verb *be*, form the negative with *was not* or *were not*; form questions by switching the order of the verb *was* or *were* with the subject.

Base Form / Simple Past			Example
be	→	was/were	**Was** Philippe de Girard French?
buy	→	bought	He **bought** the rights to the idea.
go	→	went	Camarena **went** to flea markets.
bring	→	brought	He **brought** color television to the world.

Look at the chart for more irregular verbs in the simple past.

Irregular Past Verbs											
catch	→	caught	hide	→	hid	send	→	sent
come	→	came	keep	→	kept	sleep	→	slept
fly	→	flew	lose	→	lost	tell	→	told

Practice A

15

Complete the sentences with the simple past of the verb in parentheses. Use a dictionary if necessary.

1. I _____ lost _____ (lose) my phone. May I use yours?
2. We _____ (be) at the beach last weekend.
3. She _____ (buy) a new backpack.
4. He _____ (fly) on a small plane with his family.

Practice B

Form questions or negative sentences with *did* and the verbs in parentheses.

1. You _____ (give) Sharon the book.
2. I _____ (not tell) anyone your secret.
3. Lee _____ (go) to school today?
4. They _____ (come) to your party?
5. She _____ (not bring) the water.

Writing

Describe an Object

In this lesson you will write a description of an object. A good description often includes sensory details to appeal to the reader's five senses. This helps the reader to imagine how an object sounds, smells, looks, feels, or tastes.

Writing Prompt

Write a descriptive paragraph about an object that you have used, eaten, or worn, such as a computer, an apple, or a sweater. List related sensory details in a graphic organizer. Include these details in your paragraph. Be sure to use regular and irregular verbs in the simple past correctly.

① Prewrite Begin by choosing a story to tell.

- Write the name of the object in the center oval of your graphic organizer.

- Ask yourself how this object sounds, smells, looks, feels, or tastes.

- Add details for the other senses, as appropriate.

- Think of interesting adjectives and verbs to describe your object.

16

Here's a word web created by a student named Pablo for a description of a faucet:

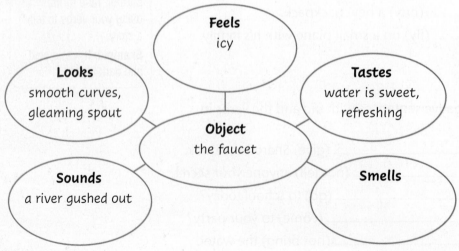

② **Draft** Use your word web to help you write a first draft.

- Remember to describe the object using different senses.
- Use a variety of adjectives and verbs to make your description vivid.
- As you write, try to help your audience visualize your object.
- Be sure to use regular and irregular verbs in the simple past correctly.

③ **Revise** Read over your draft. Look for places where the writing is unclear or needs improvement. Complete (√) the Writing Checklist to help you identify problems. Then revise your draft, using the editing and proofreading marks listed on page 401.

④ **Edit and Proofread** Check your work for errors in grammar, usage, mechanics, and spelling. Trade papers with a partner to obtain feedback. Use the Peer Review Checklist on Workbook page 16. Edit your final draft in response to feedback from your partner and your teacher.

⑤ **Publish** Prepare a clean copy of your final draft. Share your descriptive paragraph with your class. Save your work. You'll need to refer to it in the Writing Workshop at the end of the unit.

> **Writing Checklist**
>
> **Word Choice:**
> ☐ I included sensory details to describe the object.
>
> **Sentence Fluency:**
> ☐ I used regular and irregular verbs in the simple past correctly.

Here is Pablo's description. Notice how he contrasts the hot day and the cool water to make his description more vivid.

Pablo Espínola

The Faucet

It had to be 37 degrees in the kitchen. As I stood at the sink, the reflection of the sun on the faucet's metal hurt my eyes. I noticed the faucet's smooth curves, the knobs, and the gleaming spout. When I turned the cold-water knob, a river gushed out of the spout and hit the sink. Small droplets of water bounced out, leaving little wet marks along my arms. When I placed my hand on the metal spout, it felt icy from the cold water running through it. I got a glass from the cupboard and filled it. On a hot day, the water from the faucet tasted sweet and refreshing. After washing my hands and face, I felt cool and comfortable in my house on that hot, hot day.

Prepare to Read

What You Will Learn

Reading

- Vocabulary building: *Literary terms, word study*

- Reading strategy: *Visualize*

- Text type: *Literature (short story)*

Grammar

- Comparison structures: adjectives

- Comparison structures: adverbs

Writing

- Describe a place

? THE BIG QUESTION

How can change improve people's lives? Do you know someone who has a garden? What kinds of plants grow there? What kind of changes take place in a garden? How could you benefit from having a garden? Discuss with a partner.

Build Background

You will read a short story titled "Milkweeds from Nevaeh." It is realistic fiction about a special bond and a community garden. In some city neighborhoods, people plant gardens in vacant lots or empty areas of land. Each person plants flowers or vegetables in one part of the garden, and then they take care of that area.

In "Milkweeds from Nevaeh," a character named Nevaeh narrates the story, telling about the garden and her past. Short stories usually present a short sequence of events, and the main character often experiences a problem or conflict. In the story, Neveah tells why the garden, and the milkweed, are so important to her.

▲ People take care of their part of a community garden.

Vocabulary

Learn Literary Words

Literary Words

imagery
setting
simile

Imagery is figurative language used to create word pictures. These pictures, or images, appeal to the senses—sight, sound, taste, touch, smell—or to movement. Try to identify the use of imagery in the short story "Milkweeds from Nevaeh" below.

> I reached for one of the biggest milkweeds, just under its puffy pink flower, and lifted the long green leaf to reveal the underside, where a line of about a half dozen small white eggs were secured and well-hidden. Three of the eggs were nearly transparent because they were now empty. A tiny white larva lay beside each shell of the egg, their black heads slowly weaving back and forth.

Learning Strategy

Use words that you already know to learn new and essential language, or words that you must know in order to understand your schoolwork.

Notice how the words *reached* and *lifted* appeal to your sense of touch, and the words *biggest, puffy pink, long green, small white, transparent, empty, tiny white,* and *weaving back and forth* appeal to your sense of sight.

The **setting** of "Milkweeds from Nevaeh" is an old, abandoned lot in Detroit, Michigan. The setting is the time and place of the action. *Time* can be a specific year, season, or time of day. *Place* can be a specific location on a map, such as a town, state, or country. *Place* can also be a specific environment, such as a garden.

A **simile** is a comparison that uses *like* or *as*. Notice in this sentence from the story how the sight of the hatched eggs is compared to a ship.

Even though I had seen this in Mom's gardens before, the hatched eggs were still one of the greatest sights to see, **like a ship on the ocean in the distance**.

Practice
17

Work with a partner. Think of a setting such as a park. Create imagery by using sensory details and a simile to describe the setting. Write your response in your notebook. Then read your description to the class. Ask your peers and teacher for their feedback and support.

▲ Sensory details, such as "bone-chilling," could be used to describe this setting.

Listening and Speaking: Academic Words

Study the **purple** words and their meanings. You will find these words useful when talking and writing about literature. Write each word and its meaning in your notebook, then say the words aloud with a partner. After you read the short story "Milkweeds from Nevaeh," try to use these words to respond to it.

Academic Words

goal
involved
insight
reacted

goal = something you want to do in the future	⇒	She's a new and inexperienced gardener. Her **goal** is to grow prize-winning flowers.
involved = included in a project or situation	⇒	She became **involved** in a garden club at school. She goes to their meetings every Friday.
insight = something you suddenly realize that is very important or meaningful	⇒	Then I had an **insight** about the real meaning of the book.
reacted = behaved in a particular way because of what someone has said or done	⇒	Nevaeh **reacted** with joy and excitement when she saw the newly hatched eggs.

Practice 18

Work with a partner to answer these questions. Try to include the **purple** word in your answer. Write the sentences in your notebook.

1. What is one **goal** you hope to accomplish before the end of the school year?

2. What community service project would you like to become **involved** in?

3. Have you had an **insight** into how you can help your community?

4. How would you **react** if someone suggested a community garden for your neighborhood?

Women react to their prize-winning flower arrangements. ▶

Word Study: Apostrophes

As you read the story "Milkweeds from Nevaeh," you will see words that include an apostrophe ('). Use an apostrophe with a noun to show possession or to take the place of missing letters, as in a contraction.

To show possession:
- Add ' + s to the end of a singular noun.
- Add an apostrophe (') to the end of a plural noun.

> I had seen this in **Mom's gardens.** [the gardens that belonged to Mom]
> These **caterpillars' bodies** are going to grow faster than weeds. [the bodies of the caterpillars]

A contraction is two words combined into one with an apostrophe taking the place of a missing letter or letters.

I'll donate some time after school.	[I + will = I'll]
There's certainly room.	[there + is = there's]

Practice
19

Work with a partner. Read aloud the phrases in the box below. Combine the words in each phrase to make contractions or possessive nouns. Then, in your notebook, write a sentence using those words.

can not	seeds of the plants	had not
friend of Nevaeh	it is	They are

Reading Strategy   **Visualize**

When you visualize, you form pictures in your mind of what you are reading. To visualize, follow these steps:

- As you read, notice the descriptions.
- Pay attention to descriptive words and figurative language, such as similes.
- Stop from time to time and visualize the story's characters, setting, and events.

As you read "Milkweeds from Nevaeh," ask yourself what language the author is using to create a picture of the characters, setting, and events.

WB
20

Set a purpose for reading As you read, pay attention to Nevaeh's actions. In what ways do they bring about change in the story?

Milkweeds *from* Nevaeh

"Time to wake up, Nevaeh!"

I pulled the covers over my head. *Not already*, I said to myself. Saturday mornings are supposed to be for sleeping in. Yet every Saturday, rain or shine, Jorge calls up the stairs to wake me up to buy newspapers at the corner. He can't just read the internet news like everyone else. He wants to support the local businesses and buy the newspaper and coffee, too.

"Where's my little piece of heaven?" he said even louder this time. He usually has a heaven joke to tell me, because my name is *heaven* spelled backwards. Jorge always has a joke ready for any situation. He's a good foster dad that way. I can't really get mad at him for wanting to get an early start on the weekend—even though it's the same thing every Saturday.

In the eight months I've been living with Robyn and Jorge as my new **foster parents**, it's been the same thing on the walk down Grand Boulevard. It was the same scenery, same buildings, even the same cars parked on the streets. Well, this Saturday turned out to be a little different. Today we saw people shoveling dirt and hauling containers of plants into a **vacant** lot.

"It looks like the community garden is starting up again this year," said Jorge. "Last year was their first time doing it, and I guess it was successful enough to repeat with a larger **plot**. I'll have to let Robyn know. She might be able to put her tomato plants there instead of on the porch."

The garden reminded me of my last foster mom, Sonya. There was always some point in the day when I thought of her. She was the only foster mom I could think of that I ever called *Mom*.

✓ **LITERARY CHECK**

How does the **setting** help set the mood and tone in this story?

---

foster parents, adults responsible for caring for a child not born as their own
vacant, empty
plot, a piece of land used for a specific purpose

"Hi Hanna!" Jorge called out as he and Nevaeh stepped into the garden. Hanna put down a container of begonias, wiped some sweat from her eyebrow with the wrist of her work gloves, and waved to us.

"Jorge, how are you?" Her friendly face moved right down to my level. "This must be Nevaeh—I'm so glad to finally meet you."

I smiled politely. "Hi," I answered.

"How's the new garden?" asked Jorge. "Do you think Robyn can plant some tomatoes here?"

"Of course," smiled Hanna. "We have double the space this year, so there's **undoubtedly** room." Then a sudden **frown** came over her face. "But tell her that tomatoes don't do great in this rainy Detroit weather, so maybe she should keep a pot or two on her porch so they can stay drier. But I'll save her a sunny spot over there."

I smiled. Mom was always saying that about tomatoes. *The tomatoes can't get too **soaked**, so let's hope this rain stops and the sun starts shining soon!*

"Are you growing any milkweed plants?" I asked. Jorge and Hanna both turned to me.

---

undoubtedly, without doubt; certainly
frown, facial expression of unhappiness or concern
soaked, made extremely wet

Before You Go On

1. Why does Jorge always tell "heaven jokes" to Nevaeh?

2. What kind of plants does Nevaeh ask about?

 **On Your Own**

From what you've read, how is Neveah adjusting to life with her foster parents? Explain.

Reading 3 **39**

"What?" said Jorge.

"Milkweeds," said Hanna. "No, Nevaeh, I haven't gotten any yet, but I was thinking of that. Last year was our first year here, so we only grew **annuals** in case the community didn't support the garden. But they were actually super-supportive, so this year we want to add some more things . . . Now we can add . . ."

"**Perennials**," I said.

"Right!" Hanna reacted to me with surprise, and Jorge didn't know what to think of me. He was still trying to get to know me, it always seemed.

"My mom used to grow a garden every year," I said.

Jorge quickly jumped in. "Her last foster mom passed away last year," he explained.

It wasn't easy being a foster child, mainly because people were always talking about my situation and thinking they had to **pity** me.

Hanna didn't respond to Jorge. Instead, she said, "I think milkweeds are a great idea. Did you know they're the only food eaten by . . ."

"Monarch **larvae**," I said. "The butterflies will eat lots of things, but the larvae only eat the milkweed. That's why people plant it in their gardens—so monarchs will visit the garden and lay eggs so their larvae have something to eat."

"Wow," said Jorge, "Why don't we get some for the garden? We'll **donate** some milkweed plants, Hanna, if that's all right with you."

"I would love for people to get involved as much as they can," she said. "I welcome any **contribution**—especially of time."

"I'll donate some time after school," I offered. "I can do some weeding or help with planting."

And that's how I first met Hanna. Robyn and Jorge were happy that I finally started to get out of the house and enjoy my new neighborhood. It wasn't really my goal to get involved with a community garden, but it kind of just worked out that way.

"Nevaeh!" Hanna called to me one day across the garden as I was arriving for my regular Wednesday after-school shift. "The monarch eggs hatched! I haven't even checked the other plants by the Grand Boulevard gate, but look at these!"

---

annuals, plants that live a year or less from a seed
perennials, plants that regrow year after year
pity, to feel sorry for
larvae, caterpillar; immature form of an insect
donate, to give without receiving payment
contribution, offering

I reached for one of the biggest milkweeds, just under its puffy pink flower, and lifted the long green leaf to **reveal** the underside, where a line of about a half dozen small white eggs were secured and well-hidden. Three of the eggs were nearly **transparent** because they were now empty. A tiny white larva lay beside each shell of the egg, their black heads slowly weaving back and forth.

Even though I had seen this in Mom's gardens before, the hatched eggs were still one of the greatest sights to see, like a ship on the ocean in the distance. *Finally!* I always think whenever I see them. *Here they are!*

"Take my cell phone and get a picture of this!" Hanna said to me. Dylan and Leah gathered to watch the caterpillars, too. Soon the garden was as busy as a beehive.

"We can watch these caterpillars grow all summer," said Dylan.

"Well, they grow quickly. They might be full grown in . . ." Hanna said more **cautiously** than I had expected.

". . . as little as a week," I continued.

"Right, or as much as two weeks or so. Keep an eye on the garden, that's for sure," she said. "These caterpillars' bodies are going to grow faster than weeds, believe me."

---

reveal, to show
transparent, able to be seen through; clear
cautiously, carefully

✓ **LITERARY CHECK**

What sensory details are used to create **imagery** in this passage?

Before You Go On

1. What do you find out about Nevaeh's last foster mom?

2. Why are milkweed plants so important to monarch butterflies?

 On Your Own

How do you think Hanna and Nevaeh will get along? How do you know?

I walked to the Grand Boulevard gate with Hanna to check the other batch of milkweeds.

"You know, my mom used to say that she wanted to make her house like a milkweed plant for me," I said.

"Really?" asked Hanna. "How so?"

"Well, she said that her house was like the plant, and that I could grow there and get everything I needed—just like the monarch caterpillar."

"Oh, I see," said Hanna. "Then you'd become a beautiful butterfly and fly off."

"Yeah," I laughed. "I'll bet it was her way to make me feel guilty if I didn't come back to visit."

"Because she wanted to babysit for grandchildren, of course," she laughed. "Well, she seemed to have the most wonderful insight about what it's like to be a parent," said Hanna. "I'll bet you miss her."

✓ **LITERARY CHECK**
Identify a **simile** in this passage.

"She was the best mom," I said.

When we got to the gate, Robyn and Jorge were standing there, waiting to be let in. I could tell from their faces that they heard what we were saying about Mom. Robyn had an expression like she was the forgotten mother in my whole foster child story and that Hanna had jumped up a bunch of spaces in line.

That night, I went to Robyn and Jorge when they were cleaning up the dinner dishes. I told them that even though I still miss Mom and was hanging out more with Hanna than with them, they didn't need to worry. They had the most relieved reactions I've ever seen. What was funny about the whole thing was that for the first time, I felt like I wasn't the poor little foster child. I was finally helping someone feel better about something, instead of the other way around. I told them their house made a pretty good milkweed plant. And I meant it, too.

Before You Go On

1. What has changed on the milkweed plants?

2. How does Nevaeh reassure her new foster parents?

👤 On Your Own

Do you think Nevaeh is adjusting well to her new home? Explain.

Review and Practice

Reader's Theater

Act out the following scene with Jorge, Hanna, and Nevaeh.

Jorge: Hi Hanna!

Hanna: [*puts down a container of begonias and waves at Jorge and Nevaeh*]. Jorge, how are you? [*stoops down to greet Nevaeh*] This must be Nevaeh—I'm so glad to finally meet you.

Nevaeh: [*smiles politely*] Hi.

Jorge: How's the new garden? Do you think Robyn can plant some tomatoes here?

Hanna: [*smiles*] Of course. We have double the space this year, so there's undoubtedly room. [*frowning*] But tell her that tomatoes don't do great in this rainy Detroit weather, so maybe she should keep a pot or two on her porch so they can stay drier. But I'll save her a sunny spot over there.

Nevaeh: [*smiles as she thinks about her mom*] Are you growing any milkweed plants?

Jorge: [*surprised*] What?

Hanna: Milkweeds? No, Nevaeh, I haven't gotten any yet, but I was thinking of that. Last year was our first year here, so we only grew annuals in case the community didn't support the garden. But they were actually super-supportive, so this year we can add . . .

Nevaeh: [*interrupting*] Perennials.

Hanna: [*surprised*] Right!

Nevaeh: My mom used to grow a garden every year.

> ### Learning Strategy
> Speak using nonverbal cues, such as facial expressions and gestures, to show the character's feelings and actions.

Comprehension
21

Did you understand the story? If not, reread it with a partner. Then answer the questions below.

Recall

1. Who wants to plant some tomatoes?

2. What is the setting of the story?

Comprehend

3. Why is Nevaeh living with Robyn and Jorge?

4. How does Nevaeh seem to change from the beginning of the story? Explain.

Analyze

5. Why do you think the author chose the title "Milkweeds from Nevaeh?"

6. What is the main character's inner conflict? How is it resolved?

Connect

7. Would you recommend this story to others to read? Explain.

8. Describe a time in your life when you learned something. What was it? How did it make you feel?

Listening Skill

If you can't hear the speaker, you may say, "Excuse me, could you speak louder, please?"

Discussion

Discuss with a partner or in a small group.

1. Who do you think Nevaeh has the greatest bond with in her new community? Explain.

2. How would you describe Nevaeh's relationship with her new foster parents? Is it changing? Explain.

 How do you think Nevaeh is adjusting to changes in her life? Who and what is helping her adjust the most? Explain.

Response to Literature

W B
21

Write a thank-you letter from Nevaeh to Hanna. Use details and imagery from the story to help you. If possible, include a simile in your letter. Trade letters with a partner and read each other's letters aloud. Then share with the class.

Grammar

Comparison Structures: Adjectives

To compare people or things, you can use comparison structures such as comparative and superlative adjectives. A comparative adjective compares two things. A superlative adjective compares one thing to two or more things in a group. Form comparative adjectives with *-er* or *more*; form superlative adjectives with *-est* or *most*.

> These flowers are **more beautiful than** those. [after linking verb *are*]
> She seemed to have **the most wonderful** insight. [before noun *insight*]

A comparative adjective is usually followed by *than*, but if the comparison is understood, *than* is often omitted. A superlative adjective is usually preceded by *the*. Possessive pronouns can also precede superlatives.

> The garden is **drier than** last year.
> I am **younger** (than she is).
> I tossed out **the biggest** pieces of broken glass.

Practice A
22

Complete each sentence with the correct form of the comparative adjective in parentheses.

1. Oranges are _____ sweeter _____ than lemons. (sweet)

2. The black cat is _____ than the white cat. (friendly)

3. This car is _____ than our last one. (good)

4. This exercise is _____ than the first one. (easy)

5. Peg's story is more _____ than mine. (interesting)

Practice B

Complete each sentence with the correct form of the superlative adjective in parentheses.

1. My _____ oldest _____ brother lives in the city. (old)

2. The _____ way to get there is by train. (quick)

3. What do you think is the _____ place to eat? (good)

4. That is the most _____ flower I've ever seen. (beautiful)

5. My father makes the _____ cake. (sweet)

Comparison Structures: Adverbs

To compare two actions, you can use comparison structures such as comparative and superlative adverbs. For one-syllable adverbs, use *-er* and *-est*. For adverbs with two or more syllables, plus adverbs that end in *-ly*, use *more* and *most*. Some adverbs have irregular comparative and superlative forms.

Grammar Skill

Some words are both adjectives and adverbs, such as, *early / earlier / earliest* and *hard / harder / hardest.*

deeply → more → most deeply deeply	I planted my seeds **more deeply** than Isabel, but Juanita planted her seeds **most deeply**.
well → better → best	Dinner tasted **better**, but the dessert tasted the **best**.
badly → worse → worst	She felt **worse than** ever. It was **the worst** she'd ever felt.
early → earlier → earliest	We woke **earlier** than usual, but Min woke **earliest**.

Practice A
23

Complete each sentence with the correct form of the adverb in parentheses.

Example: She works ___more quickly___ (quick) than he does.

1. I study ____harder____ than my sister. (hard)
2. You can get there _____ by plane. (fast)
3. He speaks English _____ than I do. (well)
4. I'll see you _____. (late)
5. I study _____ in the library than at home. (well)

Practice B

Complete each sentence with the correct form of the adverb in parentheses.

1. She works ___more quickly___ than he does. (quickly)
2. My mother drives _____ than my father. (carefully)
3. He reacted the _____ of anyone I know. (badly)
4. She learns _____ than he does. (easily)
5. I always get there the _____. (early)

Grammar Check

✓ When forming a **superlative adverb**, when do you use *most?*

Apply

Work with a partner. Tell about something you can do well now that you couldn't in the past. Use comparative and superlative adverbs.

Example: I speak English better now than I did last year.

Writing

Describe a Place

In this unit, you have learned how to describe an event and an object. Now you will learn how to describe a place. One way to write a description of a place is to present the details in spatial order, or in order of location. For example, to describe your classroom, you might start at the back of the room and make your way toward the front, describing all the important features along the way. Words such as *inside, outside, on top of, underneath,* or *next to* can help readers visualize a place.

Writing Prompt

Write a paragraph describing a place you are familiar with, such as a room in your home, a park, or your neighborhood. List details in a graphic organizer. Present them in spatial order. Be sure to include comparison structures, such as comparative and superlative adjectives.

① **Prewrite** Begin by choosing a place to describe.
24

- Close your eyes and try to visualize the place.

- First, picture the whole scene.

- Then, visualize each part of the place, for example: the back, the middle, and the front.

- List your ideas in a graphic organizer, such as the one below.

Here's a three-column chart created by a student named Nicole.

The Garden		
Back	**Middle**	**Front**
corn stalks	tomatoes, eggplants	squash, carrots

② **Draft** Use your graphic organizer to help you write a first draft.

- Give an overview of the scene.
- Describe specific details of the place in spatial order.
- Keep in mind your purpose for writing.
- Be sure to use comparison structures correctly.

③ **Revise** Read over your draft. Look for places where the writing is unclear or needs improvement. Complete (√) the Writing Checklist to help you identify problems. Then revise your draft, using the editing and proofreading marks listed on page 401.

④ **Edit and Proofread** Check your work for errors in grammar, usage, mechanics, and spelling. Trade papers with a partner to obtain feedback. Use the Peer Review Checklist on Workbook page 24. Edit your final draft in response to feedback from your partner and your teacher.

⑤ **Publish** Prepare a clean copy of your final draft. Share your description with the class. Save your work. You'll need to refer to it in the Writing Workshop at the end of the unit.

Writing Checklist

Organization:
- ☐ I presented details in spatial order.

Word Choice:
- ☐ I used comparison structures, such as comparative and superlative adjectives correctly.

Here is Nicole's description. What does it tell us about her family?

Nicole Siley

The Garden

As I walked outside, I noticed my grandparents' garden. I noticed their garden was more beautiful than mine. There were so many colors—red, yellow, purple, green, and orange. Then I noticed how the vegetables were arranged from back to front according to the size of the plants. In the far back, there were corn stalks, the tallest plants in the garden. Next, there were the biggest tomato plants I had ever seen. They sat in the middle of the garden with the eggplants. My favorite vegetables, the squash and the carrots, were in the front rows. Looking at these vegetables made me remember all the wonderful Sunday night dinners I've shared with my family. I never imagined that looking at vegetables could trigger such pleasant memories.

Link the Readings

Critical Thinking

Look back at the readings in this unit. Think about what they have in common. They all tell about changes. Yet they do not all have the same purpose. The purpose of one reading might be to inform, while the purpose of another might be to entertain. In addition, the content of each reading relates to changes differently. Now complete the chart below.

Title of Reading	Purpose	Big Question Link
"What's for Dinner?"		It describes the ways in which new inventions and methods for growing food have changed the way we eat.
"Early Inventions"		
"Milkweeds from Nevaeh"	to entertain	

Discussion

Discuss with a partner or in a small group.

- Which invention in "What's for Dinner?" or "Early Inventions" has influenced life today the most? Are the results always positive?
- **How can change improve people's lives?** Which selection do you think answered this question the best? Explain.

Media Literacy & Projects

Work with a partner or in a small group. Choose one of these projects.

(1) Imagine you can create a dinner menu with foods from anywhere in the world. Create your perfect menu to serve to your classmates. Include an appetizer, a main course, and a dessert. Include visuals if possible. Share your menu with the class, walking them through each course and describing the food.

(2) Think of an invention that you would like to create. Illustrate your invention, showing how it works and what it does. Include descriptive labels and captions. Share your ideas with a partner.

(3) Design a vertical farm. Illustrate your farm, showing the different levels and crops that are growing. Does your farm use dirt, or is it hydroponic? Then take your classmates on a "tour," describing each level. Also explain the crop choices that you made.

(4) Create a community garden. Map out an area on posterboard. Draw and label the plants you want to include in the garden. Then take your classmates on a "tour," describing each plant.

Further Reading

Choose from these reading suggestions. Practice reading silently with increased ease for longer and longer periods.

Inventions that Changed the World, David Maule
This book looks at some of the most important inventions from ancient times to the present day. Topics include printing, mathematics, navigation, weapons, flight, communications, and computers.

City Green, DyAnne DiSalvo-Ryan
Marcy lives in the city near an empty lot. One day she has an idea to start a community garden. Not only does her idea improve the empty land, but it helps her neighborhood as well.

Genetically Modified Food, Nigel Hawkes
This book examines the relationship between people and nature. It explores the benefits to humans of natural resources and the damage that can be done. It has lots of "green" facts to make readers think.

The Story of Thomas Alva Edison, Margaret Cousins
This is the life story of the man who brought us the phonograph, motion pictures, and the electric light bulb—revolutionary inventions that forever changed the way we live.

Listening & Speaking Workshop

Team Presentation

You will give a team presentation describing a person, place, object, or experience that has changed your school or community for the better.

① Think About It

Look back over the readings in this unit. Talk in teams about change. Think of changes that have occurred in your school or community recently.

Work together to develop a list of beneficial changes that have taken place, for example:

- The new hire of an inspirational teacher
- A new community center
- The purchase of new school equipment
- The development of a new recycling plan

② Gather and Organize Information

As a team, choose a topic from your list. Then write down everything you know about that topic. Include any questions you have about it.

Research Use the library and/or the internet to get more information. You may also wish to interview school or community leaders or fellow students. Remember to use appropriate language during your interview. If you are speaking to a person you have not met before or the interview occurs in a serious setting, use formal language. Formal language includes complete sentences, correct grammar, and few contractions. If you are speaking to someone you know well, use informal language. Informal language includes more conversational words, simple phrases and sentences, and contractions. Take notes on what you find.

Order Your Notes Share your notes with the team. Discuss how the notes you've gathered could best be used in the presentation to create a picture in the minds of the audience. Write the notes in a graphic organizer, such as a T-chart (to show before and after, for example). Be sure to include sensory details. Choose a logical order in which to present this information.

Use Visuals Make or use existing visual aids such as photos, maps, and illustrations to enhance your presentation. Make sure they are large enough for audience members to see easily.

③ Practice and Present

Keep your graphic organizer nearby as you practice your presentation as a group. Speak clearly and confidently, and use your visual aids to support key ideas. Make sure each team member has a part, and work on making smooth transitions from one speaker to the next. Keep practicing until you no longer need to look at your graphic organizer.

Deliver Your Group Presentation Look at your audience as you speak. Emphasize key ideas by pointing to your visual aids. Slow down when you come to the most important points, or restate them at the end of your presentation.

④ Evaluate the Presentation

You will improve your skills as a speaker and a listener by evaluating each group presentation you give and hear. Complete (√) this checklist to help you judge your group's presentation and the group presentations of others.

- ☐ Was the team's topic clear?
- ☐ Did the speakers use sensory details to help listeners create a picture in their minds?
- ☐ Could you hear and understand each speaker easily?
- ☐ Were the transitions between speakers smooth and logical?
- ☐ Are there ways each speaker could improve the presentation?

Speaking Skill

Request assistance. Ask a friend or classmate to listen and give feedback as your team practices. Or record your rehearsal, if possible. Listen to the recording together, and find places where you can improve your presentation.

Listening Skill

As you listen, identify the team's topic. Listen for the general meaning, main ideas, and important details. After each presentation, exchange this information with a partner to confirm that you have understood it correctly.

Take notes as you listen. Write down key details, and use them to picture what the speakers are describing.

Strengthen Your Social Language

Describing a process means communicating well. Go to your Digital Resources and do the activity for this unit. This activity will help you expand your vocabulary using high-frequency English words necessary for identifying and describing people, places, objects, and processes.

Writing Workshop

Descriptive Essay

Write a Descriptive Essay

In this workshop, you will write a descriptive essay. An essay is a group of paragraphs that focus on one topic. Most essays begin with a paragraph that introduces the topic. Two or more body paragraphs develop the topic by adding ideas and details. A concluding paragraph sums up what the essay is about.

Writing Prompt

Write a five-paragraph descriptive essay about an experience or change in your life that had a big effect on you. Describe the places, people, and events surrounding this experience. Include adjectives, similes, and sensory details that will help the reader understand your experience. Use sequence words to show what happened and how you changed after this experience.

① **Prewrite** Review the paragraphs you wrote in this unit. Now brainstorm ideas. What experiences had an impact on your life, feelings, or ideas? You might write about meeting a new friend, moving to a new place, or trying a new activity. Choose an experience that you can describe clearly and vividly.

In your notebook, answer these questions:

- What was the main experience?
- What were some important details?
- What effect did this experience have on me?

After selecting a topic, use a graphic organizer such as a word web or a sequence-of-events chart to help you develop your essay. A student named Nicole wrote about going to middle school. She used a word web to gather ideas and details for her essay.

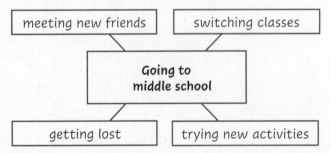

(2) Draft Use your graphic organizer and the model on pages 57–58 to help you write a first draft

- Include an introductory paragraph, three body paragraphs, and a concluding paragraph.

- Use sequence words to show order of events.

- Describe your feelings and explain how they changed.

(3) Revise Read over your draft. Think about how well you have addressed questions of purpose, audience, and genre. Your purpose is to describe. Is your description vivid? Does it help the reader to imagine your experience?

Keep these questions in mind as you revise your draft. Complete (√) the Writing Checklist below to help you identify additional issues that may need revision. Mark your changes on your draft using the editing and proofreading marks listed on page 401.

Learning Strategy

Monitor your written language production. Using a writing checklist will help you assess your work. Evaluate your essay to make sure that your message is clear and easy to understand.

Six Traits of Writing Checklist

☐ **Ideas:** Does my essay describe an experience that had an important effect on me?

☐ **Organization:** Are my ideas organized logically?

☐ **Voice:** Does my writing express who I am?

☐ **Word Choice:** Do I use words that describe events and feelings?

☐ **Sentence Fluency:** Do my sentences flow smoothly?

☐ **Conventions:** Does my writing follow the rules of grammar, usage, and mechanics?

Here are the revisions Nicole plans to make to her first draft.

A Big Step

In my town, three elementary schools ~~go~~ [combine] into one middle school. I

used to think my elementary school was the larg~~er~~ [est] school in town,

with the most students. [Now] I realize that the middle school is so much

larger! Going there has been a [new] exciting experience that has

changed me in many ways.

[At first,] I had feelings of concern about going to middle school. I ~~worried~~ [worried]

about the responsibility of getting my own locker and remembering

the combination. I also ~~worried~~ [felt nervous] about getting lost There were so many [busy]

classrooms and [long] hallways! Getting lost is a scary thing to think about [when you're young].

For a while, other things bothered me too. There were lots of

strangers. [When I started,] I didn't know many of the students or any of the teachers.

Also I had to switch classes for the first time, so I had to learn the

schedule. Different classes began on different days at different times.

It seemed very confusing!

[Finally,] I realized that everything was going to be fine. The teachers in

the school helped us find our way during the first week, so we didn't

get too lost. I began to like having my own locker to keep my stuff [private and safe].

switching classes gave everybody a chance to meet up with old friends

and to make new friends from other schools. [Also there are tons of fun clubs to join.]

Revised to improve word choice and correct use of superlative adjective.

Revised to include sequence word and correct order of adjectives.

Revised to include a transition word and to correct spelling according to spelling patterns for simple past.

Revised to improve specific details.

Revised to improve flow of ideas.

Revised to add a sequence word and specific details.

The step from elementary school to middle school changed me. I adjusted very well to the challenges. I learned that students are given more freedom as they get older but that they still have people there. *to watch over them and help them*

Best of all, middle school expanded my horizons by allowing me to experience new activities and to meet new friends.

(4) Edit and Proofread Check your work for errors in grammar, usage, mechanics, and spelling. Then trade essays with a partner and complete (√) the Peer Review Checklist below to give each other constructive feedback. Edit your final draft in response to feedback from your partner and your teacher.

W B
25

Peer Review Checklist

- ☐ Does the first paragraph introduce the topic?
- ☐ Does the concluding paragraph sum up the main ideas?
- ☐ Does the essay describe the experience clearly?
- ☐ Is the description organized chronologically?
- ☐ Is there a development in the writer's feelings before and after the experience?
- ☐ Is it clear how the experience changed the writer?
- ☐ Could changes be made to improve the essay?

Here are the changes Nicole decided to make to her final draft as a result of her peer review.

Nicole Siley

A Big Step

In my town, three elementary schools combine into one middle school. I used to think my elementary school was the largest school in town, with the most students. Now I realize that the middle school is so

much larger! Going there has been an exciting new experience that
has changed me in many ways.

At first, I had feelings of concern about going to middle school.
I worried about the responsibility of getting my own locker and
remembering the combination. I also felt nervous about getting lost.
There were so many busy classrooms and long hallways! Getting lost
is a scary thing to think about when you're young.

Revised to correct an error in mechanics.

For a while, other things bothered me, too. There were lots of
strangers. When I started, I didn't know many of the students or any
of the teachers. Also I had to switch classes for the first time, so I
had to learn the schedule. It seemed very confusing! Different classes
began on different days at different times.

Finally, I realized that everything was going to be fine. The teachers
in the school helped us find our way during the first week, so we didn't
get too lost. I began to like having my own locker to keep my stuff
private and safe. switching classes gave everybody a chance to meet
up with old friends and to make new friends from other schools. Also,
there are many tons of fun clubs to join.

Revised to improve word choice and to correct errors in mechanics.

The step from elementary school to middle school changed me. I
adjusted very well to the challenges. I learned that students are given
more freedom as they get older, but that they still have people there
to watch over them and help them. Best of all, middle school expanded
my horizons by allowing me to experience new activities and to meet
new friends.

(5) **Publish** Prepare a clean copy of your final draft. Share your
descriptive essay with the class.

26

Test Preparation

Practice

Read the following test sample. Study the tips in the boxes. Work with a partner to answer the questions.

Jing and Sarah are in Mrs. Sampson's class. They have to do a report about where refugees settle in the United States. Jing is very excited when he finds this chart. He thinks it will help them for the report.

Refugee Settlement by State in 2009

State	Rank	Number of Refugees
Arizona	4	4,320
California	1	11,278
Florida	5	4,193
Michigan	6	3,500
New York	3	4,412
Texas	2	8,212

1 Which state receives the most refugees?
- **A** Arizona
- **B** California
- **C** New York
- **D** Texas

2 Which state is ranked third?
- **A** Texas
- **B** Michigan
- **C** Florida
- **D** New York

3 Who wants Sarah to do a report?
- **A** Jing
- **B** Her father
- **C** The class
- **D** Mrs. Sampson

Taking Tests
You will often take tests that help show what you know. Study the tips below to help you improve your test-taking skills.

Tip
Eliminate answers that you know are wrong. Look at the remaining answers. Choose the best answer from those that are left.

Tip
Review the test when you are finished. You may find questions you skipped or mistakes you made.

27–30

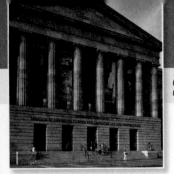

Invention and Change

The United States has always been a country of invention and change. When the first European settlers arrived in the 1500s, they called their new homeland the New World. Since then, the country has grown and changed in ways the first settlers could never have imagined. The theme of change runs throughout the work of many American artists.

Hans Hofmann, *Fermented Soil* (1965)

In *Fermented Soil*, Hans Hofmann did not paint faces or objects that you would recognize. Instead, he used thick and thin brushstrokes. He also used the flat edge of a knife to apply layers of color. Hofmann purposely used paints made from colors that come from the earth. Then he layered these colors one on top of another until he created a field of yellows, golds, and browns. Hofmann even tried to "turn" the paint with the flat knife as though he were turning dirt. The end result is a "garden" of paint on a huge canvas.

▲ Hans Hofmann, *Fermented Soil*, 1965, oil, 48 x 60 in., Smithsonian American Art Museum

When something *ferments*, it breaks down and then changes into something new. Hofmann called this work *Fermented Soil* because he began with simple brown paint. Then he had the brown paint "ferment" with other layers of color until it became something new.

▲ Samuel Colman, *Storm King on the Hudson*, 1866, oil,
32⅛ x 59⅞ in., Smithsonian American Art Museum

Samuel Colman, *Storm King on the Hudson* (1866)

In *Storm King on the Hudson*, Samuel Colman shows the
new world of steam-powered engines. These great ships
arrived on American rivers in the mid-1800s. On the left
side of this painting, steam-powered boats move down the
mighty Hudson River in New York State. The rowboats in
their path look very small and weak. In the distance, on the
right side of the canvas, the white sails of several sailboats
stand out against the sides of Storm King Mountain. Colman
wanted to show the two worlds that existed on the Hudson
River at the time: the new and the old, or the new steam-
powered ships versus boats powered by people, such as the
sailboat and rowboat.

But this change came with a price, as Colman shows in his
painting. Dirty air from the smokestacks on the steamers fills
the sky. The artist shows this in contrast with the clean white
color of the clouds in the background. Sometimes change
also signals the end of good things.

Hofmann's work captures the exciting side of change,
while Colman's painting shows both the good and the bad.
Even though Colman's painting is more realistic, both artists
capture a tension that all of us connect with change.

Discuss What You Learned

1. In what way are these artworks
   about inventing something new?

2. How do both Colman and Hofmann
   show tension in their paintings?

BIG QUESTION
How could you capture the
idea of change in an artwork?
Explain.

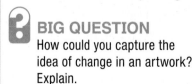

31–32

Unit 2

What are the benefits of facing challenges?

This unit is about challenges. You will read texts that describe people who faced difficult challenges and will tell how these experiences changed their lives. Reading, writing, and talking about these topics will help you practice the language you need to use in school.

Reading 1
Biography/Science

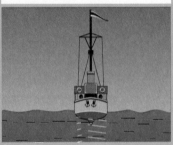

- "Deep Mapping"
- "You Can Help the Oceans"

Reading Strategy
Recognize cause and effect

Reading 2
Personal Narrative/Poem

- "Five New Words at a Time" by Yu-Lan (Mary) Ying
- "Quilt" by Janet S. Wong

Reading Strategy
Identify problems and solutions

Reading 3
Short Story/Science

- "A Dark Day with Bright Spots"
- "Do This, Not That!"

Reading Strategy
Predict

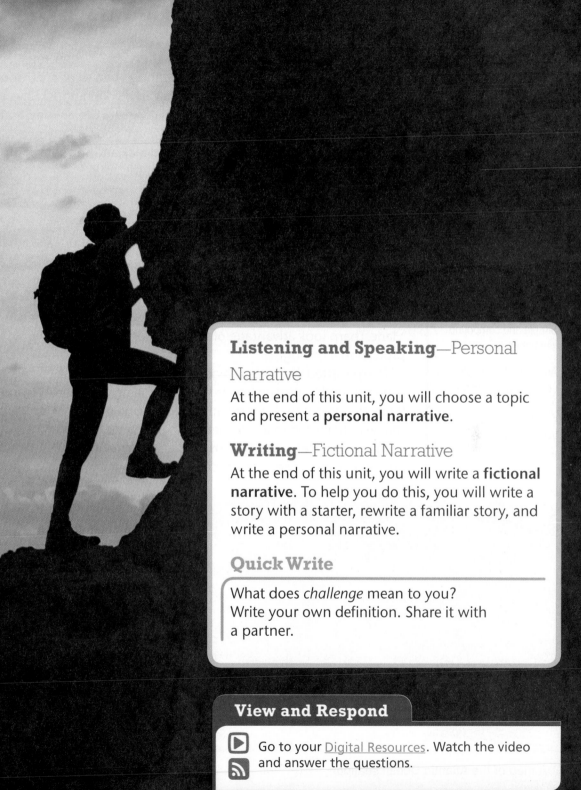

Listening and Speaking—Personal Narrative

At the end of this unit, you will choose a topic and present a **personal narrative**.

Writing—Fictional Narrative

At the end of this unit, you will write a **fictional narrative**. To help you do this, you will write a story with a starter, rewrite a familiar story, and write a personal narrative.

Quick Write

What does *challenge* mean to you? Write your own definition. Share it with a partner.

View and Respond

Go to your <u>Digital Resources</u>. Watch the video and answer the questions.

Prepare to Read

What You Will Learn

Reading

- Vocabulary building: *Context, dictionary skills, word study*

- Reading strategy: *Recognize cause and effect*

- Text type: *Informational text (science)*

Grammar

- Simple and compound sentences

- Agreement in simple and compound sentences

Writing

- Write a story with a starter

❓ THE BIG QUESTION

What are the benefits of facing challenges? When you "face a challenge," you try something even though you might fail. Some challenges are worth accepting; others can be dangerous. Have you ever accepted a difficult challenge? What was it? Did anyone try to stop you? Was the outcome beneficial? Share your experience with your peers and teacher. Ask for their feedback and support in order to develop background knowledge about this topic.

Build Background

"Deep Mapping" is a biographical science article about a woman who mapped the ocean floor.

In the 1940s, many scientific fields were closed to women. But after World War II started and many men were involved in the war effort, opportunities opened up for women. A woman named Marie Tharp took advantage of this and studied to become a professional geologist.

Tharp started working as a geologist for an oil company, but soon decided to pursue her dream of mapping the entire ocean floor. Her dream took her on an extraordinary journey of discovery that eventually led to a complete map of the seafloor in 1977.

"You Can Help the Oceans," is an informational text about how to conserve ocean resources.

Reading Skill

To help you understand the challenges that Tharp and her colleagues faced, look at the seafloor map of the Atlantic Ocean. What is most noticeable or surprising?

▲ A map of the Atlantic Ocean seafloor

Vocabulary

Listening and Speaking: Key Words

Read aloud and listen to these sentences. Use the context to figure out the meaning of the highlighted words. Use a dictionary to check your answers. Then write each word and its meaning in your notebook.

Key Words

accurate
continuous
data
depth
determine
theory

1. Her dream was to complete an accurate map of the seafloor, correct in every way and actually showing what it looked like.

2. An accurate map of the seafloor was only possible by taking continuous measurements, not one at a time.

3. Using data from deep-sea cameras, they worked together to locate airplanes that had crashed and sunk to the bottom of the ocean.

4. In order to map the ocean floor, it was necessary to take depth measurements of the water from the surface to the bottom.

5. Technology was developed to determine the exact measurements of any part of the ocean.

6. The theory of continental drift tried to explain the movement of Earth's continents and was very controversial.

Practice

WB 33

Write the sentences in your notebook. Choose a key word from the box above to complete each sentence. Then take turns reading the sentences aloud with a partner.

1. That nonstop and _____ music is so annoying!

2. Your figures don't add up. These results are not _____.

3. Is the _____ at the shallow end of the pool three feet?

4. Her idea has not been proven. It's still just a(n) _____.

5. Were you able to _____ how long it will take to get there?

6. I'm sorry to say that the _____ we collected doesn't explain what happened.

▶ The sign indicates the depth of the swimming pool.

Listening and Speaking: Academic Words

Study the **purple** words and their meanings. You will find these words useful when talking and writing about informational texts. Write each word and its meaning in your notebook, then say the words aloud with a partner. After you read "Deep Mapping" and "You Can Help the Oceans," try to use these words to respond to the texts.

Academic Words

accompanied
aid
challenge
code

accompanied = went somewhere with someone	➡	Marie Tharp, **accompanied** by Bruce Heezen, proved that the ocean floor is not a featureless blank.
aid = help or support given to someone	➡	She wouldn't have been successful without the **aid** of others.
challenge = something difficult that you need skill or ability to do	➡	Marie Tharp faced many **challenges** because women were not treated equally in the scientific community.
code = a way to use words, letters, or numbers to record information	➡	We need to interpret the **code** to understand the information.

Practice
34

Work with a partner to answer these questions. Try to include the **purple** word in your answer. Write the sentences in your notebook.

1. Who **accompanied** you on your first day of school?
2. What kind of **aid** could you give a friend preparing for a test?
3. What is a **challenge** that you have faced in your life?
4. Why is it sometimes not possible to understand **code**?

◀ Being able to write computer code is a valuable skill.

Word Study: Words with *ch* and *tch*

Ch and *tch* are consonant clusters. They sound the same but are spelled differently. Look at the words *which* and *scratch*. The final sound in each word is the same, but the words are spelled differently. English words may begin with the letters *ch*, but never with the letters *tch*. Read the examples in the chart below and pronounce each word aloud.

Spelling	Initial Position	Final Position
ch	change challenge check	reach research attach
tch		catch match

Practice 35

Fill in the missing letters of each word and check the spelling in a dictionary. Then read the sentences aloud with a partner.

1. It can be a real ———— allenge to rea ———— your goals.

2. The results of the resear ———— need to be ———— ecked again for accuracy.

3. There was one big ca ————. Tharp wasn't allowed to go on the expedition.

4. I'm going to ———— ange the picture and atta ———— it to the next page.

Reading Strategy   **Recognize Cause and Effect**

Recognizing a cause-and-effect pattern can help you better understand a text, especially informational texts. Why an event happens is a cause. What happens as a result of a cause is an effect. To recognize causes and effects, follow these steps:

- As you read, look for events in Marie Tharp's life. These may be causes. Look for things that happened as a result. These are the effects.

- Look for words and phrases the author uses to talk about causes and effects, for example, *because*, *so*, and *as a result*.

  As you read "Deep Mapping," look for causes and effects. Make sure you understand the relationship between each cause and its effect.

36

Set a purpose for reading As you read, think about the enormous challenges involved in exploring and protecting the ocean. Explorer Marie Tharp faced additional challenges because of her gender. What keeps people working toward a goal?

Deep Mapping

For thousands of years, maps only provided details about land features. Mapmakers worked hard to plot valleys, hills, mountains, and plateaus. They depicted the detailed outlines of lakes, rivers, and streams. But when they reached the oceans, mappers simply gave up. They drew huge, flat, blue spaces. This meant that maps ignored almost two-thirds of planet Earth. However, Marie Tharp, accompanied by Bruce Heezen, proved that the ocean floor is not a featureless blank. Their discoveries changed the way people think about our planet—and about the role of women in science.

Reading Skill

To help you understand the reading, study the title and headings. This will help you identify the most important ideas.

Listening Skill

As you listen to the audio, look at the pictures on pages 68–73. Use these visuals to help explain new words or ideas. Discuss these words or concepts with a partner to gain understanding.

PHYSIOGRAPHIC DIAGRAM OF THE
SOUTH ATLANTIC OCEAN
BY BRUCE C. HEEZEN AND MARIE THARP
Lamont-Doherty Geological Observatory, Columbia University   United States Naval Oceanographic Office

◀ Tharp and Heezen discovered that the ocean floor is full of ridges and valleys.

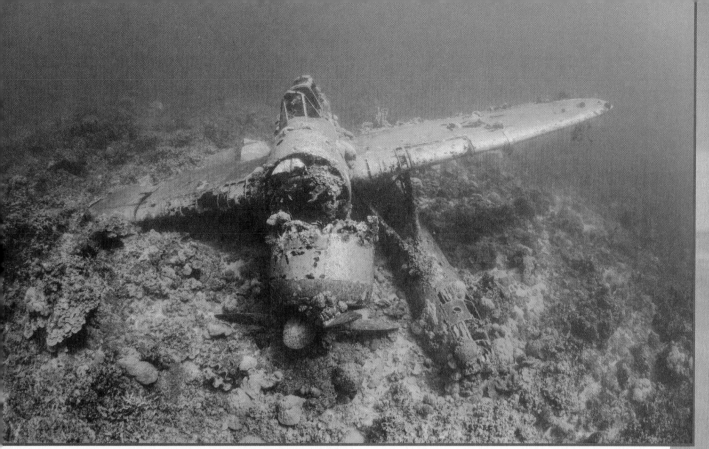

▲ Tharp and Heezen's original job was to find aircraft that had crashed into the sea.

From Land to Sea

Born in 1920, Marie Tharp faced many challenges because women were not treated equally as scientists. Throughout her career, she had to overcome unfair rules and prejudices.

When Tharp was in college, many scientific fields were closed to women. Then World War II started. Because many men were involved in the war, some **geology** departments opened their doors to women for the first time. Tharp seized the opportunity. Soon, she became a professional geologist.

At first, she worked for an oil company. But she wasn't satisfied there. When she began looking for other work, she met Bruce Heezen. They became partners on an exciting new research project. Using data from deep-sea cameras, Tharp and Heezen's job was to locate airplanes that had crashed and sunk to the bottom of the ocean.

Tharp realized that the bottom of the ocean was an unexplored world waiting to be discovered. In 1947, she began to work with Heezen on a daunting project: mapping the entire ocean floor. Tharp knew that the task would be difficult, but she also knew it would be worthwhile. Looking back, she said, "It was a once-in-a-lifetime—a once-in-the-history-of-the-world—opportunity for anyone, but especially for a woman in the 1940s."

---

geology, the study of Earth and rocks

Before You Go On

1. What were some of the challenges Marie Tharp faced?

2. According to the article, what event opened doors for women at the time?

 On Your Own

Do you think Tharp will be able to meet the challenges she set for herself? Explain.

The Power of the Ping

Tharp and Heezen needed to collect an enormous amount of new data. At the time, the only parts of the ocean floor that had been studied were areas near the coasts. They wanted to extend this knowledge to cover the whole ocean.

Their plan was ambitious. They would gather data from research boats crossing the oceans, taking depth measurements called soundings. They planned to use a new invention called a continuous echo sounder. Early depth measurements were taken using ropes with heavy weights attached. The echo sounder used electricity instead. The machine sent out an electronic sound signal called a ping. At the same time the ping went out, a four-inch strip of paper was spinning on the boat. A **stylus** marked the time the ping left the machine. The sound traveled down through the water and, when it reached the ocean floor, an echo of the sound returned to the surface. The stylus burned the paper with an electric spark to mark the time the echo returned. Pings were sent continuously as the boat moved, creating a paper code that needed to be interpreted to determine the ocean's depth at each point.

Tharp and Heezen planned to take soundings across every ocean. However, there was one big catch. They had to split up in order to begin because women were not allowed on research ships. So Heezen gathered information at sea. He then sent it to Tharp, who began the difficult job of making sense out of the **raw data**.

---

stylus, a needle
raw data, information collected directly from a source or study

▲ An echo sounder measures water depth by sending down an electronic sound and recording how long it takes for the echo to return.

Reading Skill

Take turns reading the article aloud with a partner. As you listen, use the visuals to help clarify words or ideas. Discuss these words or ideas with your partner to gain understanding.

A Deeply Surprising Discovery

Tharp spent countless hours "plotting, drawing, checking, correcting, redrawing, and rechecking" the data. Nonetheless, the picture Tharp began to form of the ocean floor was far from clear, so the results were often frustrating. After years of work, Tharp still had a confusing **hodgepodge** of results that showed disconnected chunks of the North Atlantic floor. She could make educated guesses about what the ocean looked like in the missing sections, but this solution did not satisfy her. She wanted to produce a complete and accurate map of the underwater world.

By 1952, Tharp's study of this confusing network of ocean soundings led her to a surprising discovery. The data showed a vast underwater opening in the Atlantic Ocean. This **rift** was strong evidence for the theory of continental drift. This theory suggests that Earth's continents move very slowly, appearing to wander across the planet's surface.

Many scientists, including Bruce Heezen, didn't believe this theory. Tharp was excited to share her findings with Heezen, but he dismissed her interpretation as "girl talk." Tharp didn't give in. Eventually, Heezen realized that she was correct. Their data clearly showed a gigantic ridge system that extended 40,000 miles through all the world's oceans. Their work helped convince people to accept continental drift.

---

hodgepodge, a confused mixture or jumble
rift, a deep break in Earth's crust

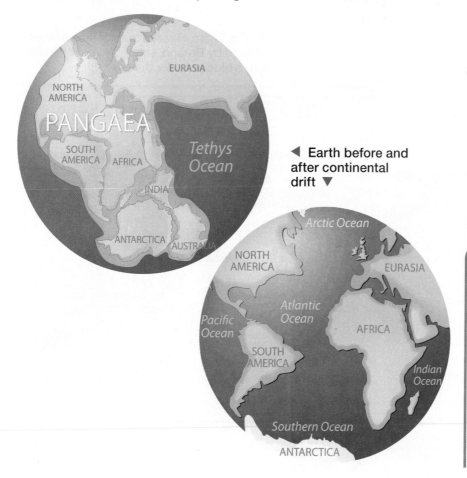

Earth before and after continental drift ▼

Before You Go On

1. What technology did the researchers use to aid their mapping?

2. What do you think is an "educated guess"?

On Your Own

What qualities about Tharp do you think contributed to her success? Explain.

An Artist Improves the Ocean Map

At last, Tharp and Heezen had enough data. They could plot a complete map of Earth's oceans. But they wanted their map to be as attractive as it was accurate. As a result, they sought the aid of Heinrich Berann.

Berann's career as a map artist would never have happened if it weren't for another bold young woman. His young daughter was disappointed by the maps she saw published in the popular magazine *National Geographic*. She decided to write a bold letter. "I've been looking at your maps," she wrote, "and my father can paint better than you can." Her letter was persuasive enough that the magazine's editors went to Austria to see Berann's art. They were so impressed, they hired him to paint for the magazine.

Berann's art was a perfect match for Tharp and Heezen's science.

A Map Changes the World

Marie Tharp's dedication proved that maps don't just describe the world. They have the power to change it. She and Heezen published a complete map of the seafloor in 1977, and people were amazed.

Looking back on her extraordinary life, Tharp wrote, "The whole world was spread out before me (or at least, the 70 percent of it covered by oceans). I had a blank canvas to fill with extraordinary possibilities, a fascinating jigsaw puzzle to piece together: mapping the world's vast hidden seafloor."

▼ The Tharp-Heezen map of the seafloor, painted by Berann, shows the spectacular forms hidden under the sea.

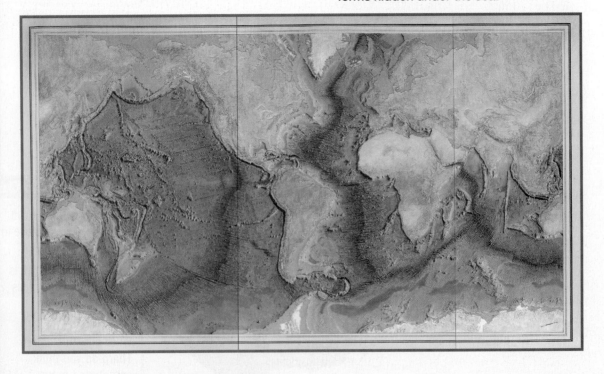

▲ Cleaning the ocean can save sea life.

You Can Help the Oceans

Marie Tharp recognized the importance of oceans. She knew that they cover 71% of Earth's surface and contain 97% of Earth's water. Her mapping helped us understand this vast resource. Today, young people around the world are working together to make sure the oceans stay safe and clean.

In Hawaii, a group of young visitors decided not to spend their vacation lying on the beach all day and playing in the surf. Instead, they joined shore clean-up crews to clear away plastic, netting, and other waste. Thanks to their hard work, the beaches were cleaner and safer for both people and animals.

Plastic in the ocean is a big problem. Experts estimate there are about 46,000 pieces of plastic in every square mile of ocean. The result is deadly. Each year, about 10,000 marine animals get tangled in this debris and die. Some young people are working hard to solve the plastic problem.

After seeing the problem firsthand, a sixteen-year-old inventor came up with a daring solution. He dreams of using ocean currents to help clean up the ocean. He founded a research team that hopes to use huge floating filters to remove plastic from the water.

Other young people focus on education. They know that the best way to keep oceans clean is not to pollute them in the first place. In Hong Kong, one class created posters to encourage people to stop using plastic shopping bags.

What will you do to protect the ocean?

Before You Go On

1. Why did the mapping scientists seek the aid of Heinrich Berann?

2. What is the young inventor's idea for cleaning up the oceans?

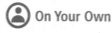 On Your Own

Why do you think people are so curious about the ocean and try so hard to protect it? Explain.

Review and Practice

Comprehension
37

Recall

1. How did mapmakers show the oceans before Tharp and Heezen's work?

2. What did Marie Tharp and Bruce Heezen do on their first project together?

Comprehend

3. What were some of the **challenges** for a woman scientist in the 1940s?

4. Why did Tharp and Heezen want to explore the oceans beyond areas near the coasts?

▲ Research ships use echo sounders to map the seafloor.

Analyze

5. How do you think the author felt about the kinds of decisions Tharp and Berann's daughter made? Explain.

6. In the first years of the mapping project, why was it necessary to make educated guesses?

Connect

7. Which of Marie Tharp's challenges was the greatest? Explain.

8. Would you recommend this article to others to read? Why or why not?

In Your Own Words

In your notebook, make a chart like the one below. Write the main idea of each section of the article. Then use this information to summarize it for a classmate. The first one is done for you.

Text Feature and Title	Main Idea
Introduction: Deep Mapping	Marie Tharp and Bruce Heezen proved that the same features we see on land are also under the ocean.
Heading: From Land to Sea	
Heading: The Power of the Ping	
Heading: A Deeply Surprising Discovery	
Heading: An Artist Improves the Ocean Map	
Heading: A Map Changes the World	
Sidebar: You Can Help the Oceans	

Discussion

Discuss with a partner or in a small group.

1. What character traits do you think were most important to do what Tharp and Heezen were able to do? Why?

2. What do you think Tharp's most important contribution to the field of science was? Explain.

 What are the benefits of facing challenges? How did Tharp benefit from facing the challenges she did? How did others? Explain.

Listening Skill

Listen carefully to your classmates. Identify the important ideas. Retell these ideas in your own words to confirm that you have understood them correctly.

Read for Fluency

It is often easier to read a text if you understand the difficult words and phrases. Work with a partner. Choose a paragraph from the reading. Identify the words and phrases you do not know or have trouble pronouncing. Look up the difficult words in a dictionary.

Take turns pronouncing the words and phrases with your partner. If necessary, ask your teacher to model the correct pronunciation. Then take turns reading the paragraph aloud and giving each other feedback.

Extension

WB
37

Work with a partner to write a front-page news headline and article about Tharp's achievement. Use an attention-grabbing headline, such as "New York Woman Maps Ocean Floors." Be sure to answer the 5Ws: *Who? What? Where? When? Why?* When you are satisfied with your article, share it with the class. Arrange your articles for the front page of a newspaper on a bulletin board.

Learning Strategy

To better acquire and understand new academic language, use and reuse these words in meaningful ways in your writing.

Grammar

Simple and Compound Sentences

A complete sentence has a subject and a predicate. The subject is what or whom the sentence is about. The predicate tells something about the subject and contains either an action verb or a linking verb.

A simple sentence contains a subject and a predicate. A simple sentence may also contain an object, a predicate adjective or predicate noun, prepositional phrases, adverbs, or adjectives.

action verb		prepositional phrase		linking verb	adjective	prepositional
subject	object			noun	adverb	phrase
They explored the outlines of lakes, rivers, and streams.				His daughter was very disappointed by the maps.		

A compound sentence joins two simple sentences or independent clauses with a conjunction. Use a comma when joining the clauses.

> They published a map of the seafloor in 1977, **and** people were amazed.
> She began looking for other work, **but** then she met Bruce Heezen.

Practice A
38

Copy the pairs of simple sentences below into your notebook. Rewrite them as compound sentences, using the conjunction in parentheses.

1. Tharp worked for an oil company. She wasn't satisfied there. (but)
   Tharp worked for an oil company, but she wasn't satisfied there.

2. The sound traveled through the water. An echo returned to the surface. (and)

3. Tharp was excited to share her findings with Heezen. He dismissed her interpretation as "girl talk." (but)

4. They wanted an attractive map. They sought help from an artist. (so)

Practice B
38

Complete the sentences with *and* or *but*. Use a comma when necessary. Identify each sentence as *simple (S)* or *compound (C)*.

1. They didn't know the exact depth _____ they knew it was more than a kilometer. _____

2. The noise was very loud _____ continuous. _____

3. She had a theory _____ presented it to us. _____

Agreement in Simple and Compound Sentences

In a sentence, the verb must agree in number with the subject. If the subject is singular, then the verb must be singular. If the subject is plural, then the verb must be plural. Be sure you are consistently using the correct form of the verb (present, past, etc.).

> singular subject and verb
>
> **SIMPLE SENTENCE: Her letter was** persuasive enough.
>
> singular subject and verb, simple past   plural subject and verb, simple past
>
> **COMPOUND SENTENCE: Tharp was** in college, but many scientific **fields were** closed.

Be careful that all nouns and pronouns agree. Each pronoun should correctly refer to its antecedent, or the noun that comes before it.

> **Tharp** was excited to share **her findings** with **Heezen**, but **he** dismissed **them** as "girl talk."
> [*Her* refers to antecedent *Tharp*; *he* refers to antecedent *Heezen*; *them* refers to antecedent *findings*.]

Practice A 39

Write the word in parentheses that best completes each sentence.

1. We opened _____our_____ books. (our / my)
2. When _____ reached the oceans, the mappers simply gave up. (he / they)
3. Women _____ not treated equally. (was / were)
4. She faced _____ own challenges. (her / his)

Practice B 39

Complete the sentences with the pronoun that matches its antecedent.

1. The researchers presented _____their_____ findings.
2. My friend Cathy left _____ bag at my house.
3. I was surprised that the teacher couldn't remember _____ name.
4. The echo sounder presents the data on _____ screen.

Grammar Skill

Sometimes a subject is separated from a verb by a phrase or clause: The **windows** on the house were **broken**. Identify the subject and make sure it agrees in number with the verb.

Grammar Check

✓ What should verbs always agree with in **simple** and **compound** **sentences**?

Apply

Write four sentences describing a member of your family. Then tell a partner about the person. Be sure your sentences follow the rules of agreement you have learned.
Example: My cousin Amelia is a ballet dancer. Her . . .

Writing

Write a Story with a Starter

At the end of this unit you will write a fictional narrative. To do this, you will need to learn some of the skills writers use to write narratives, or stories. An important aspect of a story is its setting. To describe a setting, you need to include details about the time (year, month, time of day) and place (country, state, neighborhood, home) of a story's action.

Writing Prompt

Write a fictional narrative. Begin your story with the following starter: *The view was unlike anything I had ever seen before.* Use simple and compound sentences that describe the scene and action in the story.

(1) **Prewrite** Begin by thinking of a setting for your story.

- Close your eyes and visualize the setting: Where is it? What time of day or night is it? What can you see?

- Name the setting in the top bubble of your word web.

- Add details about the time and the place in the lower bubbles.
  40

Here's a word web created by a student named Madeline. She used this story starter: *The storm had closed in on us without warning.* Then she used a word web to organize details about the setting.

Setting
the top of Mt. Everest

Details about time
without warning, only minutes before, now, just minutes later

Details about place
the summit of the mountain, the sun was shining brightly, the amazing view from the top of the world, the icy wind was howling, the snow made it impossible to see

2 Draft Use your word web to help you write a first draft.

- Use the story starter to lead into the description of the setting.
- Describe the place and the time.
- Use simple and compound sentences correctly.

3 Revise Read over your draft. Look for places where the writing is unclear or needs improvement. Complete (√) the Writing Checklist to check your work. Then revise your draft, using the editing and proofreading marks listed on page 401.

4 Edit and Proofread Check your work for errors in grammar, usage, mechanics, and spelling. Trade papers with a partner to obtain feedback. Use the Peer Review Checklist on Workbook page 40. Edit your final draft in response to feedback from your partner and your teacher.

5 Publish Prepare a clean copy of your final draft. Share your story with the class. Save your work. You'll need to refer to it in the Writing Workshop at the end of the unit.

Writing Checklist

Ideas:
☐ I used the story starter.

Word Choice:
☐ I used words that clearly establish the setting.

Conventions:
☐ I used correct agreement of subjects and verbs in simple and compound sentences.

Here is Madeline's story. Notice how she establishes the setting of her story.

Madeline Shaw

View from the Top

The storm had closed in on us without warning. We had reached the summit of the mountain only minutes before, and the sun was shining brightly. All of the climbers were exhausted, but so happy to have completed the brutal climb up Mt. Everest. Surprisingly, there was silence as everyone marveled at the amazing view from the top of the world and what we had accomplished. Now, just minutes later, everything had changed. The icy wind was howling and the snow made it impossible to see more than a few steps ahead. We could feel a sense of panic growing among us as the reality of our situation became clear. Would we ever make it back down the mountain?

Prepare to Read

What You Will Learn

Reading
- Vocabulary building: *Literary terms, word study*
- Reading strategy: *Identify problems and solutions*
- Text type: *Literature (personal narrative and poetry)*

Grammar
- Gerunds as subjects and subject complements
- Gerunds as objects

Writing
- Rewrite a familiar story

THE BIG QUESTION

What are the benefits of facing challenges? Moving to a new city, state, or country can be overwhelming. You have to say good-bye to your friends, you might have to go to a new school, and you might live among people who speak a different language or have different beliefs or customs from your own.

Have you ever moved to a new place? Where did you move? What challenges did your family face there? How was the move beneficial for your family? Use your prior experiences to discuss these questions with a partner.

▲ A family moves into their new home.

Build Background

In this section, you will read a personal narrative called **"Five New Words at a Time"** and a poem, **"Quilt."** In a personal narrative, the writer tells about something he or she experienced. In the narrative you are about to read, the writer tells about moving to a new country and having to learn a new language.

Vocabulary

Learn Literary Words

Literary Words

characters
point of view

As you have learned, a plot is a sequence of related events within a story. The people involved in those events are called **characters**. You can learn about characters' traits, feelings, and actions by paying attention to their involvement in story events, what they say, and what other characters in the story say about them.

Point of view refers to the narrator, or person telling the story. When a person tells a story using the pronouns *I, me, my,* or *we,* the story is in the first-person point of view. Personal narratives use the first-person point of view.

> **First-person point of view:**
> Today is my first day at this school. I'm nervous. I don't know English that well, and I'm afraid this will keep me from making new friends.

In other stories, the narrator uses the pronouns *he, she,* or *they* to refer to the characters. These stories are told from the third-person point of view.

> **Third-person point of view:**
> Leila was nervous on her first day of school in the United States. She missed her friends and teachers in Ecuador.

Practice
41

Write the sentences below in your notebook.
Identify the point of view in each sentence. Then change those sentences in the first-person point of view to the third person, and those sentences in the third person to the first person. Take turns reading the sentences aloud with a partner.

1. I moved to Mexico City earlier this year.
2. He didn't know what to say so he was quiet.
3. We meet every day after school.
4. "How do you like your tutor?" my teacher asked.
5. I answered, "He is very helpful."

▲ **A student works with a tutor.**

Listening and Speaking: Academic Words

Study the **purple** words and their meanings. You will find these words useful when talking and writing about literature. Write each word and its meaning in your notebook, then say the words aloud with a partner. After you read "Five New Words at a Time" and "Quilt," try to use these words to respond to the texts.

approach = a way of doing something or dealing with a problem	➡	Our teacher's **approach** was a lot of fun. She encouraged us to play word games every day.
communicate = express your thoughts or feelings so other people understand them	➡	When I came to the United States, it was difficult to **communicate** with my classmates because I did not speak English.
resources = a supply of materials used to complete a task	➡	I used **resources**, like a dictionary and a thesaurus, to complete my homework.
response = something that is said, written, or done as a reaction or reply to something else	➡	My **response** to the teacher's question was correct.

Practice

WB 42

Work with a partner to answer these questions. Try to include the **purple** word in your answer. Write the sentences in your notebook.

1. What **approach** do you use when trying to make new friends?

2. How do you **communicate** with someone who does not speak your language?

3. What kinds of **resources** do you use in school?

4. What is your **response** to the idea of an extended school year?

▲ These students use a friendly approach to make new friends at school.

Word Study: Prefixes *im-*, *over-*, *un-*, *after-*

Prefixes are groups of letters added to the beginning of base words to change their meanings. Learning how to quickly identify and pronounce prefixes will help you as you sound out words. Memorizing the meanings of prefixes will help you understand new and unfamiliar words.

Prefix	Meaning	Base Word	New Word
im-	not	perfect	imperfect
over-	too much	do	overdo
un-	not	equal	unequal
after-	after	word	afterword

Practice

43

Work with a partner. Look through "Five New Words at a Time" and find words with the prefixes shown above. Write each in your notebook, as well as a definition for each word. Then use a dictionary to check your work.

Reading Strategy Identify Problems and Solutions

Identifying problems and solutions helps you understand a text better. To identify a problem that a character must solve and its solution, follow these steps:

- What problem or problems does the person or character have?
- Think about your own experience and what you would do to solve the problem.
- Remember that there may be more than one solution to a problem.

As you read "Five New Words at Time," ask yourself what problems the characters experience. How do they try to solve their problems? Are they able to find solutions, or not?

44

Set a purpose for reading As you read, pay attention to the families described in the texts. What is the response of each family to challenging situations?

Five
New Words
at a Time
Yu-Lan (Mary) Ying

My family came to America in 1985. No one spoke a word of English. In school, I was in an English as a Second Language class with other foreign-born children. My class was so overcrowded that it was impossible for the teacher to teach English properly. I **dreaded** going to school each morning because of the fear of not understanding what people were saying and the fear of being laughed at.

At that time, my mother, Tai-Chih, worked part time in a Chinese restaurant from late afternoon till late in the night. It was her unfamiliarity with the English language that forced her to work in a Chinese-speaking environment. Although her job **exhausted** her, my mother still woke up

Reading Skill

Identify the words you don't understand as you read and ask your teachers or peers for help with those words.

dreaded, worried about
exhausted, tired

early in the morning to cook breakfast for my brother and me. Like a hen guarding her chicks, she never **neglected** us because of her **fatigue**.

So it was not surprising that very soon my mother noticed something was troubling me. When I said nothing was wrong, my mother answered, "You are my daughter. When something is bothering you, I feel it too." The pain and care in her moon-shaped eyes made me burst into the tears I had held back for so long. I explained to her the fear I had of going to school. "Learning English is not impossible," my mother said. She cheerfully suggested that the two of us work together to learn the language at home with books. The **confidence** and determination my mother had were **admirable** because English was as new to her as it was to me.

That afternoon I saw my mother in a different light as she waited for me by the school fence. Although she was the shortest of all the mothers there, her face with her welcoming smile and big, black eyes was the most promising. The afternoon sun shone brightly on her long, black hair creating an **aura** that distinguished her from others.

My mother and I immediately began reading together and memorizing five new words a day. My mother with her encouraging attitude made the routine fun and interesting. The fact that she was sacrificing her resting time before going to work so that I could learn English made me see the strength she possessed. It made me admire my mother even more.

---

neglected, failed to take care of
fatigue, tiredness
confidence, belief in oneself
admirable, worthy of respect
aura, quality or feeling

✓ LITERARY CHECK

Who are the **characters** in this story?

Listening Skill

Follow along in your book as you listen to the audio. Notice the words in bold type. To understand them, read the definitions at the bottom of the page. Knowing the meanings of these words will enhance and confirm your comprehension of the story.

Before You Go On

1. Why was Yu-Lan afraid to go to school?

2. What did her mother suggest to help Yu-Lan learn English?

👤 **On Your Own**

What do you think of Yu-Lan's mother's solution? What are the benefits? Explain.

Reading 2 **85**

Very soon, I began to comprehend what everyone was saying and people could understand me. The person solely responsible for my accomplishment and happiness was my mother. The reading also helped my mother learn English so that she was able to pass the postal entrance exam.

It has been seven years since that reading experience with my mother. She is now forty-three and in her second year at college. My brother and I have a strong sense of who we are because of the strong values my mother established for herself and her children. My admiration and **gratitude** for her are endless. That is why my mother is truly the guiding light of my life.

---

gratitude, thankfulness, appreciation

✔ **LITERARY CHECK**
From which character's **point of view** is this story told? How do you know?

About the Author

Yu-Lan (Mary) Ying received her medical degree from the University of Pittsburgh Medical School. She practices in otology and neurotology in Newark, New Jersey.

Quilt

Janet S. Wong

Our family
is a quilt

of odd **remnants**
patched together

in a strange
pattern,

threads **fraying,**
fabric wearing thin—

but made to keep
its warmth

even in bitter
cold.

---

remnants, parts of something that remain after the rest of it is gone
fraying, becoming loose

About the Poet

Janet S. Wong was educated at UCLA and Yale Law School. After several years practicing law, she began writing poetry and books for young readers. She lives in New Jersey with her husband and son.

Before You Go On

1. How did Yu-Lan's mother benefit from reading with Yu-Lan?

2. What object does the speaker of the poem compare her family to? Why?

 On Your Own

Do you identify more with the story or the poem? Explain.

Review and Practice

Reader's Theater

Act out the following scene between Yu-Lan and her mother.

Yu-Lan: This is impossible! I'll never learn English.

Mother: What's the matter? You look so upset!

Yu-Lan: Nothing, I'm fine. How was work?

Mother: I can tell you're upset. What's wrong?

Yu-Lan: Oh, Mother, I'm so frustrated! I can't learn English. It's too difficult for me.

Mother: Don't they teach you English in school?

Yu-Lan: The class is so large. The teacher has no time to answer my questions.

Mother: I'm sorry to hear that, but learning English is not impossible. I need to learn English, too. Why don't we study together? Every day we will learn five new words.

Yu-Lan: Oh, Mother, do you really think we could?

> **Speaking Skill**
>
> Speak naturally and with feeling.

Comprehension
45

Recall

1. Why was it impossible for Yu-Lan's teacher to teach English properly?

2. Why was Yu-Lan's mother forced to work in a Chinese-speaking environment?

Comprehend

3. Why was it important for Yu-Lan and her mother to learn English?

4. What do the actions of Yu-Lan's mother tell you about her character?

▲ A Chinese restaurant

Analyze

5. What did Yu-Lan's mother teach her daughter about facing challenges?

6. In the poem "Quilt," the speaker says the following about her family: *but made to keep/its warmth/even in bitter/cold.* What does this mean?

Connect

7. Have you ever had to learn another language? If so, what was your **approach**? What **resources** did you use?

8. How effective was Yu-Lan's mother's plan for learning five new words a day? How do you know? Would you recommend it?

Discussion

Discuss with a partner or in a small group.

1. Are the family relationships described in the personal narrative and in the poem similar in any way? If so, how?

2. Yu-Lan's mother encourages her daughter to learn English. Do you think it is easier to face challenges with the help and encouragement of other people? Explain.

What are the benefits of facing challenges? Have you ever helped someone meet a challenge? What did you do? How did the experience make you feel?

> ### Listening Skill
>
> Respect each speaker. Listen politely even if you disagree with the speaker's ideas.

Response to Literature [WB] 45

Can you think of a recent challenge you've had to face? Compare your experience to Yu-Lan's. Complete the right column of the chart below with information about your experience. Share your chart with your peers and teacher. Ask for their feedback about how your experience compares with Yu-Lan's.

Experience	Yu-Lan	Me
Challenge	learned to **communicate** in English	
Feelings about challenge	scared, frustrated	
Approach to challenge	read with her mother and learned five new words a day	
Outcome	both mother and daughter learned English	

Grammar

Gerunds as Subjects and Subject Complements

A gerund is the *-ing* form of the verb that functions as a noun. A gerund or gerund phrase is often the subject of a sentence. A gerund is singular. It is followed by a third-person-singular verb. A possessive noun or a possessive pronoun is often used before a gerund. Form the negative of a gerund with *not*.

> "**Learning English** is not impossible," my mother said.
> **Our reading** also helped my mother learn English.
> **Not finishing** the assignment would be bad.

A gerund can also be a subject complement. A subject complement is a noun following a linking verb that defines or describes the subject.

> My favorite pastime is **reading**. [*reading* defines subject *my favorite pastime*]

Practice A
46

Complete the subject of the sentences with the gerund form of the word or phrase in parentheses.

1. (draw) _____Drawing_____ is my favorite part of art class.

2. (piano play) _____ is Kyle's favorite pastime.

3. (eat) _____ small meals is the best thing for your health.

4. (not know) _____ the language is a challenge for new students.

5. (watch) _____ TV is a good way to learn English.

Practice B
46

Write sentences in your notebook. Use the sentences from Practice A to create sentences with the gerund as the subject complement.

1. <u>My favorite part of art class is drawing.</u>

> ## Grammar Skill
>
> The *-ing* ending occurs in many English words. Be careful not to mistake the gerund with the present progressive form or the present participle:
> **Studying** English is fun. (gerund)
> We **are studying** English. (present progressive)
> Our English class is **interesting**. (present participle)

> ## Grammar Check
>
> ✓ What are two functions of a **gerund** in a sentence?

> ## Apply
>
> Work with a partner. Think of some activities that end in *-ing* that you like to do. Take turns telling your partner about these activities, using gerunds as subjects.
> **Example:** Playing video games is my favorite thing to do.

Gerunds as Objects

Gerunds and gerund phrases are often used as the object of a verb. Gerunds are used after certain verbs. These include verbs that express preferences (*like, hate, avoid*); the verbs *begin, finish,* and *delay*; verbs that give advice (*consider, discuss, suggest*); and verbs that describe thoughts (*recall, miss, remember*).

> I dreaded **going to school** each morning.
> My mother and I began **reading together**.

Gerunds often follow prepositions and verb-preposition combinations.

> I explained to her the fear I had **of going** to school.
> She was sacrificing her time to rest **before going** to work.

> My mother **believed in taking care of** her children.
> She never **complained about having** to work hard.

Practice A
47

Complete the sentences with the gerund form of the verbs from the box.

| fly   work   hike   watch   ~~swim~~ |

1. Cindy enjoys ___swimming___ in the ocean.
2. Neal began _____ the movie an hour ago.
3. He wants to start _____ as a waiter when he grows up.
4. She doesn't like _____ on planes.
5. They finally completed _____ the mountain trail.

Practice B
47

Complete each sentence with a preposition from the box and the gerund form of the verb in parentheses.

| of   in   before   ~~about~~ |

1. He always complains ___about doing___ homework. (do)
2. It was the fear _____ what people were saying. (misunderstand)
3. The teacher believed _____ every student. (help)
4. A good breakfast is important _____ your day. (start)

Grammar Skill

A gerund with its objects, complements, and modifiers is called a gerund phrase. For example, *going to school each day* is a gerund phrase.

Grammar Check

✓ What is often used before a **gerund**?

Apply

Work with a partner. Write five sentence starters using verbs on this page. Take turns completing them with gerunds and your own ideas and opinions.
Example: I don't like taking tests.

Writing

Rewrite a Familiar Story

Stories may be written from different characters' points of view. For example, the personal narrative you just read is told from Yu-Lan's point of view. Yu-Lan describes the characters and events in the story and how she felt about them. But the same events could be narrated from another character's point of view, such as Yu-Lan's mother. How would her version of the story be different from her daughter's version?

Writing Prompt

Think about a story you know well. Rewrite it from a different character's point of view. Use the pronouns *I, me, my,* or *we* if you write in the first-person. Use *he, she,* or *they* if you write in the third-person. Try to use gerunds as the subject of a sentence, the object of a verb, and/or the object of a preposition.

(1) Prewrite Begin by choosing a story to rewrite.
48

- What point of view was used in the story you chose?
- Whose point of view will you choose to retell the story?
- How will this change the interpretation of the events?
- How will you need to change the pronouns?
- List your ideas in a T-chart.

Here's a T-chart created by a student named Austin for retelling the story about Yu-Lan from her mother's point of view:

Yu-Lan's point of view	Mother's point of view
mother unfamiliar with English— forced to work in a Chinese restaurant	like working in a Chinese restaurant because I am able to understand others
mother never neglected us	working long hours made it difficult to spend time with my children
dreaded going to school each morning	noticed Yu-Lan seemed unhappy

(2) **Draft** Use your T-chart to help you write a first draft.

- Remember to change the pronouns.

- Keep in mind the feelings and opinions of the new person telling the story.

- As you write, think about how to convey the character's point of view with your choice of words and expressions.

(3) **Revise** Read over your draft. Look for places where the writing is unclear or needs improvement. Complete (√) the Writing Checklist to check your work. Then revise your draft, using the editing and proofreading marks listed on page 401.

(4) **Edit and Proofread** Check your work for errors in grammar, usage, mechanics, and spelling. Trade papers with a partner to obtain feedback. Use the Peer Review Checklist on Workbook page 48. Edit your final draft in response to feedback from your partner and your teacher.

(5) **Publish** Prepare a clean copy of your final draft. Share your story with your class. Save your work. You'll need to refer to it in the Writing Workshop at the end of the unit.

Writing Checklist

Voice:

☐ I used a voice that captured the character's point of view.

Word Choice:

☐ I used pronouns that correctly conveyed the character's point of view.

Sentence Fluency:

☐ I used gerunds as subjects and objects.

Here is Austin's paragraph. Notice the changes in the story because of the new point of view.

Austin Saiz

Five New Words at a Time

Although we didn't speak English, my children and I moved to America in 1985. I quickly found a job at a Chinese restaurant. I like working there because I am able to understand what people are saying. But working long hours makes it difficult for me to spend time with my children. I am usually exhausted when I help them get ready for school in the morning. Even so, I noticed my daughter seemed unhappy. One day, I asked her what was wrong. She looked at me and burst into tears. She told me that learning English at school was impossible. I reassured her that learning a new language could be fun. In fact, I promised her that we would read books and learn the language together—five new words at a time.

gratitude

confidence

determination

admirable

aura

Prepare to Read

What You Will Learn

Reading

- Vocabulary building: *Literary terms, word study*

- Reading strategy: *Predict*

- Text type: *Literature/science (short story/article)*

Grammar

- Passive: Simple past; regular and irregular past participles

- Passive forms of the verb: Review

Writing

- Write a personal narrative

THE BIG QUESTION

What are the benefits of facing challenges? Imagine that you are on a camping trip. You become separated from your friends and now you are alone in the woods. What would you do? Would you panic? Would you stay calm and try to figure things out? Are you the type who can think quickly on your feet? Everyone faces challenges, but it's tough to know how each challenge will affect you until you're in the situation. Think about what you learn about yourself and others as you face real-life challenges.

Build Background

In this section, you will read the short story **"A Dark Day with Bright Spots,"** about a thirteen-year-old girl named Avni. Avni goes on a shopping trip with her Auntie Tara. While they are in the store, Auntie Tara has a medical emergency. What can Avni do to get her aunt the help she needs?

Then you will read the informational article **"Do This, Not That!"** In it, the writer describes what to do, and not to do, in some tough situations.

▲ Security cameras can capture emergencies that may happen in public places.

Vocabulary

Learn Literary Words

Literary Words

conflict
point of view

In literature, a **conflict** may involve a struggle between characters or may involve outside forces. In the story you are going to read, there are two conflicts: one is between characters. In the other conflict, a character is faced with a sudden and difficult situation and has to think quickly. The main conflict in the story begins as she faces something outside of her control and it evolves into a situation where she has to make a critical decision quickly. The way a character responds to conflicts reveals something about that character.

Learning Strategy

Noticing words you know can help you understand literary terms and concepts. For example, thinking about struggles with thoughts and feelings can help you better understand what a *conflict* is.

Noticing the **point of view** from which a story is told can help you understand it better. The story you are going to read is told in the first person, from the main character's point of view. In the story, the main character is the one who has to make a critical decision. Reading about this from her point of view will help you better understand how the situation affects her and her feelings about it.

Practice
49

Work and discuss with a partner. Read the paragraph below. Then answer the following questions: What conflict is the character experiencing? How would the story be different if it were told from Theo's point of view? Would you have more insight into the conflict he faces? Why or why not?

The sun was shining as Theo left the farm. Soon after, a large, dark cloud passed over the sun's bright rays. A chilly wind whipped across the sky. Theo pulled the collar of his jacket up around his neck and continued to trudge toward town. He was used to cold weather, but he wasn't prepared for the driving snow that showered from the sky minutes later. The road quickly became covered in white, the path to town no longer visible. Theo lost his sense of direction. Worse yet, the damp cold began to seep through his clothing.

Listening and Speaking: Academic Words

Study the purple words and their meanings. You will find these words useful when talking and writing about certain texts. Write each word and its meaning in your notebook, then say the words aloud with a partner. After you read "A Dark Day with Bright Spots" and the article "Do This, Not That!," try to use these words to respond to the texts.

Academic Words

available
display
injured
survive

available = able to be used or seen		Clothes of all colors were **available** in the store.
display = a setup in a store or other location to show things easily		The **display** in the store showed what was on sale this week.
injured = hurt		Wear a helmet when you bike, so you are less likely to be **injured** if you fall.
survive = continue to live after an accident, illness, or natural disaster		The boy and his family hoped to **survive** the storm unharmed.

 Practice 50

Work with a partner to answer these questions. Try to include the purple word in your answer. Write the sentences in your notebook.

1. When you go shopping in your community, what kinds of stores are available to you?

2. How would you describe a display you have seen recently in a store?

3. Have you or anyone you know ever been injured?

4. What advice about ways to survive would you give someone who is lost in the wilderness?

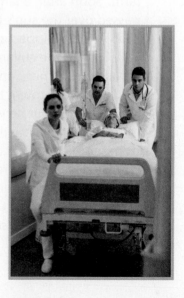

Getting quick care is important ▶ if someone is injured.

Word Study: Closed Compound Nouns

Compound nouns are formed by combining two or more nouns together. Some compound nouns are written as one word. They are called closed compound nouns. The word *basketball* is a closed compound noun. It is made up of two nouns: *basket + ball*. Look at the chart below for more examples.

Noun	+ Noun	= Compound Noun
land	mark	landmark
snake	bite	snakebite
head	ache	headache

Practice
51

Work with a partner. Use the words in the box to form a closed compound noun to complete each sentence. Then take turns reading the sentences aloud.

door	rain	prints	week
end	foot	way	bow

1. He bumped his head as he walked through the _____.

2. After the storm ended, we saw a beautiful _____ in the sky.

3. We are going on a trip to the mountains this _____.

4. I thought I was alone on the beach until I saw the _____ in the sand.

Reading Strategy | Predict

Predicting helps you better understand a text and focus on a story. Before you read, predict (or guess) what the story will be about. You can also make new predictions as you're reading. To predict, follow these steps:

- View the title and look for any headings in the story to predict what it is about.
- Stop reading from time to time and ask yourself, "What will happen next?"
- Look for clues in the story and in the illustrations. Think about what you already know. Make a prediction.

As you read "A Dark Day with Bright Spots," stop and check to see if your prediction was correct. Make a new prediction if necessary.

Set a purpose for reading As you read, think about a time someone you know faced a challenge. Did you do anything to help? How did others help? What did you learn from the experience?

A Dark Day with Bright Spots

The Worst Day Ever Begins

Shopping for clothes is probably one of my least favorite things to do. The only thing worse than looking at clothes is trying them on. Everybody has an opinion about how you look, when I'd much rather nobody paid any attention to me.

The shopping trip was Mom's idea; I had argued that my favorite pants were just fine, but she disagreed. "Absolutely not, Avni," she said.

Uh-oh. She said my name in that tone of voice which means, "Don't argue with me." I've learned to take that tone very, very seriously.

So, grumpily, I had resigned myself to a shopping trip. But half an hour before we were going to leave, she got called into work. The look on my face must have given away my joy at this very welcome **postponement** of our shopping trip because she pointed at me and said, "That doesn't mean you're getting out of this." A moment later she was on the phone to one of her sisters. She disconnected and gave me a **triumphant** look. "Auntie Tara says she'd love to take you shopping."

I groaned. I like Auntie Tara, I really do. I mean, everybody does. But out of my seven aunties, she's the one I know the least. And she has a weird way of looking at me that makes me feel very unprotected, like she can see the thoughts inside my head. Plus, we've never spent any time alone together. Looking through clothes I won't like with someone I barely know is a recipe for disaster, as far as I'm concerned.

The door buzzed and the next thing I knew, Auntie Tara was swooping around like a joyful parrot, her colorful dress flapping behind her like wings. "This will be so much fun," she said, diving toward me. I think she wanted to pinch my cheeks, but I managed to duck out of the way before she got to me. "Just the two of us!" she squawked, pretending to ignore my **sullen** glare.

---

postponement, putting off until a later time
triumphant, victorious; successful
sullen, angry or unhappy

I looked back at Mom, hoping maybe she'd rescue me after all, but she was busy getting ready for work and wasn't even looking at me. "Have fun, you two," she said, "and remember to try everything on before you buy it. Sometimes I think designers only care about what clothes look like on display and on the hangers."

"Don't worry, sister," said Auntie Tara, taking my hand in hers. "Avni and I will take care of each other."

The Brightest Store in the World

Auntie Tara's grip was as strong as a boa constrictor, and I couldn't wrest my hand free. The whole way to the store, I wanted to scream that I'm way too old for holding hands, but I didn't want to hurt her feelings. She finally let go when we got inside the store, where she clapped her hands together and cried, "Look at all the beautiful fabrics!"

To me, the store looked like a rainbow had exploded. Auntie Tara was thrilled; she raced down the aisles, grabbing things for me to try on. When she started going through a stack of bright red pants, I knew I had to say something.

"I usually prefer clothes that are a little less . . . colorful," I managed.

She stroked my cheek softly. "I know you do, sweetie, but we need to get you some clothes that will help you stand out." She put the pants in our basket.

Before You Go On

1. Why was Avni already in a bad mood before she even got to the store?

2. What does Avni's mother say to do before buying anything?

 On Your Own

Do you agree more with Avni's or her aunt's view of the shopping trip? Explain.

"I don't want to stand out," I said, putting the red pants back on the shelf. "I want to blend in so no one notices me. That's my goal."

Auntie Tara laughed and put the pants back in our basket. "And my goal is to help you change that ridiculous goal. You deserve all the attention in the world."

✓ **LITERARY CHECK**

What is Avni's **conflict** at this point in the story?

Which is exactly what I'll get if I wear any of the clothes she's picking out for me to try on. I sneaked a solid gray shirt into the basket, burying it under a blue and white striped scarf. But Auntie Tara spotted the sleeve of the shirt, pulled it out, and shook her head sadly.

"That must have gotten in there by mistake," she said, placing it back on a rack. "It's so drab and invisible."

"But I want to be invisible!" I shouted. "I get it—all these colors make you feel happy and confident. But they make me feel like a clown."

Auntie Tara didn't say anything. She just stared at me. Then all of a sudden she broke the uncomfortable silence by bursting out, "What glorious spots! They're like electric lights buzzing in the air."

That was weird even for Auntie Tara, because there was nothing with spots on it anywhere near us.

"What astonishing shapes!" she continued. I looked around again, but there was really nothing there.

Suddenly she grabbed a rack of clothes with one hand and her forehead with the other and crashed to the floor, bringing the rack with her. "Auntie!" I exclaimed. I knelt down and cleared the clothes from her face.

"Are you OK, Auntie?" I asked, though she obviously wasn't.

Her face looked pale and her eyes were closed. I couldn't tell if she was breathing. I put my hand in hers and squeezed lightly. She squeezed back and her eyes fluttered open. "Auntie?" I asked. She didn't answer.

"HELP!" I shouted. "Can someone help us!" For once, I wanted everyone to hear me. I wanted to be noticed.

Auntie closed her eyes again. I stood up but didn't let go of her hand. All my disagreements with her over the past hour were forgotten. I shouted again, but no one heard me; my voice wasn't loud enough.

Trying to think of how I could get attention, I looked around for a guard. Nobody. But I spotted the blinking light of a security camera high up in the corner. I let go of Auntie's hand and grabbed a huge handful of clothes and tossed them into the air. They rained down on us and formed a brilliant puddle of fabric. Twice, three times, I threw the bright clothes—shouting, "Help!"

It worked! Two clerks and a store guard came storming down the aisles. They looked really annoyed until they looked really alarmed.

"Don't worry, Auntie, you'll be OK," I said as I took her hand again and got ready to explain.

✓ **LITERARY CHECK**

What is Avni's **conflict** at this point in the story?

Before You Go On

1. What was Avni's goal for the shopping trip?

2. Why does Avni suddenly want to be noticed?

 On Your Own

What do you think is going to happen next? Why?

Safe at Home

A few days later, the whole family was talking after dinner. Auntie Tara was retelling the story, so of course everything was a little exaggerated.

"... and then I fell dead to the floor. My head was hit by this unbelievable pain, like it was struck by lightning. When I opened my eyes, the store lighting burned like hot coals. I heard Avni doing something **bizarre**, so I opened my eyes a tiny bit and saw clothes exploding in the air like fireworks. Avni saved me."

"I was just trying to get someone's attention," I said.

"Well, I think you saved me, whether you like it or not," said Auntie Tara, with a laugh.

"And I'm going to save everyone else by finishing the story," I said with a wink. "The security guard called the paramedics, who rushed us to the hospital. A few hours later, when Auntie was feeling a bit better, a very nice

✔ **LITERARY CHECK**

How does the author's use of first-person **point of view** help you understand Avni's changing feelings?

---

bizarre, very strange or unusual

nurse explained everything. Auntie had a kind of super-strong headache called a migraine. Those weird spots she saw in the store were a warning sign called an "aura." There are lots of different kinds of auras. Some people see zigzag lines, others get dizzy or hear a ringing in their ears. It turns out, a lot of people get migraines from bright lights—"

Auntie cut me off. "But since I've never had one before, I have to go back to the doctor next Tuesday for some tests."

"Do you want me to go with you?" I asked. "Just to keep you company?"

Auntie Tara smiled and took my hand. "That sounds wonderful. And afterwards we can get back to your shopping."

"That sounds perfect," I said. Surprising myself, I realized I really meant it. "There's a pair of red pants I want to try on."

Auntie tilted her head curiously, as if she wasn't sure whether to believe me. Since I wasn't sure either, we both broke up laughing. I guess we'll see what happens Tuesday.

Before You Go On

1. How does Auntie Tara say that she survived the emergency?

2. How did the incident in the store make Avni feel toward her aunt?

On Your Own

How do you think the experience will change Avni and Auntie Tara's relationship? Why?

Set a purpose for reading As you read the text, pay attention to the instructions given. Why do you think the writer provides information about what you should <u>not</u> do in these situations?

Do This, Not That!

Big and small emergencies happen all the time. Do you know the best way to handle them? You might be tempted to follow your instincts, or advice you've heard. But both strategies could get you into trouble. Here's what to do, and what not to do, in several different tough situations.

GETTING LOST OUTDOORS

Don't Do This: Panic.

Do This: Remember the word STOP. Each letter stands for a strategy that can help you find your way:

- **Sit** down and stay calm.
- **Think.** Ask yourself questions to calm down and consider your next moves. What direction were you traveling? Did you pass any landmarks?
- **Observe.** Look at where you are. Try to figure out which way is north. Look for footprints, paths, or other markers.
- **Plan.** Decide which way you will move. If possible, stay in open areas and travel downhill. Leave a trail behind you with sticks or rocks. That way you can always return and start over.

STALLED ELEVATOR

Don't Do This: Try to exit the elevator car or force open the doors.

Do This: Use the emergency phone or a cell phone to call for help. Press the CALL button in the elevator. Also try pressing the DOOR OPEN button, or a lower floor number. If necessary, bang on the doors and shout for help.

TOOTHACHE

Don't Do This: Wiggle the tooth. Place aspirin on the sore tooth—the aspirin can burn your gums.

Do This: Rinse with warm salt water. Place an icepack on your cheek near the tooth. Call a dentist if the pain lasts.

BUG BITE

Don't Do This: Scratch—opening the bite makes **infection** more likely.

Do This: Wash with mild soap and water. If there's a stinger in the skin, try to remove it with tweezers, a plastic card, or tape. Get treatment if your reaction is severe.

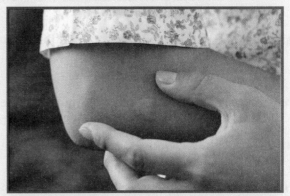

SNAKEBITE

Don't Do This: Apply a **tourniquet** and suck out the venom. The injury caused by a tourniquet can be worse than the injury from the snakebite.

Do This: Call an ambulance and Poison Control. Remove jewelry or tight clothing before swelling begins. Try to keep the bitten area from moving and keep it below heart level.

PAPER CUT

Don't Do This: Touch anything that can get into the cut and cause infection, such as soil, sand, food scraps, or garbage.

Do This: Wash the area with soap and water. Dry it by patting it with a clean cloth or paper towel. Apply a safe, medicated cream to the dried area and place a bandage over it.

---

tourniquet, something used to stop blood flow to an area

Before You Go On

1. What does the article say not to do if you get lost outdoors?
2. What is probably the biggest danger with a bug bite?

On Your Own

Which advice from the article will you remember most? Why?

Review and Practice

Reader's Theater

Act out the following scene.

Auntie Tara: . . . and then I fell dead to the floor. My head was hit by this unbelievable pain, like it was struck by lightning. When I opened my eyes, the store lighting burned like hot coals.

Avni: The security guard called the paramedics, who rushed us to the hospital. It turns out Auntie had a migraine from bright lights.

Auntie Tara: But since I've never had one before, I have to go back to the doctor next Tuesday for some tests.

Avni: Do you want me to go with you? Just to keep you company?

Auntie Tara: [smiling] That sounds wonderful. And afterwards we can get back to your shopping.

Avni: That sounds perfect. There's a pair of red pants I want to try on.

Comprehension [W|B] 53

Demonstrate your understanding of the story by responding to the questions.

Recall

1. What did Auntie Tara see before her episode?
2. How did Avni get the attention of the store employees?

Comprehend

3. Assuming Auntie Tara hadn't had her episode with the migraine, what do you think would have been the outcome of Avni's shopping trip with her? Explain.
4. From what you read, how might the shopping trip have gone if Avni's mother had taken her? Explain.

Analyze

5. Why do you think Avni seemed to change her mind about shopping at the end of the story?
6. How do you think their next shopping trip will go, assuming Auntie Tara is just fine? Explain.

▲ Auntie Tara's dress made Avni think of a parrot.

Connect

7. Would you recommend this story to someone to read? Explain.

8. Who would you want to take on a shopping trip with you: Avni or Auntie Tara? Why?

Discussion

Discuss with a partner or in a small group.

1. Would you want Avni with you in an emergency? What qualities of Avni's helped her react to the emergency the way she did? Explain.

2. Which story character did you enjoy the most? Why?

3. Which situation described in "Do This, Not That!" do you think you might encounter? Do you agree with the advice? Explain.

 What are the benefits of facing challenges? How do you think Avni benefited by saving the day for her aunt? Explain.

Response to Literature 🔖 53

Work with a partner. Imagine you are the security guard and one of the clerks at the store and that you have to write an incident report about what happened for the store manager. Discuss what details you think should be in the report to the manager. Be sure to tell the store manager what you discovered and how, and credit Avni for helping her aunt. Include words to describe Avni's quick reactions. Once you're finished with your incident report, read it aloud to each other and make any needed changes. You can use words you learned, such as *injured* and *survive*. Then, share your incident report with the class.

◀ An incident report is an official record of an event and how officials responded.

Grammar

Passive: Simple Past; Regular and Irregular Past Participles

Form the passive with a form of the verb *be* + the past participle. Regular past participles are formed by adding *-d* or *-ed* to the base form of the verb. Irregular past participles, like the one below, must be memorized.

> My hand **was held** tightly by Auntie Tara the whole way here.

Here are a few more examples of irregular past participles.

Base Form of Verb	Simple Past	Past Participle
build	built	built
have	had	had
take	took	taken

Grammar Skill

In the passive, use a *by*-phrase to indicate the performer of the action:

The disease was spread **by** mosquitoes.

When the performer of the action is unimportant or unknown, omit the *by*-phrase.

Practice A
54

Complete the sentences with the correct passive form of the verb in parentheses.

1. The class was ____separated____ into two groups. (separate)
2. Finally, after looking for hours, the lost animals were _____. (find)
3. The World Cup game was _____ by millions of people. (view)
4. The new house was _____ in only three weeks. (build)

Grammar Check

✓ How is the **passive** formed?

Practice B

Work with a partner. Rewrite the sentences below in your notebook, changing them into the passive. Use the past form of the verb.

1. Avni threw the clothes up into the air.
   <u>The clothes were thrown up into the air by Avni.</u>
2. The bright lights triggered her migraine headache.
3. They called the paramedics.
4. Avni and Auntie Tara told the family about the incident.

Apply

Work with a partner. Write sentences that describe something you did today. Use the simple past as well as the passive in the past. Share your sentences with another group of students.

Passive Forms of the Verb: Review

You can use the passive with all verb forms. The passive is always formed with a version of *be* + the past participle. Look at the different forms of the passive below.

Simple Present	*is/am/are* + past participle	The paramedics **are called**.
Simple Past	*was/were* + past participle	The paramedics **were called**.
Present Progressive	*is/am/are being* + past participle	The paramedics **are being called**.
Present Perfect	*has/have been* + past participle	The paramedics **have been called**.
Past Perfect	*had been* + past participle	The paramedics **had been called**.
Simple Future	*will be* + past participle	The paramedics **will be called**.
Be going to	*is/am/are going to be* + past participle	The paramedics **are going to be called**.

Practice A
55

Work with a partner. Rewrite the sentences below in your notebook, changing them into the passive. Use the correct form of the verb (present, past, etc.). Use the *by*-phrase if necessary.

1. Tom is explaining the process.
   <u>The process is being explained by Tom.</u>
2. The teacher collected all of the tests.
3. He has already presented the report.
4. The company will give the winner a prize.
5. She told the story with pictures.

Practice B

Work with a partner. Rewrite the sentences in your notebook. Use the form in parentheses for the passive verb.

1. The doctor was called. (simple future)
   <u>The doctor will be called.</u>
2. The test was given on Thursday. (*Be going to*)
3. The tickets were being sold by students. (simple past)
4. The new mall will be located downtown. (simple present)
5. None of us were included in the group. (past perfect)

Writing

Write a Personal Narrative

In this lesson, you will write a personal narrative from your own point of view. In your personal narrative, tell the reader about an event in your life that was memorable and meaningful to you. Most often, the event you choose to write about will involve other people, or characters. It is important to describe and develop these characters for the reader. One way to do so is through the use of dialogue, or what the characters say to each other.

Writing Prompt

Write a personal narrative. You might write a paragraph about a memorable experience you had with a friend or a classmate. Be sure to use verbs in the passive correctly.

(1) Prewrite Begin by choosing a memorable event. **W B** 56

- Decide on the time and place of your narrative.
- Who are the other characters in your narrative?
- What happened?
- What did people say about it?
- List your ideas in a graphic organizer like the one below.

Here's a three-column chart created by a student named Ari.

Who was there	What happened	What was said
me, my father, and a bobcat	We saw an injured bobcat.	"Come here quick!" "It's a bobcat." "I think it might have fallen off that ledge there. I think it was knocked out. I can see it breathing." "Hold on. I think it's waking up. Let's take a step back."

2. **Draft** Use your graphic organizer to help you write a first draft.

- Remember to establish the setting.
- Use dialogue to make the characters seem realistic.
- As you write, think about your audience.

3. **Revise** Read over your draft. Look for places where the writing is unclear or needs improvement. Complete (√) the Writing Checklist to help you identify problems. Then revise your draft, using the editing and proofreading marks listed on page 401.

4. **Edit and Proofread** Check your work for errors in grammar, usage, mechanics, and spelling. Trade papers with a partner to obtain feedback. Use the Peer Review Checklist on Workbook page 48. Edit your final draft in response to feedback from your partner and your teacher.

5. **Publish** Prepare a clean copy of your final draft. Share your personal narrative with the class. Save your work. You'll need to refer to it in the Writing Workshop at the end of the unit.

Writing Checklist

Ideas:
☐ I described a memorable event.

Voice:
☐ I tried to sound like myself.

Conventions:
☐ I used passive verbs correctly.

Here is Ari's narrative. Notice how he included passive verbs in his writing.

Ari Janoff

The Bobcat

One of my favorite things is going hiking with my dad. A lot of great trails have been developed near my house. Last weekend we went on a really long hike. I was washing my face in a stream when I heard my father cry out, "Come here quick!" When I got to my dad, he was sitting on the ground next to what looked like a big cat. But it was no ordinary cat. "It's a bobcat," my dad said. It wasn't moving, and I thought it might be dead. "I think it might have fallen off that ledge there. I think it was knocked out at first. Now, I can see it breathing," my dad explained. I was happy that the wild cat had only been injured and not killed. "Hold on," my dad said. "I think it's waking up. Let's take a step back." And just like that, the cat got on its feet, looked at us, and ran off. You never know what you'll see on a hike!

Link the Readings

Critical Thinking

Look back at the readings in this unit. Think about what they have in common. They all tell about challenges. Yet they do not all have the same purpose. The purpose of one reading might be to inform, while the purpose of another might be to entertain or persuade. In addition, the content of each reading relates to challenges differently. Complete the chart below.

Title of Reading	Purpose	Big Question Link
"Deep Mapping"		It describes the challenges a female scientist experienced as she tried to map the ocean floor.
"Five New Words at a Time"		
"A Dark Day with Bright Spots" "Do This, Not That!"	to entertain to inform	

Discussion

Discuss with a partner or in a small group.

- Compare and contrast the challenges faced by the people and story characters in this unit. How were they similar? How were they different?

- **What are the benefits of facing challenges?** How did the people and story characters in the unit benefit by facing the challenges they did? How did others benefit? Explain.

Media Literacy & Projects

Work with a partner or in a small group. Choose one of these projects.

(1) Research new ways that people can help keep our oceans healthy and clean. What other challenges are there besides pollution? Make a list of problems and solutions related to oceans and share them with your classmates.

(2) You read about Yu-Lan Ying and her challenge in adapting to a new culture. Do research to learn about other people who found themselves in a new culture and went on to make a positive difference. Choose one person and prepare an oral presentation. Use visuals. Tell the class why you chose that particular person.

(3) Survival skills courses teach people how to survive in the wilderness with little or no equipment. Research a group that offers these courses and create a brochure about it. Share your brochure with the class.

(4) Imagine you are Avni from "A Dark Day with Bright Spots." Write another section for "Do This, Not That!" about your experience with Auntie Tara. Share your work with the class.

Further Reading

Choose from these reading suggestions. Practice reading silently with increased ease for longer and longer periods.

Adrift, Steve Callahan
The amazing true survival story of a man lost on the Atlantic Ocean for 76 days before being rescued.

The Distance Between Us, Young Readers Edition, Reyna Grande
The memoir of a young Mexican girl whose family is separated by borders, but comes together in new lands and in new ways.

The World I Live In, Helen Keller
This is Helen Keller's most personal work—one that highlights her extraordinary achievements. In it, she describes what it is like to experience the world as a deaf and blind woman.

I Am Malala, Malala Yousafzai
The biography of the world's youngest Nobel Prize laureate, who has championed education in her native Pakistan.

Listening & Speaking Workshop

Personal Narrative

As you have learned, a personal narrative is a story about events in your life. You will present a personal narrative about a challenge you have faced.

① Think About It

Look back at the readings in this unit. Talk in small groups about challenges. Describe some challenges you have faced in the past.

Work together to develop a list of challenges you could tell about in a personal narrative, for example:

- A difficult class or homework assignment
- Trying to defeat a fierce sports opponent
- Relationships you've had with friends
- Issues within your neighborhood

② Gather and Organize Information

Choose a challenging experience from your group's list. Think about the setting and plot of your personal narrative. List the characters involved in your story.

Reflect Think about what made the challenge difficult. How did you meet the challenge? Why was the experience memorable? How was facing this challenge beneficial? Write down the most important points you would like to communicate to your classmates. Include specific details.

Order Your Notes List the events you want to share in chronological order.

Use Visuals Make a poster that illustrates the events in your story. Point to the poster as you tell your story. Be ready to answer questions.

③ Practice and Present

Use your list of events as the written outline for your presentation. Keep your outline nearby, but practice talking to an audience (family or friends) without reading from it word-for-word. To make your narrative richer and more interesting, use a variety of grammatical structures, sentence lengths, sentence types, and connecting words. If possible, use a tape recorder to record your storytelling. Then play back the recording and listen to yourself. Keep practicing until you are relaxed and confident, and know your presentation well.

Deliver Your Personal Narrative Remember that presentations of this type are informal. Try to create that atmosphere during your presentation. Look at your audience as you speak. Emphasize key events with your voice and actions. For example, slow down when you come to the most important events in your narrative, and point to pictures of them on your poster. Give your classmates a chance to ask questions at the end.

④ Evaluate the Presentation

You will improve your skills as a speaker and a listener by evaluating each presentation you give and hear. Complete (√) this checklist to help you judge your presentation and the presentations of your classmates.

- ☐ Did the speaker's topic get your interest?
- ☐ Was the setting clearly described?
- ☐ Did the speaker explain why the event was memorable?
- ☐ Did the speaker use formal or informal language? Was it appropriate?
- ☐ Did the speaker answer your questions?
- ☐ Could the presentation be improved?

Speaking Skill

As you speak, employ non-verbal cues, such as facial expressions and gestures, to show how you felt during this challenging experience.

Listening Skill

As you listen, identify the speaker's topic. Listen for the general meaning, main ideas, and important details. After each presentation, exchange this information with a partner to confirm that you have understood it correctly.

What else would you like to know about this challenging experience? Write down questions and ask them at the end of the presentation. When responding, provide your audience with as much information as possible.

Strengthen Your Social Language

Sharing stories with others helps to expand your English vocabulary. Go to your Digital Resources and do the activity for this unit. This activity will help you to retell simple stories and basic information, represented or supported by pictures.

Writing Workshop

Fictional Narrative

Write a Fictional Narrative

In this workshop, you will write a fictional narrative created with your imagination. A good fictional narrative has a clear setting and interesting characters. Dialogue helps bring the characters to life. The events in a fictional narrative are called the *plot*. Most events are presented in sequence and focus on a conflict that is resolved by the story's end. Another important element of a fictional narrative is the point of view from which the story is told. Sometimes, a narrator outside of the story tells what happens. Sometimes, a character in the story tells what happens.

Writing Prompt

Write a fictional narrative about someone who faces a problem and successfully meets the challenge. Try to make your characters' actions believable and their dialogue realistic. Use sensory details to establish setting. Decide on the point of view you will use. Make sure pronouns agree in gender and number.

① **Prewrite** Review your previous work in this unit. Brainstorm a list of possible challenges to write about. Invent a situation that interests you. You might write about someone who wins a contest, overcomes an illness, or stands up against injustice. Then think about your main character. What are his or her traits? From whose point of view will you tell your story? In your notebook, answer these questions:

- Where does the story take place?

- Who is the main character and what kind of person is he or she?

- What kind of problem does he or she face?

- How does the main character meet the challenge?

W B
57

List your ideas in a graphic organizer like the one below.
Here is a graphic organizer created by a student named Austin.

Characters	Setting	Problem	Solution
Julia Melissa	School auditorium Julia's house	Julia wins the part Has trouble learning the role	Melissa helps Julia practice Great performance!

② **Draft** Use your graphic organizer and the model on page 120 to help you write a first draft.

- Remember to establish a setting for your story.

- Tell the story events in chronological order.

- Use transitions to keep the ideas flowing smoothly.

- Keep the point of view consistent and use correct pronoun agreement.

- Use dialogue to bring the characters to life.

- Make sure pronouns agree with their antecedents.

③ **Revise** Read over your draft. Think about how well you have addressed questions of purpose, audience, and genre. Your purpose is to entertain. Is your story entertaining? Is it appropriate in content and tone for the intended audience? Does your story include all the elements of a narrative?

Keep these questions in mind as you revise your draft. Complete (√) the Writing Checklist below to help you identify additional issues that may need revision. Mark your changes on your draft using the editing and proofreading marks listed on page 401.

Six Traits of Writing Checklist
☐ **Ideas:** Did I establish the setting? Did I present the events in chronological order?
☐ **Organization:** Are my ideas organized logically so that my writing has coherence?
☐ **Voice:** Does my writing have energy and personality? Did I use dialogue to bring the characters to life?
☐ **Word Choice:** Did I choose precise words in order to create vivid images?
☐ **Sentence Fluency:** Did I use transitions in an effective way? Did I vary my use of simple, compound, and complex sentences?
☐ **Conventions:** Is my point of view consistent? Do my pronouns agree in gender and number?

Here are the revisions Austin plans to make to his first draft.

A Challenge and Success!

The New York streets were bustling with people as ~~I~~ (Julia) made ~~my~~ (her) way to the audition. Lucky charm in hand, ~~I~~ (she) entered the auditorium of the performing arts academy where ~~I~~ (she) attended school. The room was filled with other students rehearsing lines, dancing, and singing.

Julia tried her best. (but) ~~S~~he didn't think the director looked too impressed with her performance. (In fact,) ~~S~~he was shocked and thrilled a week later, when she learned that she had (been awarded) the leading role!

(The part was long and difficult.) One day, after rehearsing alone in her room, Julia began to doubt she would ever learn her lines. "I don't even know a page, she exclaimed. She repeated her lines over and over.

"I think I've got it!" she shouted Then, a minute later, she cried, "Darn, I forgot them again." She threw her script ~~in~~ (on) the floor and wondered, "Should I just drop out? NO! It would upset Mom and Dad so much."

(The phone rang.) "Hello?" Julia said tiredly.

"JULIA, JULIA, OH, MY GOSH! How are you?" said her friend melissa.

"Stressed!" Julia answered.

"Why?" Melissa demanded.

Julia confessed all her fears.

Edited to change point of view and adjust pronoun agreement.

Revised to create a compound sentence, add a transition word, and use passive verb.

Edited to include a descriptive detail.

Revised to correct an error in use of preposition.

Revised to include a new detail.

"Don't worry," Melissa said. "Why don't I come over everyday to help you."

Julia thought about it. Then she admitted, "That would be great!"

"DEAL!" Melissa said.

Had rehearsing with Melissa really helped? On opening night, Julia was so nervous she almost couldn't breathe. After two hours, the last line of the show was ~~sayed~~ said. Julia had done it! As she stood up to a standing ovation, she made eye contact with Melissa in the crowd and smiled a big thank-you.

Melissa silently mouthed the words, "You're welcome." Julia felt a rush of happiness and gratitude as she took her bow.

Revised to improve narrative flow and to correct spelling and use of preposition.

(4) **Edit and Proofread** Check your work for errors in grammar, usage, mechanics, and spelling. Then trade stories with a partner and complete (√) the Peer Review Checklist below to give each other constructive feedback. Edit your final draft in response to feedback from your partner and your teacher.

W B
57

Peer Review Checklist

- ☐ Did the story sustain my interest?
- ☐ Is the story line engaging?
- ☐ Is the action well paced?
- ☐ Is the setting specific and believable?
- ☐ Are the characters interesting? Are they well developed?
- ☐ Could changes be made to improve the story?

Here are the changes Austin decided to make to his final draft.

Austin Saiz

A Challenge and Success!

The New York streets were bustling with people as Julia made her way to the audition. Lucky charm in hand, she entered the auditorium of the performing arts academy where she attended school. The room was filled with other students rehearsing lines, dancing, and singing.

Julia tried her best, but she didn't think the director looked too impressed with her performance. In fact, she was shocked and thrilled a week later, when she learned that she had been awarded the leading role!

The part was long and difficult. One day, after rehearsing alone in her room, Julia began to doubt she would ever learn her lines. "I don't even know a page," she exclaimed. She repeated her lines over and over.

> *Revised to correct errors in punctuation.*

"I think I've got it!" she shouted. Then, a minute later, she cried, "Darn, I forgot them again." She threw her script on the floor and wondered, "Should I just drop out? NO! It would upset Mom and Dad so much."

The phone rang. "Hello?" Julia said tiredly.

"JULIA, JULIA, OH, MY GOSH! How are you?" said her friend melissa.

"Stressed!" Julia answered.

"Why?" Melissa demanded.

Julia confessed all her fears.

> *Revised to correct errors in punctuation, spelling, and capitalization.*

"Don't worry," Melissa said. "Why don't I come over everyday to help you?"

Julia thought about it. Then she admitted "That would be great!"

"DEAL!" Melissa said.

On opening night, Julia was so nervous she almost couldn't breathe. Had rehearsing with Melissa really helped? After two hours, the last line of the show was said. Julia had done it! As she stood up to a standing ovation, she made eye contact with Melissa in the crowd and smiled a big thank-you.

Melissa silently mouthed the words, "You're welcome." Julia felt a rush of happiness and gratitude as she took her bow.

---

(5) Publish Prepare a clean copy of your final draft. Share your story with the class.

58

Test Preparation

Practice

Read the following test questions. Study the tips in the boxes. Work with a partner to decide on the correct answers. Then circle the correct letter.

1 Where is the sign found?

   A   In a car

   B   In a store

   C   By the road

   D   By the door

2 A square is a quadrilateral. It is a rhombus because it has four congruent _____. It is a rectangle because it has four 90° angles. All squares are rectangles and rhombi, but all rhombi and rectangles are not squares.

   A   geometry

   B   similar

   C   sides

   D   shapes

WB
59–62

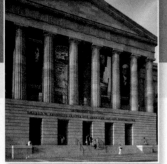

Smithsonian American Art Museum

The Challenge of Illness

Most people face illness at some point in their lives. Sometimes medicine alone cannot heal them. People need help from family and friends as well as their own personal strength to get well. American artists often celebrate the spirit that moves people to recover from disease or injury.

Alice Eugenia Ligon, *Embroidered Garment* (about 1949)

Alice Eugenia Ligon had to go to the hospital for a medical problem in 1949. Later, she turned the symbol of her illness—her hospital gown—into a holiday present and work of art for her children. She gives the viewer this information by sewing the story in green thread in the bottom left corner of the gown, under the second rainbow. Using every blank area, she also embroidered dozens of religious, patriotic, and personal phrases and images on the gown that held great meaning to her. This piece of folk art celebrates Ligon's ability to face the challenge of her illness and turn it into something positive. If she had to sit and heal, then she could also sit and create!

Alice Eugenia Ligon, *Embroidered Garment*, about 1949, muslin, cotton, 43¾ x 38½ in., Smithsonian American Art Museum ▶

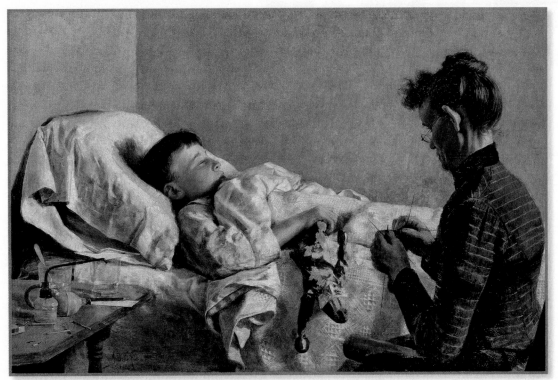

▲ J. Bond Francisco, *The Sick Child,* 1893, oil, 32 x 48 in., Smithsonian American Art Museum

J. Bond Francisco, *The Sick Child* (1893)

In J. Bond Francisco's *The Sick Child,* a mother sits nervously in her chair. She knits and stares through her glasses at a boy resting in bed. The boy holds a toy clown, which stands out in the center of the painting. It's uncertain if the boy will have enough strength to continue to hold on to the clown. It looks as if it might fall to the floor. Francisco leaves it unclear whether the boy will survive his illness. The mother faces the challenge the best way that she knows how: sitting by her son's side and keeping busy to pass the long hours.

Francisco painted *The Sick Child* at a time when medicine was still very limited. Unfortunately, many parents in the 1800s experienced the horror of watching a child die. This made it easy for them to understand the subject matter of Francisco's painting. Thousands of doctors' offices across the United States hung a copy of *The Sick Child* in their waiting rooms, which made Francisco's painting very well known.

Both artworks celebrate the human need to face challenges and to reach out to family during troubled times.

Discuss What You Learned

1. What creates an air of uncertainty in Francisco's painting?

2. How does each of these artworks celebrate the spirit that helps people to recover from illness? In what ways are they similar and different?

 BIG QUESTION
What other kinds of challenges do people face besides illness, and how could they be shown in an artwork?

63–64

How are relationships with others important?

THE BIG QUESTION

This unit is about relationships. You will read an informational text and literature about different kinds of relationships and how they change the lives of the people involved. Reading about these topics will give you practice using academic language and will help you become a better student.

Reading 1
Novel

from *Salsa Stories*, "Aguinaldo" by Lulu Delacre

Reading Strategy
Analyze cultural context

Reading 2
Social Studies

"Inspiring Peace"

Reading Strategy
Compare and contrast

Reading 3
Legend

from *Blue Willow* by Pam Conrad

Reading Strategy
Identify with a character

Listening and Speaking—How-to Demonstration

At the end of this unit, you will choose a topic and deliver a **how-to demonstration** about it.

Writing—Expository Essay

At the end of this unit, you will write an **expository essay**. To help you do this, you will write a paragraph with instructions, a critique, and a paragraph that compares and contrasts.

Quick Write

List different kinds of relationships that you have with other people. Circle the three relationships that are the most important to you.

View and Respond

Go to your <u>Digital Resources</u>. Watch the video and answer the questions.

Prepare to Read

What You Will Learn

Reading
- Vocabulary building: *Literary terms, word study*
- Reading strategy: *Recognize cultural context*
- Text type: *Literature (novel excerpt)*

Grammar
- Imperatives
- Embedded questions

Writing
- Write instructions

❓ THE BIG QUESTION

How are relationships with others important? There is an old saying that when you help someone, you are really helping yourself. What do you think that means? Do you think it is important to reach out to others? Discuss with a partner and recall a time when you helped someone else.

Build Background

In this section, you will read **"Aguinaldo,"** an excerpt from the novel **Salsa Stories**. It is about a young Puerto Rican girl named Marilia. Her class is going on a field trip to a nursing home where her classmates plan to deliver surprise Christmas gifts, or *aguinaldos*, to the elderly people who live there. However, Marilia is afraid to participate; her only grandmother died in a nursing home the year before, and the thought of returning to one makes her sad.

Currently, more than 1.5 million elderly in the U.S.A. live in nursing homes, or places where elderly people live. Some of them cannot care for themselves. They receive medical care, healthy meals, opportunities to participate in organized activities, and companionship. According to the United Nations, the number of elderly people around the world is growing quickly. As of 2015, one in eight people globally is older than 60, and by 2030 it is projected to be one in six people.

▲ Visiting an elderly nursing-home resident

Vocabulary

Learn Literary Words

Literary Words

foreshadowing
irony

Foreshadowing is an author's use of clues to hint at what might happen later in a story. Writers use foreshadowing to engage readers in wondering about what might happen and to create suspense.

Irony is the difference between what the reader expects to happen and what actually happens in a story. Writers include ironic situations in stories to create surprise and amusement. Read the example of irony below.

Jonathan didn't want to study in France, but his parents thought it would be beneficial for him to experience another culture. After saying good-bye to his parents at the airport, Jonathan made a mental list of all the reasons why he *should not* be flying to France: He didn't speak the language, none of his friends lived there, he didn't even like French food.

* * *

Three months later, Jonathan decided to call his parents—it wouldn't hurt to ask. He was nervous as he listened to the phone ring. His mother answered. "Hi, Mom. Do you think I could stay here for the rest of the school year?"

What is ironic about Jonathan's situation?

Practice
65

In a small group, discuss a movie you have seen that has an ironic situation. Describe the difference between what you thought would happen and what actually happened. Also, describe any foreshadowing that may have been used.

Listening and Speaking: Academic Words

Study the purple words and their meanings. You will find these words useful when talking and writing about literature. Write each word and its meaning in your notebook, then say the words aloud with a partner. After you read "Aguinaldo," the excerpt from *Salsa Stories*, try to use these words to respond to the text.

Academic Words

distributes
positive
reluctant
residents

distributes = gives something to different people or places	→	Our class **distributes** gifts to needy people each year.
positive = good or useful	→	Simonese enjoyed her visit to the nursing home. It was a **positive** experience.
reluctant = feeling uncomfortable about doing something	→	Aaliyah was **reluctant** about visiting the nursing home.
residents = people who live in a place	→	The **residents** of the nursing home were happy to have visitors.

Practice 66

Work with a partner to answer these questions. Try to include the purple word in your answer. Write the sentences in your notebook.

1. Is there a shelter in your area that distributes food or clothing to the needy? Have you ever volunteered to work there?

2. Do you think volunteering is a positive use of your time? Why or why not?

3. Have you ever been reluctant about the opportunity to volunteer? Explain.

4. What are some ways that the residents of your community volunteer to make it a better place to live?

These volunteers make a positive impact by keeping school grounds clean. ▶

Word Study: Spelling s- Blends

A consonant blend in a word is made up of two or three consonant letters that stand for the sounds each letter stands for, blended together. Identifying blends that begin with *s-* can help you say and spell unfamiliar words with them. Read the *s-* blends and examples in the chart below.

sw- /sw/	sp- /sp/	st- /st/	str- /str/
swept	**sp**ecial	**st**ay	**str**anger
swim	**sp**ace	**st**omach	**str**ong

Practice
67

Work with a partner. Read the sentences aloud. Complete the word in each sentence with the correct *s-* blend.

1. We are _____ending the day at the nursing home.
2. The building is across the _____eet.
3. The woman told me _____ories about her childhood.
4. I _____allowed the juice.
5. She _____ared at the card.

Reading Strategy | Recognize Cultural Context

Recognizing the cultural context of a story or text helps you visualize and understand what's happening. Cultural context includes the beliefs, art, ideas, and values of a particular community. To recognize cultural context, follow these steps as you read:

- Pay attention to the setting and to the characters and their backgrounds.
- Think about what you already know about Puerto Rico and the people who live there.
- Notice details about the main character's school, relationships between students and teachers, traditions for holidays, practices and leisure activities, meals, attitudes about others, and feelings about family.
- Think about your background. How is it similar and different? How does comparing story details with your own life help you better appreciate the story?

As you read "Aguinaldo," think about why the story is called this. Consider the cultural context. Think about and compare the ideas and traditions to your own.

68

Set a purpose for reading As you read, notice how Marilia's views about the nursing home change. What are the reasons for this change?

from Salsa Stories
Aguinaldo 🎧
Lulu Delacre

*On New Year's Day, a neighbor gives Carmen Teresa a blank notebook. Although she is grateful for the gift, Carmen Teresa has no idea how to fill it. Her guests suggest she use it to record family stories. When she agrees, her family members eagerly share their childhood experiences. This excerpt is **Tía** Marilia's tale.*

When I was growing up in Puerto Rico, I went to a small, Catholic girls' school. Every December, Sister Antonia, our religion teacher, insisted that students visit the nursing home in Santurce. Bringing Christmas cheer to the old and **infirm** was an experience she felt all students should have.

"I'm not going," I whispered to my friend Margarita.

"You have to, Marilia," she said. "Everyone has to go."

All of my classmates looked forward to the trip. But ever since my only grandma died in a nursing home, the thought of going back to one made me feel sad. I didn't want to go.

As I sat at my desk making the Christmas card that I would give to a resident, I tried to figure out how I could skip this **field trip**. Maybe they

---

Tía, aunt
infirm, weak or sick
field trip, trip students take with their classmates and teacher

would let me help at the library. Maybe I could write a special book report at school while they were out. Or better yet, I could wake up ill and stay home from school. As soon as the recess bell rang, I ran over to the library to try out my first plan.

"**Hola**, Marilia," **Señora** Collazo greeted me.

"Hola, Señora Collazo," I said, smiling sweetly. "I came to ask you if I could stay here tomorrow to help you paint posters for the book fair. I really don't mind spending the whole day at the library."

"Aren't you going on a field trip tomorrow?" Señora Collazo asked.

"My class is going. But I could be excused if you need my help." The librarian thanked me and said that if I wanted to help I could join the other students who had already volunteered to stay after school to do the posters. Biting my lip, I left the library in a hurry. It was time to try my second plan.

I marched right back to my classroom. Sister Antonia was grading papers at her desk as I went in.

"Sister Antonia," I said softly.

"Yes, Marilia," Sister Antonia answered.

I stared for a moment at the buckles of my shoes. Then without looking up, I took a deep breath, swept back my black curls, and asked, "May I stay in school tomorrow to do an extra book report?"

"I'm afraid not, Marilia," Sister Antonia said firmly. "Tomorrow is our trip to the nursing home. But if you want to do an extra book report, you can do it over the weekend."

---

hola, *hello*
Señora, *Mrs.*

Listening Skill

As you listen to the audio, look at the illustrations on pages 130–137. Use these visuals to help explain new words or ideas. Discuss these words or concepts with a partner to gain understanding.

Before You Go On

1. What do students have to do every December? How does Marilia react to this?

2. What happens to the two plans Marilia comes up with to get out of going? What do you think will happen next?

On Your Own

From what you read or know, why do you think Marilia doesn't want to go? Explain.

I glanced across the room to the trays of *besitos de coco*, the coconut sweets that my class had prepared to bring to the nursing-home residents as an *aguinaldo*: *Aguinaldos*, surprise Christmas gifts, were fun to receive. But still, I wasn't going, so it wasn't my concern. I whispered thank you to the sister, and left.

That evening at dinnertime, I put my third plan into action. To my parents' surprise, I had two big helpings of rice and kidney beans, two helpings of dessert, and three glasses of **mango** juice. I *never* ate so much. I figured that with all this food, I was sure to get **indigestion**. I went to bed and waited. I tossed and turned. I waited for several hours expecting a stomachache any second, but instead, the heavy meal made me tired and I fell sound asleep.

"Marilia, get dressed!" Mami called early the next morning. "We have to leave soon for school!"

How unlucky. I woke up feeling quite well. There was only one thing left to do. I ran to the bathroom, let the hot water run, and drank a full glass of it. Then I went back to bed.

"Marilia." Mami came in. "Get up! What is going on with you?"

"I feel warm, Mami," I **mumbled**.

Mami looked with **concern**. She touched my forehead and my neck. She left the room and in a few minutes came back with the **thermometer** in her hand. I opened my mouth and she slipped it under my tongue.

---

mango, sweet tropical fruit
indigestion, stomach pains from eating too much food
mumbled, spoke quietly and unclearly
concern, worry
thermometer, instrument that measures
   the temperature of your body

When the time was up, Mami pulled the thermometer out and read it.

"One hundred and six degrees?" she exclaimed. "That's impossible. You look perfectly fine to me."

After a little questioning, I confessed what I had done. I told Mami how much I didn't want to go on the field trip.

"You know, Marilia," she advised, "you might enjoy yourself after all. Besides, I've already promised Sister Antonia two trays of **tembleque** to bring as an *aguinaldo* to the residents of the home."

There was no way out. I had to go.

In the big lobby of the nursing home, paper streamers hung from the tall windows. The residents were **scattered** everywhere. Sister Antonia took out her guitar and at the sound of the first bar we began to sing a medley of carols. Meanwhile, the residents clapped and sang along while a student passed around our cards for us to give to them later. As I watched how happy our music made the residents, memories of my grandma rushed to me, making me **dizzy** with sadness. Suddenly, I saw that everybody was visiting with their residents. I was alone. I didn't feel like joining one of the groups. Maybe I could quietly slip away until the visit was over. I hoped it would be soon. Then I noticed a chair against the yellow wall. I sat there still holding the card I had made.

---

tembleque, dessert made from coconut milk
scattered, spread out
dizzy, unsteady

Before You Go On

1. What *aguinaldos* does Marilia's class plan to distribute to the residents of the nursing home?

2. How does Marilia feel when she goes to the nursing home? Why?

On Your Own

How would you feel about being at the nursing home if you were Marilia? Explain.

Across the room there was a frail old lady in a wheelchair. She was alone, too. I looked at my card again. It was rather pretty. I had painted it with shades of blue and gold. Maybe I could just hand it to her and leave. It might brighten her day. So **gingerly**, I crossed the lobby and stood next to her.

"Who is there?" the old lady asked as she **coquettishly** fixed her silver bun with the light touch of her **manicured** hand.

"My name is Marilia," I said. "I brought you a card."

"*Dios te bendiga*," the old woman said. "God bless you."

She reached for the card but her hand was nowhere near it. Her gaze was lost in the distance, and I knelt down to place the card in her hand. It was then that I saw the big clouds in her eyes. She was blind. *What was the use of a card if you couldn't see it?* I felt cheated. I stood up to go back to my chair.

"My name is Elenita," she said as I tried to slip away. "Tell me, Marilia, what does your card look like?"

I knelt down beside her and, in as **vivid** detail as I could, described the three **wise men** I had drawn. Then, Elenita's curious fingers **caressed** every inch of the card. She couldn't have enjoyed it more if she had seen it.

---

gingerly, cautiously
coquettishly, in a feminine way
manicured, professionally cared for
vivid, clear, specific
wise men, kings who came to see the baby Jesus
caressed, felt in a gentle way

When the coconut sweets were passed around, she **mischievously** asked for two.

"I bet you are not supposed to eat one of these," she giggled.

"No," I replied. "Sister Antonia told us that the sweets were just for residents."

"Well," she whispered. "Nobody said I couldn't give you one of *mine*."

I liked Elenita. I placed the *besito de coco* in my mouth and **relished** it even more. Especially since I wasn't supposed to have it. I enjoyed being her partner in mischief. After all, she asked me if I liked music and if I knew how to dance.

"Ay," I said, "I love to listen to music and dance."

Then she told me how, when she was young, she had been a great dancer.

"I used to dance so well that men would line up for a chance to dance with me. I had many, many **suitors** at one time," she said. "I had suitors that **serenaded** me in the evening and others that brought me flowers. But I didn't go out with all of them. You have to be selective, you know."

Too soon we were interrupted by Sister Antonia. It was time to get on the bus and return to school. I didn't want to leave.

---

mischievously, playfully
relished, enjoyed
suitors, men who want to marry a woman
serenaded, sang a romantic song to

✓ **LITERARY CHECK**

What is the **irony** of Marilia's trip to the nursing home?

Before You Go On

1. Why does Elenita ask Marilia to describe the card?

2. What are *besitos de coco*? What are they made of?

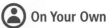 **On Your Own**

How would you feel about Elenita if you were Marilia? Explain.

"Thank you for the card, Marilia," Elenita said. She opened her hand and **gestured** for me to give her mine. "I'll keep this card to remember you by."

"I'm sorry you can't see it," I said as I squeezed her hand. For a moment it felt as warm and giving as my own grandma's. "I wish I had brought you a better *aguinaldo*."

"The best *aguinaldo*," Elenita said, "was your visit, Marilia."

As I left, I felt light and warm and peaceful. On the bus ride back, I told my friend Margarita all about our visit. I couldn't wait to come back next year. I already knew what I would bring Elenita. I would make her a **collage**. That way she would be able to feel the many textures of my picture, even if she couldn't see it. And maybe I could make a picture of her dancing. I knew she had been very pretty when she was young.

"Are you going to wait until next Christmas to give her your collage?" Margarita asked.

I thought for a moment. "Maybe Mami could bring me back sooner," I said.

As I looked out the window, I remembered how good Elenita's hand felt to touch. It's funny how sometimes things change unexpectedly. Just that morning I didn't want to go at all. But then, I couldn't wait to visit my new friend again. We had gone to the nursing home to give *aguinaldos*. And what a very special *aguinaldo* I had been given—Elenita's friendship.

LITERARY CHECK

Look back at the story. Identify one instance of **foreshadowing**.

---

gestured, made a motion
collage, work of art made by sticking pictures, photographs, cloth, etc.
    onto a surface

Marilia's Besitos de Coco

(Coconut Kisses)

3¼ cups fresh frozen grated
    coconut, firmly packed

1 cup brown sugar, firmly packed

8 **tbs.** all-purpose flour

¼ **tsp.** salt

4 tbs. butter, at room temperature

3 **lg.** egg yolks

½ tsp. vanilla

Preheat oven to 350°F. Place grated coconut in a bowl. Add brown sugar, flour, salt, butter, yolks, and vanilla. Mix well. Grease a 9- by 13-inch glass baking dish. Take mixture by the tablespoon, shape into balls, and arrange in baking dish. Bake for about 35 minutes or until golden. Let cool in baking dish for 10 minutes. With a small spatula, remove *besitos* carefully and place upside down onto platter. Let cool completely and turn over.

Makes about 35.

tbs., short for tablespoon, which is a large spoon used for
    measuring food
tsp., short for teaspoon, which is a small spoon used for
    measuring food
lg., large

About the Author

Lulu Delacre was born in Puerto Rico to Argentine parents. She showed an early interest in drawing and attended painting classes in Argentina when she was ten. Later, she studied fine arts in Puerto Rico and France. The stories in her books, which she both writes and illustrates, are inspired by her cultural heritage.

Before You Go On

1. What *aguinaldo* does Marilia say she was given at the nursing home?

2. Why does Marilia have positive feelings when she leaves the nursing home?

On Your Own

How do you know that Marilia has changed her mind about visiting the nursing home? Explain.

Review and Practice

Reader's Theater

Act out the following scene between Marilia and her mother.

Mami: [*reading a thermometer*] One hundred and six degrees! You don't look that sick. Marilia, what's going on?

Marilia: Mami, I don't want to go on the field trip to the nursing home.

Mami: Why not?

Marilia: [*sounding sad*] It reminds me of Grandma. I miss her.

Mami: I know, I miss her, too. But Marilia, you might enjoy your trip to the nursing home more than you think.

Marilia: [*shaking her head "no"*] I don't think so, Mami.

Mami: Besides, we have to bring *aguinaldos* for the residents. Now, get ready. We have to leave soon.

Marilia: [*sounding defeated*] Okay, Mami, I'm coming.

> **Learning Strategy**
>
> Use appropriate gestures and facial expressions for your character. Use the [*stage directions*] in brackets to help you.

Comprehension
69

Recall

1. In what area of the world do the story characters live?

2. What reason does Marilia give for what she's going to bring next year?

Comprehend

3. How do you know that Marilia is **reluctant** to go on the field trip?

4. How do you know that Marilia changed her mind about the field trip?

Analyze

5. Why does the school have this field trip every year, and why does Sister Antonia think it is a **positive** experience? Use details from the story to explain.

6. Why do you think Marilia chose this experience to put in Carmen Teresa's notebook? What did she want to share with her family about the nursing home **residents**?

Connect

7. Do you have elderly friends? How are they important to you?

8. Describe a special recipe that you like to share with friends.

Discussion

Discuss with a partner or in a small group.

1. How are Marilia and Elenita similar? Explain.

2. How do you think Marilia's experience at the nursing home might affect her the next time she is very reluctant to do something?

 How are relationships with others important? In what ways did Marilia help herself by reaching out to Elenita? Has someone ever reached out to you when you needed a friend? Explain.

Response to Literature

69

Marilia dreads having to go on the school field trip to the nursing home. Prior to leaving, she discusses her fears with her mother.

Work with a partner. Write a dialogue that occurs between Marilia and her mother after the field trip. In it, include Marilia's description of events—what she saw at the nursing home, what she did there, and who she met. Include her plans to return to the nursing home. Ask your peers and teacher for their feedback about your dialogue. Then perform your dialogue for the class.

Listening Skill

Respect each speaker. Listen politely, even if you disagree with the speaker's ideas.

Learning Strategy

When writing a dialogue between two story characters, work with a partner to be sure each part of the dialogue makes sense. Ask yourself: *Is there a question? If so, does the other story character answer it? Does the dialogue seem natural? If not, which words can I change?*

Grammar

Imperatives

You can use an imperative to give a command or make a request with *please*. An imperative is always in the simple present. The subject is *you*, but it is not stated.

Give a Command Marilia, **get dressed! Don't tell** me you're sick!
Give Instructions **Place** grated coconut in a bowl. Carefully **break** the eggs.
Make a Request or Offer Please **take** a *besito de coco*. OR **Take** a *besito de coco*, please.

Use "let's" before the verb to make a suggestion that includes yourself.

We will go to the nursing home. **Let's not forget** the *aguinaldos*!

Grammar Skill

When an adverb is used with an imperative, it usually comes before the imperative.

Grammar Check

✓ What is the subject of an **imperative**?

Practice A 70

Work with a partner. Rewrite the sentences as imperatives in your notebook.

1. You must go to the nursing home. *Go to the nursing home.*
2. You should go to the zoo to see the panda.
3. You can't cross the street now!
4. We should order some pizza.
5. You shouldn't forget to study for the test.
6. You need to slow down—you're going too fast!

Practice B

Change each sentence in Practice A to an imperative using "Let's (not)" to make a suggestion. Write the sentences in your notebook.

Example: Go to the nursing home. *Let's go to the nursing home.*

Apply

Work with a partner. Using imperatives, give your partner instructions to do something or directions to go somewhere.

Example: Take some bread. Put some butter on it . . .

Embedded Questions

An embedded question is a type of noun clause. It can be the subject or object of the sentence. Begin embedded information questions with a question word. Begin embedded *yes / no* questions with *if* or *whether*.

> **INFORMATION QUESTION: What would I bring Elenita?**
> **EMBEDDED QUESTION: I already knew what I would bring Elenita.** [object]
> **EMBEDDED QUESTION: What I would bring Elenita would make her happy.** [subject]
> ***YES / NO* QUESTION: Could I stay here tomorrow?**
> **EMBEDDED QUESTION: I came to ask you if I could stay here tomorrow.**

Practice A
71

Work with a partner. Change the questions in parentheses to noun clauses, or embedded questions, to complete the sentences.

1. (Where do you live?) Please tell me *where you live*_____.
2. (Who are they?) Do you know _____?
3. (When did he leave?) I wonder _____.
4. (Who is coming?) I need to know _____.
5. (What are we doing in class?) _____ is easy.
6. (What did she say?) _____ made me upset.

Practice B

Change each *yes / no* question into a sentence with an embedded question. Write the sentences with the embedded questions in your notebook.

1. (Is he more tired than you are?)
   I want to know whether he is more tired than you are.
2. (Are you finished with the book?)
3. (Can I see that next?)
4. (Is it Maggie's turn, or mine?)
5. (Do you have the assignment?)

Writing

Write Instructions

At the end of this unit you will write an expository essay. Expository writing explains or informs. Writing instructions is one kind of expository writing. Instructions explain how to do or make something. For example, the recipe on page 137 explains how to make *besitos de coco*. First, the recipe lists the ingredients, such as coconut and brown sugar. Then a clear sequence of steps tells how to mix the ingredients together. Finally, the recipe explains how to cook the treats. When describing a sequence of steps, writers use sequence words, such as *first, then, next,* and *finally,* to keep the order clear.

Writing Prompt

Write a set of instructions. Be sure to write about something you know how to do well, such as baking cookies or using an MP3 player. Be sure to use imperatives and embedded questions correctly.

① **Prewrite** Begin by choosing something you know how to do.

72

- Write the name of the activity you will write instructions about.
- Think about how to explain the activity. What equipment or tools do you need? What are the steps in the activity?
- List your ideas in a sequence chart.
- Decide which sequence words to use with each step.

Here's a sequence chart created by a student named Haley. She is explaining how to find volunteer opportunities.

> **First:** Do an internet search with the key word <u>volunteer</u> and your zip code.

> **Then:** Collect information about each place that interests you.

> **Next:** Call your friends and ask them if they are interested in volunteering.

> **Finally:** Choose a place to volunteer and call or visit to find out more.

(2) **Draft** Use your sequence chart to help you write a draft.

- Keep in mind your purpose for writing.

- Remember to explain the steps in the correct order.

- Use imperatives and embedded questions correctly.

- Make sure to use sequence words.

(3) **Revise** Read over your draft. Look for places where the writing is unclear or needs improvement. Complete (√) the Writing Checklist to help you identify problems. Then revise your draft, using the editing and proofreading marks listed on page 401.

(4) **Edit and Proofread** Check your work for errors in grammar, usage, mechanics, and spelling. Trade papers with a partner to obtain feedback. Use the Peer Review Checklist on Workbook page 72. Edit your final draft in response to feedback from your partner and your teacher.

(5) **Publish** Prepare a clean copy of your final draft. Share your instructions with the class. Save your work. You'll need to refer to it in the Writing Workshop at the end of the unit.

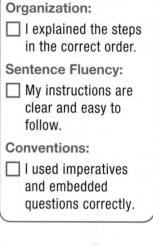

Writing Checklist

Organization:
☐ I explained the steps in the correct order.

Sentence Fluency:
☐ My instructions are clear and easy to follow.

Conventions:
☐ I used imperatives and embedded questions correctly.

Here is Haley's paragraph about how to find volunteer opportunities.

Haley Coy

How to Find Volunteer Opportunities in Your Area

Volunteering is a great way to help your community. One way to find a volunteer opportunity is to look on the internet. To do this you will need a computer with internet access, a pen or a pencil, and a phone. First, do a search. Use the key word "volunteer" and your zip code to find nearby places in which to *volunteer*, such as nursing homes, hospitals, food banks, and homeless shelters. Next, collect information about each place that interests you. Be sure to find out what skills or experience you need in order to volunteer at these places. Then call your friends and ask them if they are interested in volunteering, too. It'll be fun to volunteer together. After you decide on a place to volunteer, write down the address, telephone number, and the name of a person to contact. Finally, call or visit the organization to find out more about it.

Prepare to Read

What You Will Learn

Reading

• Vocabulary building: *Context, dictionary skills, word study*

• Reading strategy: *Compare and contrast*

• Text type: *Informational text (social studies)*

Grammar

• Complex sentences

• Agreement in complex sentences

Writing

• Write a critique

THE BIG QUESTION

How are relationships with others important? Think about one of your friends. What beliefs do you share with him or her? What beliefs don't you share? Sometimes a difference in beliefs can cause conflict between people. Was this ever true for you and your friend? How did you resolve the conflict? Discuss with a partner. Share your ideas with your peers and teacher. Ask for their feedback and support in order to develop background knowledge about this topic.

Build Background

In this section, you will read the informational article, **"Inspiring Peace."** The Seeds of Peace camp unites teenagers from around the world to encourage leadership. For example, the camp brings teenagers from the Middle East together to confront the conflict that has defined the region for more than seventy years. In doing so, the camp hopes to teach these future leaders the communication and leadership skills they will need to interact with each other, to work toward peace, and to develop lasting relationships with one another.

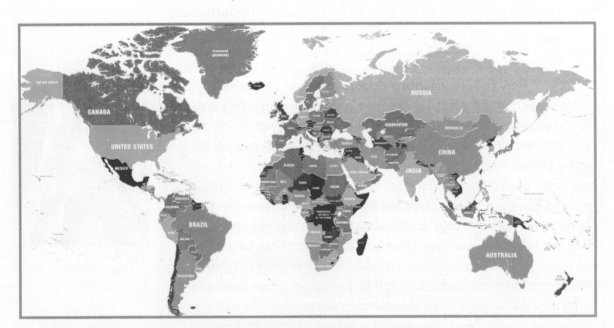

▲ Campers attend the Seeds of Peace camp in Maine from locations all around the world, including the Middle East.

Vocabulary

Listening and Speaking: Key Words

Key Words

barriers
confront
cultivate
enemy
political
violence

Read aloud and listen to these sentences. Use the context to figure out the meaning of the highlighted words. Use a dictionary to check your answers. Then write each word and its meaning in your notebook.

1. There were personal barriers that kept the girls from becoming friends.
2. If you confront your fears, they often go away.
3. Campers cultivate their friendships by building trust.
4. Ynon is from Israel, and paired with a Palestinian camper, once thought to be an enemy.
5. The students debate about political issues that relate to government and the rights of people.
6. The fighting between the countries has continued for more than seventy years. The violence in that region is frightening.

Practice [W B] 73

Choose a key word from the box above to complete each sentence. Then take turns reading the sentences aloud with a partner.

1. The president works hard to _____ relationships with other world leaders.
2. The voters could not overlook the _____ differences of the two candidates.
3. There are _____ that make it difficult to achieve world peace.
4. The leaders did not want to _____ each other about their differing beliefs.
5. _____ erupted when the citizens of one country attacked those of another.
6. She no longer considers a citizen from the warring nation to be a(n) _____.

▲ Students have a political debate.

Listening and Speaking: Academic Words

Study the **purple** words and their meanings. You will find these words useful when talking and writing about informational texts. Write each word and its meaning in your notebook, then say the words aloud with a partner. After you read "Inspiring Peace," try to use these words to respond to the text.

assumed = thought that something was true without having proof	➡	I **assumed** the test would be easy to pass because I studied hard.
focus = pay special attention to a particular person or thing instead of others	➡	It was noisy in the library. I had to **focus** very hard on the textbook to study for the test.
individuals = certain people; not a whole group	➡	A few **individuals** passed the test easily, but for most students it was difficult.
similarities = the qualities of being similar, or the same	➡	There are **similarities** in all people. We are all alike in some ways.

Practice
74

Work with a partner to answer these questions. Try to include the **purple** word in your answer. Write the sentences in your notebook.

1. Have you ever **assumed** that a class would be easier than it actually was? Explain.

2. What is your main **focus** at school?

3. What qualities make some **individuals** easier to work with than others? Why?

4. What are some **similarities** of two countries that are familiar to you?

▲ Some **individuals** work better in group situations than others.

Word Study: Suffixes -er, -or

A suffix is a letter or group of letters placed at the end of a base word. Adding a suffix changes the meaning of the base word.

The most common meaning of the suffixes -er and -or is "one who." For example, a learner is one who learns; a visitor is one who visits. The only way to know which of these two-suffixes to use is to check the dictionary. Remember, if a base word ends with an e, drop the e before adding the suffix. Study the examples in the chart below.

Base Word	+ Suffix	= New Word
travel	-er	travel**er**
bake	-er	bak**er**
act	-or	act**or**
educate	-or	educat**or**

Practice 75

Copy the sentences below into your notebook. Complete each sentence by adding -er or -or to the word in parentheses. Use a dictionary if necessary. Have a partner check your work.

1. The camp _____ led the students in a variety of activities. (counsel)
2. Each student was allowed to invite one _____ to the camp. (visit)
3. A _____ encouraged students to discuss political issues. (facilitate)
4. Each _____ presented a persuasive argument. (debate)
5. Each _____ performed during cultural night: from singing to dancing. (camp)
6. Everyone found out that Andrea is a good _____. (sing)

Reading Strategy   Compare and Contrast

Comparing and contrasting help you better understand what you read. When you compare, you look for similarities. When you contrast, you look for differences. To compare and contrast, follow these steps as you read:

- How are the people and their experiences similar? How are they different?
- Relate what you're reading to your own experiences. How are they similar and different?

As you read "Inspiring Peace," compare and contrast the campers and the regions they come from.

WB 76

Set a purpose for reading As you read, look for examples of ways the groups of teenagers deal with conflicts that affect their relationships.

Inspiring Peace

▲ Campers lead each other through the course by providing the blindfolded person with directions.

Imagine you are at summer camp. You are close to the top of an 8-foot-high structure made of poles and ropes. You are blindfolded. A fellow camper acts as your coach. He gives you careful instructions so that you can make your way to the ground safely. He tells you exactly where to place your right foot, then your left foot, and then each one of your hands. As you **descend**, you listen carefully and follow his instructions precisely. One false step and you could fall!

"Move your foot a quarter-inch to the left," your teammate **coaches**. "No, that's too much. Go back to the right just a bit . . . ." Finally, your foot makes contact with the rope. You're safe—for the moment. Your heart is pounding, but you are not afraid. You trust your teammate to guide you.

Now imagine that your teammate belongs to a group of people who, back home, you consider your enemy.

This is not a **hypothetical** situation. In the summer of 2017, a teen named Ynon at Seeds of Peace in Maine, U.S.A., was on the camp's ropes course, blindfolded. Ynon is from Kriyat Yono in Israel. To safely descend through the course, he had to rely on instructions from a fellow camper who is Palestinian. The Israeli and Palestinian governments have been engaged in political **conflict**, which has often resulted in violence, since 1948.

Like many campers, Ynon and his teammate were working to develop communication and trust, skills that will help them grow as individuals. However, Ynon and his teammate, like all the campers at Seeds of Peace, had a more **ambitious** mission: They were training to be leaders who hope to cultivate understanding and peace in their local communities.

---

descend, move down to a lower location
coaches, advises or suggests
hypothetical, made up or suggested; not real
conflict, disagreement or argument
ambitious, determined and committed

◀ The camp has been in operation for more than 25 years.

A Unique Camp

Seeds of Peace was established in 1993 by a **journalist** named John Wallach, who believed that in order for enemies to make peace, they needed to see each other as human beings. When children are born into communities that are in conflict with others, they often learn to fear those in the opposing community. They seldom have an accurate understanding of the individuals on the other side of the conflict because they are exposed mostly to images and words that make the "others" seem less human.

"I believe that over time, attitudes can change," Wallach explained. "If you begin to know your enemy, if you begin to hear your enemy, if you begin to understand your enemy, it's **inevitable** that you will begin to feel some **empathy**."

For that to happen, Wallach knew it would be **essential** for people on both sides of a conflict to work together, recreate together, and share stories. What better way to break down the barriers to communication than to bring together the young generation—the generation that will be the future leaders? And where better to do this than a summer camp in a beautiful rural location?

In its first year, the Seeds of Peace camp was small, hosting 46 teenage boys from the Middle East. In some ways, it was a typical summer camp: The boys shared meals, swam, went boating on the nearby lake, and played sports. But there was a more urgent purpose underlying the fun because the camp's mission was "to inspire and cultivate new generations of global leaders in communities divided by conflict."

---

journalist, reporter; person who writes or reports for the media
inevitable, certain to happen; unavoidable
empathy, ability to understand and share the feelings of others
essential, necessary

Before You Go On

1. What kinds of things do the campers at Seeds of Peace focus on?

2. Why might it be difficult to trust someone from a region with which your community or nation has political differences?

 **On Your Own**

How would you compare this camp to others you know about? Explain.

Most campers at Seed of Peace are between 14 and 16 years old. They are assigned to their bunks based on the "conflict region" they come from. For example, Israeli and Arab teens are assigned to one cabin; Indian and Pakistani teens are assigned to another.

▲ Discussions between groups can be difficult at times.

For creative activities, swimming, evening programs, and meals, all the campers interact with each other. But once a day, campers are divided into their "conflict groups" for two-hour dialogue sessions that are led by professional **facilitators**. In these sessions, the goal is for the campers to have honest, open conversations in which they confront issues that their communities face. No topic is **off-limits**. Campers often disagree and, sometimes, the conversations become heated or emotional.

The facilitators help the campers stay on track as they participate in these sessions. One way they do this is to help campers talk about actual experiences and avoid stereotyping. Stereotyping happens when over-generalized, untrue statements are made about a group of people. For example, it would be stereotyping to say that one group of people is more athletic than another. Stereotyping is a way that "enemy" groups avoid learning about each other. It keeps the people in each group from being able to see each other as fellow humans.

By learning how to communicate better and sharing stories and **perspectives**, the campers take steps toward change. When the teens **engage** in open, honest conversations about their experiences, they are often able to see that real people with real feelings exist on *both* sides of the conflict. The teens build understanding of the issues that divide their communities, too.

The camp also launched a program focused on tensions that have arisen among teens from the United States. This program brings teens of diverse backgrounds together from all over the United States in an effort to help them see each other as real people, respect each other's differences, and build confidence in themselves.

Said Jack, a camper from Maine, "Seeds of Peace gave me the confidence to believe that I can do something for the world. Every one of us has the ability, but very few ever use it. I want to be one of those few."

facilitators, people who aid in a process to make it easier for those involved
off-limits, not allowed
perspectives, ways of thinking about something that is influenced by the type of person you are and/or your experiences
engage, to participate in an activity

Hope for the Future

Now, more than 25 years after Seeds of Peace was established, conflict still rages in the Middle East and throughout the world, but campers are **optimistic** about their power to bring peace to their homelands. Explained Husam, a Palestinian from East Jerusalem, "We are born in this place and running away is not a solution. We should not give up. We should face this issue and try to solve it."

In 2018, former U.S. Vice President Joseph Biden expressed his support at the Seeds of Peace 25th anniversary celebration. In his address, he said, "There's so much power, so much potential in today's young people. This new generation is the most talented and tolerant in history. All over the world, the young people you're bringing together are seizing new ways to lead change. They're going to win, mark my words."

---

optimistic, believing that good things will happen in the future

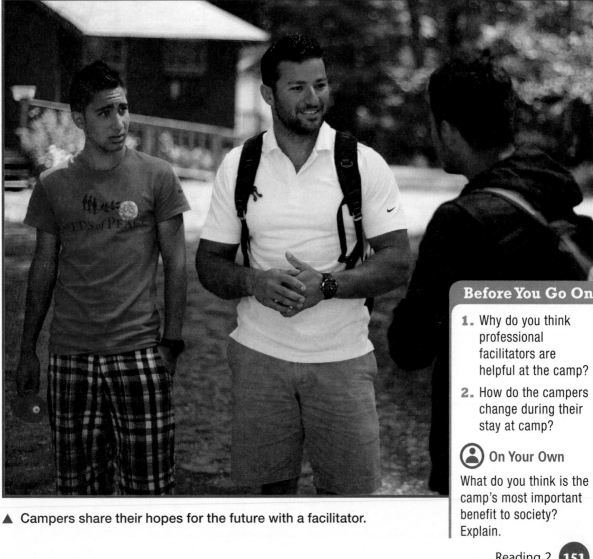

▲ Campers share their hopes for the future with a facilitator.

Before You Go On

1. Why do you think professional facilitators are helpful at the camp?

2. How do the campers change during their stay at camp?

On Your Own

What do you think is the camp's most important benefit to society? Explain.

Reading 2   151

Review and Practice

Comprehension 77

Recall

1. Who founded Seeds of Peace? Why?
2. Who goes to Seeds of Peace?

Comprehend

3. In what ways does the camp encourage interaction among campers?
4. How do the campers' interactions help resolve situations that perplex world leaders?

Analyze

5. Why do you think the camp is called "Seeds of Peace"?
6. Why do you think the campers feel tense about some of the political discussions that occur in their dialogue sessions?

▲ Seeds of Peace campers spend time doing outdoor activities.

Connect

7. Do you think a camp is a good place to bring **individuals** with opposing views together? Explain.
8. Who do you think might benefit from going to the camp? Explain.

In Your Own Words

Work with a partner to complete the chart. Try to use as many new vocabulary words as possible. Using this information, demonstrate your comprehension of the article by summarizing it for your partner.

Seeds of Peace	
Location	Maine
Campers	
Activities	
Goals	

Discussion

Discuss with a partner or in a small group.

1. What kind of **similarities** and differences do campers see in their lives and situations? How can examining these help the cause of peace?

2. Do you think Seeds of Peace can make a difference in the world? Why or why not?

 How are relationships with others important? Describe a time when you met someone who incorrectly **assumed** that your views were similar to his or her own. Did you try to understand that person's way of thinking? Were you able to get along?

Listening Skill

Implicit ideas are ideas that are not stated directly. Listen to your classmates for implicit ideas. Notice their facial expressions, word choice, and intonation.

Read for Fluency

It is often easier to read a text if you understand the difficult words and phrases. Work with a partner. Choose a paragraph from the reading. Identify the words and phrases you do not know or have trouble pronouncing. Look up the difficult words in a dictionary.

Take turns pronouncing the words and phrases with your partner. If necessary, ask your teacher to model the correct pronunciation. Then take turns reading the paragraph aloud and giving each other feedback on your reading.

Learning Strategy

To better acquire and understand new academic language, use and reuse these words in meaningful ways in your speaking and writing.

Extension 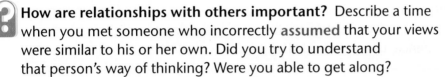 77

The relationship between Arabs and Israelis is frequently in the news. Work with a partner. Find two articles about current events happening in this region. Use newspapers, news magazines, or the internet. Summarize each article, and present the information to your classmates.

Grammar

Complex Sentences

A complex sentence is a sentence that has a main, or independent, clause and one or more subordinate, or dependent, clauses. A subordinate clause is not a complete sentence; it "depends" on the independent clause. A subordinate clause often begins with a subordinating conjunction. Some common subordinating conjunctions are *after, although, because, before, for, once, since, that, though, until, whether,* and *while.* When a clause with a subordinating conjunction begins the sentence, use a comma after it.

> **Grammar Skill**
>
> Remember that a conjunction is a connecting word.

main clause	subordinate clause
Campers from both sides of a conflict work together **because** barriers can then be broken down.

subordinate clause   main clause

As you descend, you listen carefully and follow his instructions precisely.

main clause   subordinate clause

The facilitators help them stay on track **as** they participate in these sessions.

Practice A
78

Match the main clauses on the left with the appropriate subordinate clauses on the right to make complex sentences.

> **Grammar Check**
>
> ✓ When are commas used with clauses in **complex sentences**?

1. Yolanda eats a lot of yogurt	although it was raining.
2. My father stepped on the paint	while we were driving home.
3. Randy went swimming	after she cleared the table.
4. Aimee washed the dishes	because it's healthy.
5. A cat ran in front of our car	before it was dry.

> **Apply**
>
> Work with a partner. Switch the clauses in Practice A so that the subordinate clause comes first.
> **Example:** Because yogurt is healthy, Yolanda eats a lot of it.

Practice B

Add the correct subordinating conjunction to make a complex sentence. Not all of the words will be used.

once	although	until	~~because~~	whether

1. We enrolled in the camp ____because____ our friends did.

2. _____ the camp just opened, it was already booked.

3. _____ we open the gifts, we can put out the cake.

4. We will be doing the assignment today _____ it is due tomorrow or not.

Agreement in Complex Sentences

Make sure that you use verb forms consistently in complex sentences. Both the main and the subordinate clauses should usually refer to the same time (such as past or present). For example, if the main clause is in the past, the subordinate clause should also be in the past.

Pronouns should agree with their antecedents in number and gender.

Grammar Skill

Remember that complex sentences have two clauses.

Past	Before **Leah could finish** her question, Ben **was** ready to answer. [verbs in both clauses are in the past; *her* refers to *Leah*]
Present	You **can't** just **make us** leave because it**'s ours**. [verbs in both clauses are in the present; *ours* refers to *us*] A bunk counselor **encourages the campers** to ignore boundaries as **they make** friends with **their** neighbors. [verbs in both clauses are in the present; *they* and *their* refer to the *campers*]

Practice A
79

Work with a partner. Circle the correct word or phrase to complete each sentence.

1. He assumed they agreed because (he was /(they were)) friends.
2. The food was delicious even though (it was / they were) spicy.
3. We worked quickly since a storm (is / was) coming.
4. His parents drove Tom to school until (he / they) could ride the new school bus.
5. Since it was snowing so hard, all the cars (are / were) covered.
6. Before Sarah called her parents, (they / she) finished her homework.

Grammar Check

✓ What do pronouns **agree** with in **complex sentences**?

Apply

Write five simple sentences. Then add a subordinating conjunction. With a partner, finish the complex sentences.

Example: I like the idea of the camp. (because) I like the idea of the camp because it focuses on building trust.

Practice B

Rewrite each sentence in your notebook to make the pronoun and its antecedent agree.

1. We can't think about your homework until we finish <u>yours</u>.
   We can't think about your homework until we finish ours.
2. Dad can bring you the pitcher, but you have to return it to <u>her</u>.
3. We chose the best foods that <u>is</u> at the buffet.
4. There are three ways around the park if you look for <u>it</u>.
5. As Dan locked the door, <u>they</u> turned the key.
6. The lamp in the room was on until he turned <u>them</u> off.

Writing

Write a Critique

A critique is a type of expository writing in which you judge something based on standards, or a level of quality. You list the standards, and explain why they were or were not met. For example, imagine that you like video games that include a lot of action. If a friend asked your opinion of two video games, you could judge them based on this standard: a lot of action.

Writing Prompt

Write a paragraph to critique a story, movie, video game, or place you have visited. Did you enjoy it or was it disappointing? Decide on the standards you'll use to evaluate it. Use main and subordinate clauses in complex sentences correctly.

1. **Prewrite** Begin by choosing a topic.

80

- Think of a story or movie you saw recently, or a place that you visited, such as a restaurant or an amusement park.

- Ask yourself what you liked or did not like about the experience.

- Make a list of the standards that you would use to evaluate it.

- Identify the standards met and not met.

- List your ideas in a graphic organizer.

Here's a graphic organizer created by a student named Nicole for a critique of an after-school program:

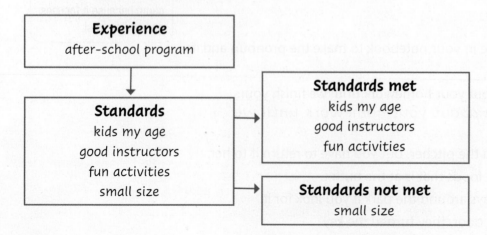

(2) **Draft** Use a graphic organizer to write a first draft.

- Identify your standards for evaluation; were they met?
- Explain why your experience did or did not meet the standards.
- What viewpoint do you want your reader to have, based on your critique?
- Use complex sentences.

(3) **Revise** Read over your draft. Look for places where the writing is unclear or needs improvement. Complete (✓) the Writing Checklist to help you identify problems. Then revise your draft, using the editing and proofreading marks listed on page 401.

(4) **Edit and Proofread** Check your work for errors in grammar, usage, mechanics, and spelling. Trade papers with a partner to obtain feedback. Use the Peer Review Checklist on Workbook page 80. Edit your final draft in response to feedback from your partner and your teacher.

(5) **Publish** Prepare a clean copy of your final draft. Share your critique with your class. Save your work. You'll need to refer to it in the Writing Workshop at the end of the unit.

Here is Nicole's critique of an after-school program. Notice how Nicole clearly identifies her standards for evaluating the program.

> **Writing Checklist**
>
> **Ideas:**
> ☐ I clearly identified the standards I used to judge my experience.
>
> **Conventions:**
> ☐ I made sure that pronouns and verbs agree in complex sentences.

Nicole Siley

The Community Arts Center's After-School Program

Last year, I attended an after-school program at the Community Arts Center in my town. It had many of the qualities I was hoping it would have: kids my age, good instructors, and fun activities. Many of my classmates attended. Because many students from other schools also came, I was able to make new friends, and we still keep in touch with one another. Unfortunately, a lot of kids—more than 100—signed up for the program. Our instructors, however, kept things moving and made the program fun. There were many activities to choose from, such as painting, drawing, dancing, and acting. I took a painting class. I learned how to paint and took a trip to the art museum. Even though it was crowded, I'm going to sign up for the after-school program again this year.

Prepare to Read

What You Will Learn

Reading

• Vocabulary building: *Literary terms, word study*

• Reading strategy: *Identify with a character*

• Text type: *Literature (legend excerpt)*

Grammar

• Transitions

• Adjectives

Writing

• Write to compare and contrast

THE BIG QUESTION

How are relationships with others important? As you know, people can be involved in different kinds of relationships. Work with a partner. Use your prior experiences to discuss the relationships you have had with others, such as friends, classmates, and teammates. Answer the following questions: How and when did each relationship begin? What makes you value each relationship? How would you feel if you could not experience these relationships?

Build Background

In this section, you will read an excerpt from a legend called **Blue Willow**. A legend is a story that is often based on fact. However, over time, details in legends move further away from factual events to describe people and actions that are more fictional than real.

The *Blue Willow* legend helps to explain the Blue Willow china pattern, which always includes a willow tree, a bridge, and a moon pavilion, or a decorative building. Plates with this pattern were produced in England during the eighteenth century—a time when the English were inspired by Chinese culture.

Set in ancient China, the legend describes the relationship between Kung Shi Fair, the daughter of a wealthy merchant, and a village fisherman named Chang the Good. The couple wants to marry, but the merchant will not grant his permission. This causes a series of events that no one could have anticipated.

◀ A plate with a Blue Willow pattern

Vocabulary

Learn Literary Words

Long before there were books, there were stories. Storytelling was a form of entertainment in ancient cultures. Stories were passed along by word of mouth from one generation to the next. This is called the **oral tradition**.

A **legend** is one kind of story that was originally shared by oral tradition. Because people told the stories to each other and did not write them down, details of the stories often changed.

Character motivation is the reason for a character's thoughts, feelings, actions, or speech. Characters are often motivated by needs, such as food and shelter. They are also motivated by feelings, such as fear, love, and pride. Knowing characters' motives helps the reader understand the characters and the story better. Read the passage below. What is Lisa's motivation?

Lisa longingly looked out the window. This was the fourth day in a row that she had stayed after school to work on her science project. "I'd rather be with my friends," Lisa thought to herself as she sighed loudly. She turned her head from the window. Out of the corner of her eye, she caught a glimpse of the science-fair poster. She focused on the words printed in bright red letters: *Grand Prize Winner—$200.* All thoughts of her friends faded as Lisa got back to work.

Practice
81

Work with a partner. Narrate, or tell, a story that you know about from books, movies, or television. Try to identify the main characters' motivations.

Listening and Speaking: Academic Words

Study the **purple** words and their meanings. You will find these words useful when talking and writing about literature. Write each word and its meaning in your notebook, then say the words aloud with a partner. After you read the excerpt from *Blue Willow*, try to use these words to respond to the text.

Academic Words

authoritative
consent
encounter
reaction

authoritative = respected and trusted as being true, or making people respect or obey you	➡	My mother makes the rules in our home. She is the most **authoritative** member of our family.
consent = permission to do something	➡	We have to get her **consent** before we can leave the house with friends.
encounter = an occasion when you meet someone without planning to	➡	I had an unexpected **encounter** with my friend at the mall.
reaction = the way you behave in response to someone or something	➡	My friend and I had the same **reaction**. We were both surprised and happy to see each other.

Practice
82

Work with a partner to answer the questions. Try to include the **purple** word in your answer. Write the sentences in your notebook.

1. In your opinion, who is the most **authoritative** person in your school?

2. Do you have to receive your teacher's **consent** before leaving the classroom?

3. Whom did you have an **encounter** with at school today?

4. What **reaction** did you have to an event at school today?

▲ Two students have an encounter at school.

Word Study: Synonyms

Synonyms are words that have the same or nearly the same meaning. The words *clever* and *intelligent*, *glisten* and *shine*, and *toss* and *throw* are synonyms. Writers often choose one synonym over another to express a specific idea or emotion. Look at the chart below for examples.

Synonym	Meaning	Sentence
claim (verb)	to say something without proof or evidence	They **claimed** to have heard the leopard cries.
state (verb)	to say something in a strong and formal way	Her father **stated** that she could not marry him.

Practice
83

Work with a partner. In your notebook, make a chart like the one above with twelve rows and three columns. Copy the three headings. Write the pairs of synonyms in order. Then, use a dictionary or thesaurus to find and write the meaning of each synonym. Write a sentence for each one.

drift/float	look/gaze	shriek/yell
special/unusual	startle/surprise	love/adore

Reading Strategy | **Identify with a Character**

Identifying with a character helps you better understand and enjoy a story. When you identify with a character, you can better appreciate that character's feelings, motivations, and actions. To identify with a character, follow these steps as you read:

- Think about the character's actions. What does he or she do?
- How do you think the character feels?
- Think about your own experiences. How would you feel? Would you act in the same way as the character?

As you read the excerpt from the legend *Blue Willow*, imagine how you would feel if you were the main character. Think about the things you would do differently.

84

Set a purpose for reading As you read, notice how Kung Shi Fair's relationship with Chang the Good affects her father. How does his reaction affect the young couple's relationship?

from

Blue Willow

PAM CONRAD

Many years ago, there was a river called Wen that flowed past a small and peaceful village.

On one side of the Wen River, in a large mansion, lived a wealthy **merchant**.

Everyone knew that he had one daughter, Kung Shi Fair. She was a beautiful girl with hands as small as starfish, feet as swift as **sandpipers**, and hair as black as the ink on her father's **scrolls**. As she grew, the people of the village wondered who she would marry, because they all knew that the merchant always gave her whatever she asked for.

One day Kung Shi Fair was sitting in her **moon pavilion** when she saw something glistening on the bank of the river. She made her way to the water. When she got there, she saw it was only a broken shell. She picked it up, then looked up and saw for the first time a boat and a young man pulling his dripping nets out of the water.

merchant, person who makes money by selling things
sandpipers, wading birds
scrolls, books written on long sheets of papers that roll up
moon pavilion, decorative building

This was Chang the Good who lived across the river. He was a young fisherman.

Now Kung Shi Fair and Chang the Good were both startled to see each other. The fish spilled out of his nets. The shell dropped from Kung Shi Fair's hand. Tossing the nets on the floor of his boat, Chang the Good picked up his oars, and he rowed across the river to her.

When he reached the shore, Kung Shi Fair watched as he pulled the boat onto the land. She came close and touched his nets. "How beautiful," she said.

"I made them myself," he told her, thinking he, as well, had never seen something so beautiful this close.

"And what a wonderful bird!" she exclaimed as the cormorant held out its wings to dry in the breeze.

"I fish with her. She dives for fish and—because I have trained her so well—she brings the fish to me."

"You are very clever," she said, turning her gaze full on him.

"Can I tell you something?" he asked her softly.

She nodded, silent.

"One morning I came down to the river, thinking my boat would be **anchored** where I had left it, but the **currents** had taken it away. All day long I searched along the river for my boat. Then, when I had given up hope, I came upon a **cove**, and there it was, drifting toward me. My heart swelled with love."

---

anchored, kept in place by a heavy weight that is connected to the boat and dropped into the water

currents, moving waters

cove, small area of water that is surrounded by land

Listening Skill

Follow along in your book as you listen to the audio. Notice the words in bold type. To understand them, read the definitions at the bottom of the page. Knowing the meanings of these words will help you better understand the legend.

Before You Go On

1. Who is Kung Shi Fair? Who is Chang the Good?

2. How do Kung Shi Fair and Chang the Good meet?

On Your Own

Based on the story so far, what do you predict about the relationship between Kung Shi Fair and Chang the Good?

Kung Shi Fair tilted her head. "And so?"

"And so, this is how I felt just now, seeing you here on the bank of the river."

Kung Shi Fair frowned. "My boat has never been in the river," she said. "So I have never lost a boat, or found one." Then she smiled at him. "But I came to the river just now thinking I saw something glistening on its bank, and now I know I came for you."

But it so happened that Kung Shi Fair's father was watching from the window of his mansion. He watched as his daughter led the fisherman across the stone footbridge, and he watched her lead Chang the Good to her moon pavilion.

That night he said nothing to his daughter about what he had seen. They were drinking their tea, sitting quietly, when one of the **servants** came **panting** onto the **veranda**.

"There is terrible news, Master. It seems there is a wild **leopard on a rampage**."

"This is frightening," the merchant said. "You must tell me if you hear news of the leopard coming in this direction."

The merchant looked at his daughter. "Perhaps, until the leopard is caught, you should not go down into your moon pavilion."

Kung Shi Fair laughed, "Don't be silly, silly father. My pavilion is perfectly safe."

* * *

The next day and every day after that, when the work of the fishing was through, Kung Shi Fair and Chang the Good would meet on the shore. First they would go to the pavilion. Then they would trail peony petals down the path to the bridge, where they would sit and talk, and eat mulberries beneath the cool willow tree.

Finally, after many days of this, Chang the Good came with a bundle.

"I have something to show you," he said.

Very carefully, he unfastened the knot and opened his bundle on the floor before her. There were **brooches** and necklaces, bracelets, and pendants hung not on gold chains as she was used to, but on rough silk cords dull with wear.

He told her, "These belonged to my mother, who died when I was very young."

"And this was her own ring," Chang the Good was saying, and he slipped a small **jade** ring onto her thumb.

---

servants, people who are paid to clean someone's house, cook food, etc.
panting, breathing quickly with short, noisy breaths
veranda, porch with a roof
leopard, large wild cat with black spots
on a rampage, behaving wildly or violently
brooches, pieces of jewelry
jade, green stone

Before You Go On

1. What news does the servant have for the merchant?

2. What is in the bundle Chang the Good shows Kung Shi Fair? Why are its contents special?

On Your Own

From what just happened in the story and your own experiences, what do you think is going to happen next? Why?

"Beautiful," Kung Shi Fair told him.

"I want you to have them," he told her. "I want you to be my wife."

Kung Shi Fair held very still.

"Yes, I would like this, too," she said. "But I must tell my father."

* * *

That night Kung Shi Fair went to her father. She said to him, "I would marry now, Father."

And he answered, "Not yet, my daughter, not yet."

"But, Father, you have always been so good to me. And this is what I want more than anything. If not now, then when?"

"When I find a copper coin in my path," he said.

Kung Shi Fair ran from the room to hide her tears, past the servant who was coming to tell the merchant that the leopard was terribly close.

Chang the Good could not be **discouraged**. Sitting in Kung Shi Fair's moon pavilion, he thought of a plan. He did not stay that day for he had special work to do, and he told Kung Shi Fair to sit by her window at dawn.

The next morning, Kung Shi Fair leaned on the window. Her father was preparing to go to a meeting concerning the rampaging leopard.

She saw the servants bring the carriage around to him, and just as her father was about to climb on, he looked down and saw coins **strewn** at his feet—hundreds of little copper coins. He looked up at his daughter in the window.

She saw no anger in his face, just sadness. She smiled kindly at him. "Now, Father? Can I now?"

He shook his head. "Not yet, my daughter, not yet."

Her smile turned to tears. "Then when, Father? Oh, then when?"

"When there's a rainbow over the stone bridge that leads to your moon pavilion," he told her, and he drove away.

Later the servants claimed to have heard Kung Shi Fair's sad crying that morning, even above winds that whistled over the river's surface. They decided she had gone to find Chang the Good, to tell him his plan had failed.

The village women later whispered about how she went down to the bank of the tumbling Wen River, to her boat. She had watched many times as Chang the Good had sailed away, and now—hoping she could remember how—she awkwardly pushed her boat into the **surging** river.

✓ **LITERARY CHECK**

What do you think is the merchant's **motivation** in refusing to let the couple marry? What makes you think so?

---

discouraged, persuaded to lose the confidence
   needed to do something
strewn, lying
surging, quickly moving

Turning her face into the wind, she steered bravely through the river's foam and **rapids**. When she was halfway across the river, the wind ripped the fig leaf sails from their mast, and the cassia bark **hull** snapped apart, tipping the merchant's beautiful daughter into the **torrential** river. For a few moments her silken robe could be seen floating near the surface, and then it was gone.

In the village, Chang the Good had gone to the meeting to hear the news about the rampaging leopard. Everyone was frightened that the leopard would come and kill their families. Then the merchant spoke to them.

"While the storm is raging," he said, "we must go out, seek the leopard, and **slay** him before he comes to our village again."

"Yes!" "Yes!" the villagers cried. "Kill the leopard now!"

---

rapids, fast-moving waters
hull, body of the boat
torrential, quickly flowing
slay, kill

Before You Go On

1. What happens when her father refuses to let her marry the first time? The second time?

2. Why do the villagers decide what they do about the leopard?

On Your Own

Are you able to relate to Kung Shi Fair's feelings? Explain.

Reading 3   167

Chang the Good had thoughts only for Kung Shi Fair. He had no heart for a hunt. Without being seen, he stepped out into the rain. He thought to himself how once the winds calmed, he would sail over and see her and ask her how things had gone with her father and the coins.

Meanwhile the swords were brought out and the bows and arrows, the spears and the clubs, and everyone received a weapon. The villagers poured out of the hall, and they took to the rain-slick road, in search of the leopard.

It was dark when the winds finally calmed and the river slowed its fury. The cormorant perched on the back of Chang the Good's boat, as he eased it into the river. Chang the Good gave it a final push and jumped in. Slowly and carefully, he made his way across, peering into the darkness of the pavilion to see if Kung Shi Fair waited for him. But there was no sign of her.

He pulled his boat ashore and called, "Kung Shi!" There was silence.

He ran to the pavilion and threw back the rain-soaked silks, "Kung Shi!"

Frightened, he turned towards her father's house that was dark and lifeless. His feet barely touched the ground. He ran from room to room, calling her name and hearing the silence answer. He knew something terrible had happened.

Slowly he left the house. The song of small green frogs carried him to the stone bridge and he decided to sit there and wait for her.

Suddenly the cormorant flapped her wings, **shrieked**, and dived into the water and disappeared. Then she flew straight up and landed beside Chang the Good. She dropped what she was carrying into her master's hand.

It was a small, jade thumb ring.

Chang the Good saw it and at that moment, he knew. He jumped up, and his eyes searched the shore for the cassia boat and he knew. He saw the whole story before him and threw back his head. He knew it was too late.

Just as the moon began to slip into sight, the **weary** villagers were returning home empty-handed. As they came back toward the village, they heard a sound coming from across the water near the merchant's house. "The leopard!" they whispered. At that, three of them jumped into a boat and sailed silently across the river to the place where the sound came from.

Now for many years after, the villagers tried to describe to each other what the sound was like. Most thought it sounded like the ragings of a leopard before it **strikes**. Later they all knew it was the sound of Chang the Good, crying his heart into the night.

Silently the boat slipped onto the riverbank, and the three men crept up the shore. In the moonlight they saw their enemy. In one thrust they all shot arrows, threw spears, and sent clubs sailing through the wailing air. Their mark was made, and Chang the Good **toppled** into the river beneath the bridge.

If this was the end of the story, it would probably have been forgotten by now, it was so long ago. But because the merchant was so heartbroken, he cried his **sorrows** to whomever would listen to him, and the entire village soon knew he had kept his daughter away from the man she loved.

It was some time later, while the last leaves were still on the willow, that there was a cloudburst in the late afternoon. The merchant heard the villagers cry out, and he went to the window.

His heart leapt at the sight, for just above the footbridge that led to his daughter's pavilion, there appeared a most wondrous rainbow of every color. While the villagers and the merchant watched, two **swallows** fluttered above the willow tree and kissed.

---

shrieked, yelled in a high-pitched voice
weary, very tired
strikes, attacks
toppled, fell
sorrows, feelings of grief and sadness
swallows, small birds

About the Author

Pam Conrad (1948–1996) wrote stories for both children and adults. Before her death, she authored twenty-nine books. Often she used her own experiences as inspiration for many of her award-winning tales.

✓ LITERARY CHECK

This **legend** was originally shared with others as part of the **oral tradition**. Retell the story to a partner. How does your oral version differ from the written story?

Before You Go On

1. How does Chang the Good find out what happened to Kung Shi Fair?

2. What happens to Chang the Good at the end of the story?

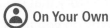 On Your Own

Did the story end as you thought it would? Why or why not? What is ironic about it?

Review and Practice

Reader's Theater

Act out the following scene between Kung Shi Fair and Chang the Good.

Kung Shi Fair: These nets are beautiful.

Chang the Good: I made them myself. I use them to catch fish.

Kung Shi Fair: And this lovely bird! What kind of bird is it?

Chang the Good: It's a cormorant. She's very smart! I have taught her how to catch fish and bring them to me.

Kung Shi Fair: Then it is you who is smart!

Chang the Good: Can I tell you something? One morning the currents took away my boat during the night. I searched for my boat all day long. Finally, I found it in a small cove. My heart was filled with joy.

Kung Shi Fair: Why are you telling me this?

Chang the Good: Because that is how I felt when I saw you.

Comprehension
85

Recall

1. Why do the people of the village wonder who Kung Shi Fair will marry?

2. What do the villagers mistake Chang the Good's crying for?

Comprehend

3. What is the significance of the willow tree, the bridge, and the moon pavilion in the story?

4. If the villagers know that her father will give her anything she asks for, why doesn't Kung Shi Fair marry Chang the Good right away?

Analyze

5. Why do you think this story kept being told? What is it about the story that made people want to share it over and over again?

6. Why do you think the author chooses to share the *Blue Willow* legend with others in the form of a written story?

▲ A copper coin

Connect

7. What would you tell someone about this legend? Would you recommend it? Why or why not?

8. If you were Kung Shi Fair, what would be your **reaction** to her father's refusals? Why?

Listening Skill

Think about what you are hearing. Does it make sense? If not, seek clarification. Ask the speaker to repeat or further explain his or her answer.

Discussion

Discuss with a partner or in a small group. Ask your peers and teacher for their feedback about your ideas.

1. Could the merchant have prevented his daughter's death? If so, how?

2. In your opinion, was the merchant right to refuse to give his **consent** to his daughter's marriage? Why or why not?

How are relationships with others important? What kind of daughter was Kung Shi Fair? What kind of father was the merchant? If you were a friend of Kung Shi Fair's, what would you have advised her to do? If you were a friend of the father's, what advice would you have given him?

Response to Literature

Reading Skill

Make sure you understand sequence words commonly found in instructions, such as *first*, *next*, *then*, and *finally*. These words help you to understand how to complete a task.

Because legends were often shared orally, many versions of the *Blue Willow* legend exist. Work with a partner. First, find an account that is different from the one you read in class. Use library resources or the internet. Then compare both stories. Add information to the chart below about the characters, settings, story events, and conclusions. Finally, share this information with your classmates. How many different versions were presented?

Blue Willow				
Version	**Setting**	**Characters**	**Story Events**	**Conclusion**
Pam Conrad's				
Internet				

Grammar

Transitions

Transitions help your reader follow your line of thought. Transitions can signal contrast, a cause-and-effect relationship, similarities, or additional information. When a transition connects two sentences, use a period. When it connects two independent clauses, use a semicolon (;). Use a comma when a transition begins a sentence or clause. Don't use a comma with most one-word transitions when they appear midsentence. When a transitional phrase appears midsentence, offset it with commas.

Grammar Skill

Remember that a clause is a group of words with a subject and a verb that is part of a complete sentence.

Contrast ideas	Kung Shi Fair loved Chang. **However,** she didn't want to hurt her father.	Show similarities	She dropped the shell. **Similarly,** Chang spilled the fish from his net.
Show cause-and-effect	Her father disapproved of Chang; Chang, **as a result,** decided on a plan.	Add information	The storm was raging; **in addition,** the leopard was on a rampage.

Practice A
86

Work with a partner. Complete each sentence with a transition from the word box, using each only once. More than one answer may be possible. Use a comma where necessary.

| as a result   consequently   ~~instead~~   on the other hand   therefore |

1. He's not studying English. _____Instead,_____ he's studying French.

2. She works hard during the week. _____ she takes weekends off.

3. Marta's father is very authoritative. _____ he's also very loving.

4. Sandra doesn't eat well; _____ she is often sick.

5. Children are very curious. _____ they get in a lot of trouble.

Grammar Check

✓ When are commas used with **transitions?**

Practice B

Work with a partner. In your notebook, rewrite the two sentences, connecting them with the transition in parentheses.

1. Sidney runs every day. He swims twice a week. (in addition)

2. Joe loves cheeseburgers. His brother loves cheeseburgers. (likewise)

3. Bill can't come. He doesn't like parties. (besides)

4. We really enjoyed the play. We're seeing it again tonight. (in fact)

Apply

Work with a partner. Look at the reading. Find sentences that you can combine with transitional words and phrases.

Adjectives

Adjectives describe nouns. There are different categories of adjectives, which describe different qualities. When you use adjectives before a noun, place them in the order shown in the chart below.

Determiner	Opinion	Size	Age	Shape	Color	Material	Origin	Purpose	Noun
some	nice	small	new	round	white	plastic	store-bought	golf	balls

When you use adjectives from the same category, separate them with commas.

> The refugees want to have **successful, positive** lives. [both *opinions*]

A compound adjective is formed when two or more words work together to modify the same noun. The first word modifies the second, and the two together modify the noun. Some common compound adjectives are written as one word, but some are hyphenated.

> This true story is much better than any **make-believe** story.

Grammar Skill

When a noun is used to describe another noun, it functions as an adjective, for example, *toy store*, *paper doll*.

Practice A
87

Put the adjectives in the correct order. Use commas where necessary.

1. I just bought (new, several, interesting) books to read.
   several interesting, new

2. Anna ate (delicious, huge, a) plate of mussels.

3. Julio likes the (old, lovely, charming) house.

4. Yoko finished (colorful, tiny, a) painting.

5. Rob is going to stay in (mountain, quiet, a, relaxing) cabin.

Grammar Check

✓ Which type of **adjective** comes first: one that describes an object's size or its shape?

Practice B

Draw a line from the sentence starter on the left to the phrase it goes with on the right. Underline the compound adjectives.

1. Don't go the wrong way down	a ten-dollar bill.
2. Last night we watched	a middle-aged man.
3. As change, the clerk handed me	a three-hour movie.
4. Our teacher is	a <u>one-way</u> street.

Apply

Work with a partner. Find three compound adjectives in the reading. Write sentences with them in your notebook.

Writing

Write to Compare and Contrast

A compare-and-contrast paragraph addresses the similarities and differences between two people, places, or things. For example, you can compare and contrast two friends. First, write down the ways your friends are similar and different. Then write your paragraph. Begin by identifying the friends. Next, tell how your friends are the same. Then write about how they are different. Include specific examples that show their similarities and differences.

Writing Prompt

Write a paragraph that compares and contrasts two people, places, or things that you know well. Be sure to correctly use adjectives to describe and to use transitions to indicate similarities and differences or to add information.

(1) **Prewrite** Begin by choosing the people, places, or things you want to write about.
88

- Think of ways they are similar or different.

- Which ideas go together? Are some ideas about physical appearance, for example, and others about personality?

- List your ideas in a Venn diagram like this one.

Here's a Venn diagram created by a student named Austin about the legend.

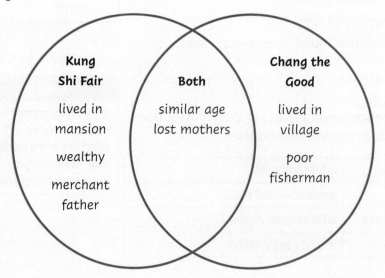

Kung Shi Fair

lived in mansion

wealthy

merchant father

Both

similar age

lost mothers

Chang the Good

lived in village

poor

fisherman

② **Draft** Use your Venn diagram to help you write a first draft.

- First, explain who or what you are comparing.
- Then describe the similarities and differences.
- Make sure to include specific examples.
- Use transitions to compare and contrast and to add information.
- Use adjectives to describe.

③ **Revise** Read over your draft. Look for places where the writing is unclear or needs improvement. Complete (√) the Writing Checklist to help you identify problems. Then revise your draft, using the editing and proofreading marks listed on page 401.

④ **Edit and Proofread** Check your work for errors in grammar, usage, mechanics, and spelling. Trade papers with a partner to obtain feedback. Use the Peer Review Checklist on Workbook page 88. Edit your final draft in response to feedback from your partner and your teacher.

⑤ **Publish** Prepare a clean copy of your final draft. Share your compare-and-contrast paragraph with the class. Save your work. You'll need to refer to it in the Writing Workshop at the end of the unit.

Here is Austin's paragraph. Notice how he used transitions to signal similarities and differences and to add information in his paragraph.

Austin Saiz

Blue Willow

Kung Shi Fair and Chang the Good are the two main characters in <u>Blue Willow</u>. They are similar in some ways, but they are also very different. First, both characters are similar in age. Also, at the time they meet, both Kung Shi Fair and Chang the Good have lost their mothers. Kung Shi Fair lives with her wealthy father in a mansion near the Wen River. Chang the Good also lives near the Wen River. However, Chang the Good lives in the village. His family isn't wealthy at all. In fact, he's a poor fisherman. Despite the differences in their backgrounds and lifestyles, Kung Shi Fair and Chang the Good see something good in each other and fall in love. Kung Shi Fair's father is against the marriage. As a result, both lovers die tragically. They meet again and are happy after death.

Link the Readings

Critical Thinking

Look back at the readings in this unit. Think about what they have in common. They all tell about relationships. Yet they do not all have the same purpose. The purpose of one reading might be to inform, while the purpose of another might be to entertain. In addition, the content of each reading relates to relationships differently. Now, complete the chart.

Title of Reading	Purpose	Big Question Link
from *Salsa Stories*, "Aguinaldo"		A young girl makes a new friend.
"Inspiring Peace"	to inform	
from *Blue Willow*		

Discussion

Discuss with a partner or in a small group.

• Which unit selection had the greatest impact on you? Why?

How are relationships with others important? What do you think is important about each relationship in the readings? What are the most important relationships in your life? What makes them important to you?

Media Literacy & Projects

Work with a partner or in a small group. Choose one of these projects.

(1) Think about foods that are part of your family's tradition. Write two or three of your favorite family recipes on note cards. Include a list of the ingredients and instructions about what to do. Share the recipes with your classmates. Describe why your recipes are special. Then combine your recipes to make a class cookbook. Use the internet to find photos for your cookbook.

(2) Make a diary entry and drawing by Marilia about her next visit to Elenita after she gives her the collage mentioned in the story.

(3) You read about Seeds of Peace. Write an informational brochure that describes the camp's mission, location, and programs. The brochure should help people understand what makes this camp special. Then share it with the class.

(4) In the legend *Blue Willow*, both Kung Shi Fair and Chang the Good die tragically. Rewrite the final scenes of the legend to include a description of their lives together had they lived. Illustrate your new ending. Then share it with the class.

Further Reading

Choose from these reading suggestions. Practice reading silently with increased ease for longer and longer periods.

Under the Royal Palms: A Childhood in Cuba, Alma Flor Ada
The author recollects growing up in Cuba and the many people who touched her life, including her grandmother, an uncle, and a dance teacher who helped her through a difficult year at school.

Shabanu: Daughter of the Wind, Suzanne Fisher Staples
Life is both sweet and cruel to strong-willed Shabanu, whose home is a windswept desert of Pakistan. When a tragic encounter with a wealthy landowner ruins the marriage plans of her older sister, Shabanu is asked to sacrifice everything she's dreamed of.

A Jar of Dreams, Yoshiko Uchida
Rinko is an 11-year-old Japanese American growing up in California in the 1930s. She wants to fit in with the other kids around her, but everyone makes her feel different because she is Japanese. When her aunt Waka visits from Japan, she teaches Rinko about the importance of her culture, and helps her realize her own strengths.

Listening & Speaking Workshop

How-To Demonstration

You will give a presentation that explains a process.

① Think About It

Have you ever shown a friend or family member how to do something? Think about everyday tasks you know how to do well, such as doing a homework assignment or using a cell phone or other device. What do you have to do to complete or use it? How would you explain the steps in the process to someone else? Review the use of imperative verbs to give commands and instructions.

Work in a team to develop a list of activities that you know something about. Think of interesting activities that you could demonstrate in class. For example:

- How to make a favorite snack
- How to download a smartphone app
- How to use a digital camera
- How to ride a skateboard

② Gather and Organize Information

Choose an activity from your team's list. Begin by thinking about how you learned to do it. Then make a list of the steps involved. Remember to include small steps that are obvious to you but that might not occur to someone else. Write down any remaining questions you may want to address.

Research Go to the library, talk to an adult, or search the internet for more information. Look for answers to your questions. Take notes on what you find.

Order Your Notes Revise your list of steps based on your research. Then write each step on a separate note card. Think about the best order in which to present the steps. Arrange your note cards in this order, and then number them.

Use Visuals Find or make props you can use to show key steps in your demonstration. You can also create posters, models, or other visuals to help you.

③ Practice and Present

Practice your demonstration until you know it well. Begin by telling your audience what you will demonstrate for them. Glance at your note cards while you speak, but don't read from them. Use your visuals and props to help you explain or act out each step. If possible, ask friends or family members to listen and give you feedback. Can they hear and understand what you are saying? Keep practicing until you feel relaxed and confident.

Deliver Your How-To Demonstration Make sure your note cards are in order and your visuals are ready before you begin. Look at your audience as you speak. Think about each step as you explain it. Emphasize imperative verbs by changing the tone of your voice. Slow down when you come to the most important points. At the end of the demonstration, give your audience a chance to ask questions.

④ Evaluate the Presentation

You will improve your skills as a speaker and a listener by evaluating each demonstration you give and hear. Complete (√) the checklist to help you judge your demonstration and the demonstrations of your classmates.

- ☐ Did the speaker present the process in a clear sequence?
- ☐ Do you feel that you were given enough information to complete the activity on your own?
- ☐ Did the speaker use props and other visuals effectively?
- ☐ Did the speaker answer your questions?
- ☐ Are there ways the demonstration could be improved?

Speaking Skills

Highlight the most important words on your note cards so that you can see them easily.

Use ordinal numbers (*first, second, third . . .*) and sequence words (*before, next, then, finally*) to clearly explain the order of steps.

Listening Skills

Watch and listen carefully. Give the speaker your full attention.

Monitor what you are hearing. Does it make sense? Would you be able to explain the steps to someone else? If not, seek clarification. Write down questions and ask them at the end of the demonstration. When responding, give as much information as possible.

Strengthen Your Social Language

In social contexts as well as in some of your content-area classes, you will need to ask for and give information. Go to your Digital Resources and do the activity for this unit. This activity will help you acquire key structures, expressions, and words needed for extended speaking assignments and in everyday academic and social contexts.

Writing Workshop

Expository Essay

Write an Expository Essay

In this workshop, you will write an expository essay. An expository essay is a group of paragraphs that gives information about a topic. A good expository essay begins with a paragraph that introduces the writer's topic and purpose. The writer develops the topic in two or more body paragraphs. Each body paragraph presents a main idea supported by facts and details. A concluding paragraph sums up the important information in the essay.

Writing Prompt

Choose one of the paragraphs you wrote for this unit and expand it into a five-paragraph essay. Be sure to use complex sentences correctly.

(1) **Prewrite** Review your previous work in this unit. Choose one of your paragraphs. Now brainstorm ideas for your essay. How can you develop the ideas from your paragraph? In your notebook, answer these questions:

WB
89

- What is the main topic?

- What kind of information am I going to add?

- How can I organize the information into paragraphs?

- What kind of research do I need to do about the topic and where will I find the information?

List your ideas in a graphic organizer such as a Venn diagram, T-chart, or three-column chart. A student named Katie decided to compare and contrast how three different animal species relate to their offspring. Here is her three-column chart:

Bald Eagle	Bottlenose Dolphin	Meerkat
bird species	mammal species	mammal species
both father and mother sit on and guard eggs	mother raises offspring	young raised communally by
eggs hatch after about 35 days	young stay with mother for up to 6 years	females in colony
young stay with parents until able to care for selves—about 14 weeks		young leave burrow at 21 days old
		group continues to protect young

(2) Draft Use your graphic organizer and the model on pages 183–184 to help you write a first draft.

- Remember to introduce your topic in the first paragraph.

- Support your information with facts and specific details.

- Sum up the important information in your concluding paragraph.

- Be sure to use complex sentences correctly.

(3) Revise Read over your draft. Think about how well you have addressed questions of purpose, audience, and genre. Your purpose is to inform. Is your essay clearly organized? Is it appropriate in content and tone for the intended audience?

Keep these questions in mind as you revise your draft. Complete (√) the Writing Checklist below to help you identify additional issues that may need revision. Mark your changes on your draft using the editing and proofreading marks listed on page 401.

Six Traits of Writing Checklist

☐ **Ideas:** Does my essay present interesting information about the topic?

☐ **Organization:** Do I present information in an order that makes sense?

☐ **Voice:** Does my writing show my knowledge of the topic?

☐ **Word Choice:** Do I use transitions to compare and contrast and otherwise connect ideas?

☐ **Sentence Fluency:** Do I vary my use of simple, compound, and complex sentences in order to achieve sentence fluency?

☐ **Conventions:** Does my writing follow the rules of grammar, usage, mechanics and spelling?

Here are the revisions Katie plans to make to her first draft.

Animal Parents and Their Young

Many animals in the wild care for their young. ~~Then~~ until their offspring

However can survive on their own. Animals have different ways of raising

Revised to use a complex sentence and a transition word.

their young. The bald eagle, the bottlenose dolphin, and the meerkat are examples of animals that care for their young in different ways.

The bald eagle is the national bird of the united States. The male and female of this species share the duty of incubating the eggs. While one parent watches the eggs the other looks for nesting material or food. Incubation lasts about thirty-five days. Once The eaglets are hatched. They continue to live with their parents for eight to fourteen weeks. By then, the eaglets can fend for themselves.

Revised to create a complex sentence.

The bottlenose dolphin is a marine mammal that lives mostly in tropical waters. Usually, a female dolphin will have a baby, called a calf, about every three years. A calf lives with its mother for up to six years. Male bottlenose dolphins are not involved in raising their offspring. During this time, a calf is taught how to find food and survive.

Revised to improve logical sequence of ideas.

A meerkat is a small African mongoose that lives in communal burrows. The male meerkat like the male bottlenose dolphin does not get involved in raising its young. Instead, the young are communally raised with the assistance of other females. After about twenty-one days, the young leave the burrow but They are still cared for by the group In fact, female "babysitter" meerkats act as lookouts near the burrow to protect the young from predators.

Edited to introduce a comparison and to create a compound sentence.

All three of these animal species brood their young. However, different animals live with their parents for different periods of time.

In addition∧

∧ The young of some species are raised by both parents, ∧ The young of
    and

other species are raised by one parent or by the group. The examples

of the bald eagle the bottlenose dolphin, and the meerkat show

in how animal species care for their offspring
similarities and differences.
                      ∧

Revised to introduce a transition, create a compound sentence, and reinforce the main idea of the essay.

(4) Edit and Proofread Check your work for errors in grammar, usage, mechanics, and spelling. Then trade essays with a partner and complete (√) the Peer Review Checklist below to give each other constructive feedback. Edit your final draft in response to feedback from your partner and your teacher.

89

Peer Review Checklist

☐ Was the essay clearly organized?
☐ Was the information interesting?
☐ Did I understand the topic better after reading it?
☐ Did the first paragraph introduce the topic?
☐ Did the concluding paragraph sum up the main points?
☐ Could changes be made to improve the essay?

Here are the changes Katie decided to make to her final draft as a result of her peer review.

Katie Veneziano

Animal Parents and Their Young

Many animals in the wild care for their young until their offspring can survive on their own. However, animals have different ways of raising their young. The bald eagle, the bottlenose dolphin, and the meerkat are examples of animals that care for their young in different ways.

The bald eagle is the national bird of the united States. The male and female of this species share the duty of incubating the eggs. While one parent watches the eggs the other looks for nesting material or food. Incubation lasts about thirty-five days. Once the eaglets are hatched, they continue to live with their parents for eight to fourteen weeks. By then, the eaglets can fend for themselves.

Revised to correct errors in mechanics and punctuation.

The bottlenose dolphin is a marine mammal that lives mostly in temperate and tropical waters. Usually, a female dolphin will have a baby, called a calf, about every three years. A calf lives with its mother for up to six years. During this time, a calf is taught how to find food and survive. Male bottlenose dolphins are not involved in raising their offspring.

Revised to improve factual accuracy.

A meerkat is a small African mongoose that lives in communal burrows. The male meerkat, like the male bottlenose dolphin, does not get involved in raising its young. Instead, the young are communally raised with the assistance of other females. After about twenty-one days, the young leave the burrow, but they are still cared for by the group. In fact, female "babysitter" meerkats act as lookouts near the burrow to protect the young from predators.

All three of these animal species brood their young. However, different animals live with their parents for different periods of time. In addition, the young of some species are raised by both parents, and the young of other species are raised by one parent or by the group. The examples of the bald eagle, the bottlenose dolphin, and the meerkat show similarities and differences in how animal species care for their offspring.

Revised to correct errors in punctuation.

(5) Publish Prepare a clean copy of your final draft. Share your essay with the class.

90

Test Preparation

Practice

Read the following test sample. Study the tips in the boxes. Work with a partner to answer the questions.

The Red River War

1   In the mid-1800s, the United States <u>expanded</u> west. Native Americans living on land that belonged to the United States were forced to leave their homes. The tribes were moved to reservations. The reservations were not like the homes the Native Americans left behind. The government gave them food. They trained to be farmers. But this was not the life that many of the Native Americans wanted.

2   In 1874, some of the Native Americans were not on reservations. A few attacked a group of buffalo hunters in Texas. The army then declared war on all Native Americans who were not on reservations. Leaders of the tribes were sent to Florida. The Native Americans did not have leaders on the reservations. Soldiers hunted any Native American in the area. Native Americans were forced onto the reservations or killed.

3   In 1875, the army negotiated with the last group of Native Americans outside of the reservations. Their leader, Quanah Parker, led his people to Fort Sill, ending the war.

1 What is the purpose of the selection?
   A   To inform the reader about an important event
   B   To persuade the reader to visit Fort Sill
   C   To explain to the reader how to live in peace
   D   To describe to the reader life on the reservations

2 In the selection, what does <u>expanded</u> mean?
   A   lived
   B   hunted
   C   spread
   D   traveled

Taking Tests
You will often take tests that help show what you know. Study the tips below to help you improve your test-taking skills.

Tip
Do not skip around when taking a test. Skipping around makes it very easy to mark an answer on the wrong line or to forget to return to answer a question.

Tip
Do not think the test has a trick question. Reread the question to be sure you understand it correctly.

91–94

Smithsonian American Art Museum

Embracing Family, Friends, and Neighbors

All people have relationships in their lives. The way you act with a parent may be different from the way you act with a friend. But both relationships may offer something important to your life. American artists have used all sorts of media to capture this idea.

Franz Kline, *Merce C* (1961)

In this large oil painting, Franz Kline painted bold black brushstrokes against a white background. Kline wanted the painting to celebrate the talent of his friend Merce Cunningham, a dancer and choreographer. Kline uses only two colors, black and white, in *Merce C*, but the viewer feels motion and excitement anyway. Kline probably used his whole body to create the wide brushstrokes, which push against the border of the canvas. He even lets spatters and drops of black paint show on the canvas. Kline did this to celebrate the unexpected movements Cunningham made in his dances. Although this may not look like a traditional portrait of his friend, Kline's painting captures a very physical grace. Some people think it looks like dancers moving.

Franz Kline, *Merce C*, ▶
1961, oil, 93 x 74⅝ in.,
Smithsonian American Art Museum

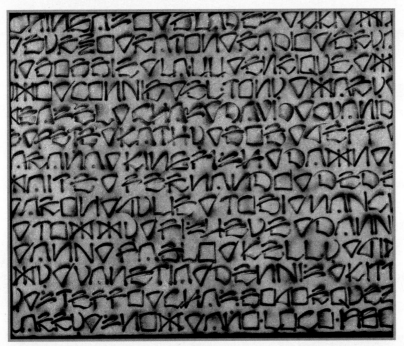

▲ Charles "Chaz" Bojórquez, *Placa/Rollcall*, 1980, acrylic, 68¼ x 83⅛ in., Smithsonian American Art Museum

Charles "Chaz" Bojórquez, *Placa/Rollcall* (1980)

In *Placa/Rollcall*, artist Charles "Chaz" Bojórquez uses stylized letters to create a painting. His painting is a wall of words that celebrates the names of his family, friends, and mentors, or teachers.

Bojórquez grew up in East Los Angeles, California. Gangs there often wrote graffiti on public places to list their members' names. Bojórquez turns this practice around. He celebrates people who have made a positive contribution to his life. He created his own secret alphabet to do it. For example, Bojórquez's *Y* is a triangle with a dot underneath it. He starts in the upper-left corner with his girlfriend's name and ends in the lower-right corner with the date. Once you adjust to the patterns in the lettering, you can find many names you'll recognize, including Tony, Tommy, Fernando, and Connie. Bojórquez sprayed the names against a huge 7-foot-wide gray-colored canvas so the painting would look like a wall or *placa* (Spanish for "plaque") of honor.

These two artists show how important caring relationships are, either in their own lives or in the lives of the people around them.

Discuss What You Learned

1. In what way does a wall of words honor people's lives? Do you know about other walls of words that do this?

2. In what way are these artworks different from those you might expect to see about friends and family relationships? Explain.

? BIG QUESTION
What kind of artwork would you create to celebrate the relationships in your life?

95–96

What does home mean?

This unit is about home. You will read texts about the homes immigrants lived in long ago, a young girl who feels most at home in a special personal space, and the feelings people experience when they are far from home. Reading, writing, and talking about these topics will give you practice using academic language and will help you become a better student.

Reading 1 Social Studies	Reading 2 Novel	Reading 3 Poetry

• "97 Orchard Street" • "The Pros and Cons of Tenement Life" **Reading Strategy** Use visuals	from *A Tree Grows in Brooklyn* by Betty Smith **Reading Strategy** Summarize	*The Lotus Seed* by Sherry Garland **Reading Strategy** Analyze text structure

Listening and Speaking—TV News Show

At the end of this unit, you will choose a topic and deliver a **TV news show** about it.

Writing—Expository Essay

At the end of this unit you'll write an **expository essay** about a topic that interests you. To help you write your essay, you'll write paragraphs for a magazine article, a plot summary, and a response to literature.

Quick Write

In your notebook, write a few sentences that describe your home or one you know about or think is a perfect home for you. Share them with a partner.

View and Respond

Go to your Digital Resources. Watch the video and answer the questions.

Prepare to Read

What You Will Learn

Reading

• Vocabulary building: *Context, dictionary skills, word study*

• Reading strategy: *Use visuals*

• Text type: *Informational text (social studies)*

Grammar

• Adjectival clauses: subject relative pronouns

• Adjectival clauses: object relative pronouns

Writing

• Write a magazine article

❓ THE BIG QUESTION

What does home mean? Why might people leave their home country? What do you know about immigrants that came to the United States in the mid-1800s to early 1900s? Use your prior knowledge to take the quiz below. Then share your answers with a partner.

1. All immigrants came from Europe. True / False

2. Immigrants came to the U.S.A. for different reasons. True / False

3. Most immigrants found high-paying jobs. True / False

4. Immigrants in large cities often lived in large houses with lots of space. True / False

Build Background

"97 Orchard Street" is an informational article. It provides factual information about a tenement museum located in New York City. The article is followed by **"The Pros and Cons of Tenement Life."** It lists both the advantages and disadvantages of living in tenements.

A tenement is a large building that is divided into many apartments. At the turn of the twentieth century, many immigrants from around the world left their homelands to come to the United States. They came to find jobs, to escape violence and discrimination, to get an education, or to own property.

After they arrived, many poor immigrants lived in tenements. Often as many as eight to ten people lived in one small apartment, many of which did not have running water or indoor plumbing. This led to unsanitary conditions. In addition, the tenements themselves were often in disrepair and unsafe.

◄ Immigrants arriving on Ellis Island, near New York City

Vocabulary

Listening and Speaking: Key Words

Read and listen to these sentences. Use the context to figure out the meaning of the highlighted words. Use a dictionary to check your definitions. Then write each word and its meaning in your notebook.

Key Words

exhibit
inspector
mission
neighborhood
preserved
tenement

1. The museum exhibit displays children's toys from the 1800s.
2. The fire inspector decided it was safe for people to live in the building.
3. The museum's mission is to provide its visitors with historical information about immigrants and how they lived.
4. There are many people who live in that area, or neighborhood.
5. The museum preserved the old buildings, or kept them from being destroyed.
6. Eight people lived together in one small apartment within the tenement.

Practice 97

Write the sentences in your notebook. Choose a key word from the box above to complete each sentence. Then take turns reading the sentences aloud with a partner.

1. That family just moved into the apartment building across the street. They are new to the _____.
2. Early tools and inventions are displayed in the science _____.
3. The old wedding dress looks new. It has been carefully _____.
4. For safety, the _____ advised the building's owner to install lights in the stairways immediately.
5. The crowded _____ was home to many families.
6. The school's _____ was to help immigrants learn English quickly.

▲ An inspector's job is to make sure a building is safe.

Listening and Speaking: Academic Words

Study the purple words and their meanings. You will find these words useful when talking and writing about informational texts. Write each word and its meaning in your notebook. After you read "97 Orchard Street" and "The Pros and Cons of Tenement Life," try to use these words to respond to the texts.

benefit = something that helps you or gives you an advantage	⮕	One **benefit** of living in a small town is that you know your neighbors.
community = all the people living in one place	⮕	New York City's SoHo district is known as a **community** of artists.
immigrants = people who enter another country in order to live there	⮕	In the early 1900s, many **immigrants** left their homelands and came to the United States.
incentive = something that encourages or motivates	⮕	The trainer uses food as an **incentive** for the dog as she teaches it tricks.

Practice 98

Work with a partner to answer these questions. Try to include the purple word in your answer. Write the sentences in your notebook.

1. What is one benefit of living in your town or city?
2. How would you describe your community?
3. Do you know any immigrants? Where are they from?
4. What kind of incentive do you need to study for a test?

◀ These community members enjoy the convenience of local shops.

Word Study: Silent Letters

In English there are certain letter combinations in which one letter is "silent." It is important to know these combinations when spelling many words. Some common combinations are listed in the chart below. Try to pronounce each word aloud.

Words with Silent Letters	Letter Combination	Sound	Silent Letter
campai**gn**	gn	/n/	g
de**bt**	bt	/t/	b
cli**mb**	mb	/m/	b
knot	kn	/n/	k

 Practice
99

Work with a partner. Take turns pronouncing and spelling the words in the box below. Then underline the letter combinations *gn*, *bt*, *mb*, and *kn* and circle the letter that is silent.

align	doubtful	knife	lamb	comb	foreign	know	limb

Reading Strategy   Use Visuals

Using visuals helps you understand the text better. Visuals include art, photographs, illustrations, diagrams, charts, maps, etc. Many informational texts have visuals. To use visuals, follow these steps:

- Look at the visual. Ask yourself, "What does the visual show? How does it help me understand the reading?"
- Read the captions that describe the visuals. Also, notice the titles, headings, and labels as they may help you identify the visuals.
- Think about how the visual contributes to your understanding of the text. Does it give extra information or explain something? How does it help you?

As you read "97 Orchard Street," pay close attention to the visuals. What do they show? How do they help you understand the text better?

100

Set a purpose for reading As you read, think about what it was like for immigrants to live in tenements. How do you think immigrants made the tenements feel like home?

97 Orchard Street 🎧

Have you ever visited New York City and seen the Statue of Liberty? Have you ever walked through Ellis Island and strolled around Castle Clinton? These **landmarks symbolize** the welcoming of immigrants to a new life. But did you ever wonder what happened *after* immigrants arrived in the United States? We suggest you make one more stop on the Immigrant Heritage Trail—97 Orchard Street.

At this New York City address, you will find a tenement building. It is located in the most famous immigrant neighborhood in America. Built in 1863, this structure is the first home of urban poor and immigrant people to be preserved in the United States. **Restored** and run by the Lower East Side Tenement Museum, the building allows us to travel back in time. Visitors can see firsthand the immigrant experience at the turn of the twentieth century.

---

landmarks, buildings or important, historical places
symbolize, represent
restored, made to look like it used to

The Lower East Side
Tenement Museum ▶

The only way to explore the museum is through a guided tour. Carefully restored apartments reflect the lives of residents from different historical periods and cultures. You will hear the stories of immigrant families who struggled to make a life in America.

Learn about the impact of **economic depressions** on the Gumpertz family in the 1870s. Discover the imaginative ways this family made their way through hard times. A visit to the Levines' apartment illustrates the Lower East Side's connection to the nation's **garment industry**. It also shows the impact this type of work had on immigrant families.

▲ An unrestored tenement apartment

In one museum exhibit, a costumed woman portrays immigrant Victoria Confino. This is a hands-on experience. You can touch any items in the apartment and try on **period clothing**. Victoria will answer any questions about life in 1916.

An unrestored apartment in the building drives home the nineteenth-century **reform movement**'s **campaign** for improved housing. Here you can participate in a program that lets you role-play. You can pretend to be a housing inspector: Determine what is acceptable housing at different times, and learn how people fought for better housing. Visitors also learn about housing rights today and how to report housing problems.

---

economic depressions, times when many people are out of work
garment industry, businesses that make clothes
period clothing, clothes that were worn long ago
reform movement, movement intended to bring about change
campaign, series of actions intended to achieve a particular result

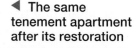

◀ The same tenement apartment after its restoration

Before You Go On

1. What is located at 97 Orchard Street?

2. What will you see and hear there?

 On Your Own

Would you want to visit the tenement museum? Why or why not?

▲ A New York City Lower East Side street scene in the early 1900s

The museum offers public tours and school tours. More than 25,000 schoolchildren each year participate in the site's original programs, which use history to teach **tolerance**. You can also take part in discussions of current issues such as immigration, labor, and **social welfare**. And walking tours of the Lower East Side describe the neighborhood's role as the nation's most famous gateway for immigrants.

An important part of the museum's mission is addressing current social issues by looking back at history. For example, immigrant students who visit the museum today use the diaries and letters of past immigrants to learn English.

To help unite the diverse community surrounding it, the museum has organized the Lower East Side Community Preservation Project. The project helps community leaders identify and restore local historic places. It is working currently to create historical markers at sites around the neighborhood. The sites represent the different groups who have lived in the neighborhood since the 1800s.

---

tolerance, the acceptance of other people and cultures as they are
social welfare, a government program that gives assistance to the poor

The Pros and Cons of Tenement Life 🎧

Pros (+):

Closeness to work: Tenement residents had a difficult time finding transportation to bring them to work. Living and working close together made life easier.

Fraternity: Immigrants sharing the same backgrounds often lived in the same neighborhoods. In this way, they found support in **fraternal organizations**. These groups offered help in finding jobs and places to live.

Assimilation: Living among people of the same background helped immigrants cope with the American way of life.

Amusements: Coney Island, **nickelodeons**, and dance halls offered nearby, inexpensive ways to have fun and relax. Taking strolls to see store windows and riding the trolley provided entertainment, too.

Cons (−):

Disease and poor sanitation: There was a high death rate among immigrants who lived in tenements. Health officials blamed this on overflowing garbage and lack of proper **sanitary facilities**.

Lack of outside air and ventilation: Prior to 1879, rooms in tenements were not required by law to have access to outside air. That meant that residents had to endure **sweltering** heat during the summer.

Darkness: One social worker nearly tripped over children sleeping in a tenement's dark hallway. Eventually, building owners were forced to install lights near the stairs.

Fire hazards: Wooden staircases, few windows, and overcrowding turned many tenements into death traps when a fire started.

---

fraternal organizations, groups of people, usually men, who consider each other brothers and support and help one another
nickelodeons, early movie theaters where a ticket cost five cents
sanitary facilities, services and equipment that keep buildings and streets clean
sweltering, extremely hot

Before You Go On

1. What is the Lower East Side Community Preservation Project? What is its goal? How does it help the community?

2. In what ways were some tenements dangerous to live in?

👤 On Your Own

Do you think the benefits of tenement life outweighed the disadvantages? Why or why not?

Review and Practice

Comprehension
101

Recall

1. When was the tenement at 97 Orchard Street built?

2. What is the only way to explore the museum?

Comprehend

3. What were some **incentives** for **immigrants** to come to the United States?

4. What were some of the struggles immigrants faced in a new **community** in the United States?

Analyze

5. How does the museum help resolve current social issues?

6. What do you think was the author's purpose for writing this text?

Connect

7. Do you think the immigration experience in the United States is easier or harder today than it was 100 years ago? Explain.

8. Would you like to visit 97 Orchard Street? Which programs or exhibits would you enjoy? Explain.

▲ Nearby places like Coney Island in New York offered tenement residents inexpensive ways to have fun.

In Your Own Words

Complete the chart with information from the article "97 Orchard Street." Then, using the chart, demonstrate your comprehension of the article by summarizing it for your partner. What cultural and historical experiences do visitors find out about there?

"97 Orchard Street"	
Subject	**Details**
Community location	97 Orchard Street, New York City
Exhibits	
Activities and programs	

Discussion

Discuss with a partner or in a small group.

1. Based on what you read about it, would you recommend the museum or any of its programs to others? Why or why not?

2. Do you think city planners will always keep this building as a museum? What would you argue to keep it that way?

 What does home mean? Do you think it is difficult to create a new home in a new country? Why or why not?

Read for Fluency

Read for Fluency

It is often easier to read a text if you understand the difficult words and phrases. Work with a partner. Choose a paragraph from the reading. Identify the words and phrases you do not know or have trouble pronouncing. Look up the difficult words in a dictionary.

Take turns pronouncing the words and phrases with your partner. If necessary, ask your teacher to model the correct pronunciation. Take turns reading the paragraph aloud and giving each other feedback.

Extension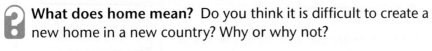

Work with a partner to write a critique in your notebook. You have already written one in Unit 3 (see pages 156–157). And, you've discussed whether you would recommend the museum. Now, you are going to write a critique of the museum at 97 Orchard Street for your school or local newspaper. Tell readers why you recommend a visit there (or not). Give reasons and examples to support your position. Use the T-chart to help you list ideas in your notebook. Note that if you do not recommend the museum, you can adjust the chart to reflect that. Include a visual. Then, take turns reading your critiques aloud to the class.

What to See and Do at 97 Orchard Street

Highlight	Details
Levines' apartment	Find out about the Lower East Side's connection to the garment industry.

Listening Skill

Think about what each speaker says and whether you agree or disagree. Try to focus on what the speaker is saying as you do this. Wait until the speaker finishes. Then, briefly summarize what the speaker said and tell whether you agree or disagree and why.

Grammar

Adjectival Clauses: Subject Relative Pronouns

An adjectival clause describes a noun or noun phrase. A relative pronoun begins an adjectival clause. The relative pronouns *who, whom,* and *that* are used to describe people; *that* or *which* is used to describe things. A relative pronoun may be a subject or object in adjectival clauses.

There are two kinds of adjectival clauses: restrictive and nonrestrictive. A restrictive clause is essential to the meaning of the sentence, and commas are not used. A nonrestrictive clause gives additional information. It is not essential to the meaning of the sentence, and commas are used.

> We especially enjoyed one program **that** lets you role-play. [The clause is *restrictive*. It is essential to the meaning since it tells which program they enjoyed.]
> We enjoyed all of the programs, **which** were very exciting. [The clause is *nonrestrictive*. It is not essential to the meaning and just adds information.]

Practice A

Complete each sentence with the subject relative pronoun *who, that,* or *which*. Then write *R* for "restrictive" or *N* for "nonrestrictive." The first one is done for you.

1. The backpack _that_ has a red sticker is mine. _R_
2. New Zealand, _____ is east of Australia, is a wonderful country to visit. _____
3. He's the man _____ bought the house next door. _____
4. I can lend you the sunglasses _____ are on the table over there. _____

Practice B

In your notebook, combine the two sentences into one, using the correct relative pronoun. The first one is done for you.

1. Carlos is my best friend. Carlos is the star of the basketball team.
   Carlos, who is my best friend, is the star of the basketball team.
2. Can you give me the box? It's in the closet.
3. I read his latest book. It was really long.
4. I liked your friends. They came to the party.

Grammar Skill

The verb in the adjectival clause must agree with the relative pronoun's antecedent. If the antecedent is singular, the verb must be singular. If the antecedent is plural, the verb must be plural. The relative pronoun itself does not change form, whether its antecedent is singular or plural, masculine or feminine.

Grammar Check

✓ Which **subject relative pronouns** are used to describe things?

Apply

Write three sentences about a vacation you have taken, using the relative pronouns *who, that,* and *which.* Then tell a partner about the place.

Example: I've been to Staunton, which is a small historic city in Virginia.

Adjectival Clauses: Object Relative Pronouns

A relative pronoun may be a subject or object in adjectival clauses. In this lesson, the focus is on relative pronouns as objects in adjectival clauses. Use the object relative pronoun *whom* to describe people; use *that* and *which* to describe things; use *where* to describe a place; use *when* to describe a time; and use *whose* to show possession.

> The tour guide, **whom I learned a lot from,** was an immigrant.
> They had an interesting **program that I participated in.**
> I participated in a program **that I enjoyed.**
> I visited an unrestored apartment **where I role-played an inspector.**
> I went to the museum on Thursday, **when it wasn't so crowded.**
> We learned about the Levines, **whose apartment we visited.**

Identify a pronoun's antecedent so you know which relative pronoun to use. In the example below, you need a pronoun to refer to housing rights. The pronouns *which* or *that* can be used.

> People fought for housing rights. We have **housing rights** today. →
> People fought for housing rights, **which** we have today.

Practice A
103

Work with a partner. Complete each sentence with an appropriate object relative pronoun. Add commas where needed.

1. They made us lunch, <u>which</u> we enjoyed.
2. The meeting _____ I went to was interesting.
3. The man _____ I was telling you about is over there.
4. Sandy went to the beach _____ there are a lot of sharks.

Practice B

In your notebook, combine the two sentences into one, using an appropriate object relative pronoun. The first one is done for you.

1. We went to the beach. We had a lovely picnic.
   <u>We went to the beach where we had a lovely picnic.</u>
2. I'm helping my neighbors. Their cat is home alone.
3. We have a birdfeeder. I made it myself.
4. These are the photos. We took them on our last vacation.

Writing

Write a Magazine Article

In expository writing, you present factual information. You are going to write a magazine article, one form of exposition. The article should immediately get your reader's attention: you can do this by asking the reader a question or posing an interesting detail that draws the reader in. Your article should answer the 5Ws: *Who? What? Where? When?* and *Why?* Think about how the article you just read answered these questions.

Writing Prompt

Write a magazine article about an event in your community. You could write about a museum exhibit, a sporting event, or a concert. Be sure to use adjective clauses correctly in your writing.

(1) **Prewrite** Begin by choosing a recent event in your community.

W B
104

- Write the name of the event at the top of the page in your notebook.

- Think about answers to the 5Ws.

- List your answers in a graphic organizer, such as a chart.

Here's a chart created by a student named Blaise. She is writing an article about an exhibit at the Museum of Science in Boston, Massachusetts.

Who?	anyone who is curious about the way things work
What?	the lightning exhibit
Where?	Museum of Science in Boston, Massachusetts
When?	whenever the museum is open to visitors
Why?	Staff members describe how lightning is made. Then they replicate the process right in front of you!

② **Draft** Use your chart to help you write a first draft.

- Remember to answer the 5W questions.
- Use adjectival clauses to combine sentences.
- Be sure to get your reader's attention.

③ **Revise** Read over your draft. Look for places where the writing is unclear or needs improvement. Complete (√) the Writing Checklist to help you identify problems. Then revise your draft, using the editing and proofreading marks listed on page 401.

④ **Edit and Proofread** Check your work for errors in grammar, usage, mechanics, and spelling. Trade papers with a partner to obtain feedback. Use the Peer Review Checklist on Workbook page 104. Edit your final draft in response to feedback from your partner and your teacher.

⑤ **Publish** Prepare a clean copy of your final draft. Share your magazine article with the class. Save your work. You'll need to refer to it in the Writing Workshop at the end of the unit.

Writing Checklist
Ideas:
☐ I answered the 5Ws in my article.
Sentence Fluency:
☐ I combined sentences using adjectival clauses.
Conventions:
☐ I used subject and object relative pronouns correctly.

Here is Blaise's paragraph about a museum exhibit. Notice how she answers the 5W questions and uses content-based vocabulary.

Blaise Yafcak

A Museum Worth Visiting

Anyone who is curious about the way things work in nature should visit the lightning exhibit at the Museum of Science in Boston, Massachusetts. The Museum of Science is one of the most exciting science museums in the country; and the lightning exhibit, which is on permanent display, is a highlight of any tour. Visitors to Boston, residents of the city, kids, teenagers, and adults will all find the exhibit fascinating. It is located in a large amphitheater, where museum staff members describe how lightning is made. They explain how positive charges in the ground can be attracted to and collide with negative charges in a rain cloud. These collisions are what you see during a lightning storm. After the lesson, the museum staff actually replicates the process of colliding charges right in front of you! This thrilling exhibit can be seen whenever the museum is open to visitors. Check the museum's website for hours of admission.

Prepare to Read

What You Will Learn

Reading

- Vocabulary building: *Literary terms, word study*

- Reading strategy: *Summarize*

- Text type: *Literature (novel excerpt)*

Grammar

- Adjectives and adjectival phrases

- Adverbs and adverbial phrases

Writing

- Write a plot summary

THE BIG QUESTION

What does home mean? We all have ideas of what makes home special for us. Maybe it's your mother's cooking. Maybe it's your room. Maybe it's the wonderful old tree in the backyard. Then again, maybe home is wherever you make it. Maybe home can be anywhere, as long as you are able to feel safe and comfortable and among the things you love. Discuss what "home" means with a partner.

Build Background

You are going to read an excerpt from the 1943 novel **A Tree Grows in Brooklyn** by Betty Smith. The story is about Francie, an immigrant girl who lives in a tenement apartment building with her brother and immigrant parents. Despite the difficulties the family experiences in daily life, Francie finds comfort in reading and endures the hardships of her life by going out on her fire escape where a large ailanthus tree grows. The tree serves as a symbol of both Francie's endurance and the solace and comfort she finds sitting and reading among its branches and leaves. In this excerpt, Francie gets a book at the library and brings it home to read on the fire escape.

▲ Fire escapes in New York, U.S.A.

Vocabulary

Learn Literary Words

Literary Words

flashback
setting

Authors will sometimes use a flashback to provide the reader with more information. A flashback is something that happened earlier in the story or in a character's past. A flashback can help the reader to better understand the characters or why something is happening at a certain time in the story.

> She remembered that the first author had been Abbott. She had been reading a book a day for a long time now and she was still in the B's. Already she had read about bees and buffaloes, Bermuda vacations and Byzantine architecture.

Learning Strategy

Use words that you already know to learn new and essential language, or words that you must know in order to understand your schoolwork.

What questions does the passage leave you with? Why do you think the author would include this flashback?

The setting of a story or a scene in it can help you understand the characters better. Notice details the author uses to describe this scene from the story. The author describes a place that is special to the main character Francie. What is the place like? How does this description help you understand Francie better?

> She arranged glass, bowl and book on the window sill and climbed out on the fire-escape. Once out there, she was living in a tree. No one upstairs, downstairs or across the way could see her. But she could look out through the leaves and see everything.

Practice 105

In a small group, reread the passages above. Discuss with a partner what you learned about the main character Francie from the flashback and from the description of a favorite place of hers in the story. Talk about what more you want to know about Francie.

Listening and Speaking: Academic Words

Study the **purple** words and their meanings. You will find these words useful when talking and writing about literature. Write each word and its meaning in your notebook, then say the words aloud with a partner. After you read the excerpt from *A Tree Grows in Brooklyn*, try to use these words to respond to the text.

Academic Words

determination
guidance
indicate
occurs

determination = having a firm purpose	➡	It was her **determination** that caused her to win the race.
guidance = advice or recommendation	➡	She went to the librarian for **guidance** when she could not find what she wanted.
indicate = say or do something that shows what you want or intend to do	➡	Students **indicate** that they have finished a test by putting their pencils on top of their papers.
occurs = happens	➡	The same situation **occurs** each time I visit the library.

Practice 106

Work with a partner to answer these questions. Try to include the **purple** word in your answer. Write the sentences in your notebook.

1. What do you wish you had enough **determination** to do?

2. What kind of **guidance** would you ask for when visiting a library?

3. In what ways do you **indicate** to others how you feel about them?

4. Can you name an event that **occurs** in your town year after year?

▲ Libraries are a tranquil place to study, but some visitors may require guidance to find what they need.

Word Study: Homophones

Homophones are words that sound the same but are spelled differently and have different meanings. For example, compare and contrast the words *see* and *sea*. *Sea* is a noun. *See* is a verb. Both words sound the same, but have different spellings and meanings.

| **sea** = a large area of salty water | The stormy *sea* has huge waves. |
| **see** = to perceive something with your eyes | The boy was sad to *see* the sun go down. |

Practice
107

Work with a partner. Read the sentences aloud. Then use one of the homophones in parentheses to complete each sentence. You can use a dictionary to help you.

1. (read/reed)

    a. The _____ of the plant grows in marshy areas.

    b. Our teacher asked us to _____ for a half hour each night.

2. (seem/seam)

    a. The _____ of the coat needed to be sewed.

    b. Tonight's homework does not _____ like a problem for the students to finish on time.

3. (made/maid)

    a. The kids _____ a big mural for the wall with their new paints.

    b. The _____ cleaned up the hotel room after the guests left.

Reading Strategy | Summarize

Summarizing the main events of a story helps you follow what's happening. Doing this will help you make predictions about what might happen and be more engaged with a story. To summarize a story, follow these steps:

- Stop reading from time to time and summarize what's happened so far.
- Take notes. Underline important details in your book.
- Use your own words to write a few sentences about what's happened in your notebook.

As you read the excerpt, summarize often and think about what might happen next.

108

Set a purpose for reading As you read, think about Francie's experience living in an immigrant neighborhood in Brooklyn. How does she use her environment to help herself feel at home there?

from A Tree Grows in Brooklyn

by Betty Smith

The library was a little old **shabby** place. Francie thought it was beautiful. The feeling she had about it was as good as the feeling she had about church. She pushed open the door and went in. She liked the combined smell of worn leather **bindings**, library paste and freshly-inked stamping pads better than she liked the smell of burning incense at high mass. Francie thought that all the books in the world were in that library and she had a plan about reading all the books in the world. She was reading a book a day in alphabetical order and not skipping the **dry** ones. She remembered that the first author had been Abbott. She had been reading a book a day for a long time now and she was still in the B's. Already she had read about bees and buffaloes, Bermuda vacations and Byzantine architecture. For all

> **Reading Skill**
>
> Identify the words you don't understand as you read and ask your teachers or peers for help with those words.

---

shabby, in poor condition
bindings, coverings for hardcover books
dry, dull

of her **enthusiasm**, she had to **admit** that some of the B's had been **hard going**. But Francie was a reader. She read everything she could find: trash, classics, time tables and the grocer's price list. Some of the reading had been wonderful; the Louisa Alcott books for example. She planned to read all the books over again when she had finished with the Z's.

Saturdays were different. She treated herself by reading a book not in the alphabetical sequence. On that day she asked the librarian to **recommend** a book.

After Francie had come in and closed the door quietly behind her—the way you were supposed to do in the library—she looked quickly at the little golden-brown pottery jug which stood at the end of the librarian's desk. It was a season **indicator**. In the fall it held a few sprigs of bittersweet and at Christmas time it held holly. She knew spring was coming, even if there was snow on the ground, when she saw pussy willow in the bowl. And today, on this summer Saturday of 1912, what was the bowl holding? She moved her eyes slowly up the jug past the thin green stems and little round leaves and saw . . . nasturtiums! Red, yellow, gold and ivory-white. A head pain caught her between the eyes at the taking in of such a wonderful sight. It was something to be remembered all her life.

---

enthusiasm, joy
admit, confess
hard going, difficult
recommend, suggest
indicator, something to tell the state or level of something

Before You Go On

1. How did Francie plan to read "all the books in the world"?

2. How is Saturday at the library different for Francie?

On Your Own

Why do you think Francie spends so much time reading? Explain.

"When I get big," she thought, "I will have such a brown bowl and in hot August there will be nasturtiums in it."

She put her hand on the edge of the polished desk liking the way it felt. She looked at the neat row of freshly-sharpened pencils, the clean green square of blotter, the fat white jar of creamy paste, the precise stack of cards and the returned books waiting to be put back on the shelves. The remarkable pencil with the date slug above its point was by itself near the blotter's edge.

"Yes, when I get big and have my own home, no **plush** chairs and **lace** curtains for me. And *no* rubber plants. I'll have a desk like this in my **parlor** and white walls and a clean green blotter every Saturday night and a row of shining yellow pencils always sharpened for writing and a golden-brown bowl with a flower or some leaves or berries always in it and books . . . books . . . books. . . ." . . . .

She stood at the desk a long time before the librarian deigned to attend to her. "Yes?" inquired that lady **pettishly** . . . .

"Could you recommend a good book for a girl?"

"How old?"

---

plush, luxurious
lace, delicately knitted fabric
parlor, living room
pettishly, with a childish bad temper

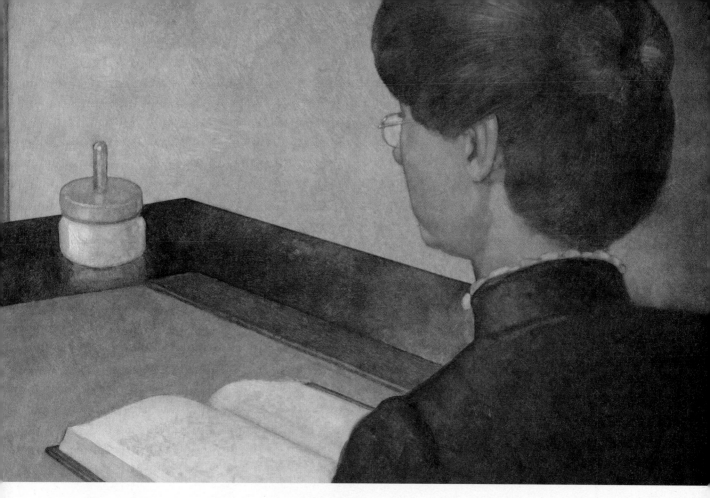

"She is eleven."

Each week Francie made the same request and each week the librarian asked the same question. A name on a card meant nothing to her and since she never looked up into a child's face, she never did get to know the little girl who took a book out every day and two on Saturday. A smile would have meant a lot to Francie and a friendly comment would have made her so happy. She loved the library and was **anxious** to **worship** the lady in charge. But the librarian had other things on her mind. She hated children anyhow.

Francie **trembled** in **anticipation** as the woman reached under the desk. She saw the title as the book came up: *If I Were King* by McCarthy. Wonderful! Last week it had been *Beverly of Graustark* and the same two weeks before that. She had had the McCarthy book only twice. The librarian recommended these two books over and over again. Maybe they were the only ones she herself had read; maybe they were on a recommended list; maybe she had discovered that they were **sure fire** as far as eleven-year-old girls were concerned.

---

anxious, wanting something very much
worship, honor, especially in a religious way
tremble, shake with emotion
anticipation, waiting for and expecting
sure fire, certain to succeed

Before You Go On

1. How does Francie feel about being in the library? Explain.

2. How do Francie's visions of the future show what is important to her?

 On Your Own

Did anything surprise you about the librarian? Explain.

Francie held the books close and hurried home, resisting the **temptation** to sit on the first **stoop** she came to, to start reading.

Home at last and now it was the time she had been looking forward to all week: fire-escape-sitting time. She put a small rug on the fire-escape and got the pillow from her bed and propped it against the bars. Luckily there was ice in the icebox. She chipped off a small piece and put it in a glass of water. The pink-and-white peppermint wafers bought that morning were arranged in a little bowl, cracked, but of a pretty blue color. She arranged glass, bowl and book on the window sill and climbed out on the fire-escape. Once out there, she was living in a tree. No one upstairs, downstairs or across the way could see her. But she could look out through the leaves and see everything.

It was a sunny afternoon. A lazy warm wind carried a warm sea smell. The leaves of the tree made fugitive patterns on the white pillow-case. . . .

Francie breathed the warm air, watched the dancing leaf shadows, ate the candy and took sips of the cooled water in-between reading the book.

If I were King, Love,

Ah, if I were King. . . .

The story of François Villon was more wonderful each time she read it. Sometimes she worried for fear the book would be lost in the library and she'd never be able to read it again. She had once started copying the book in a two-cent notebook. She wanted to own a book so badly and she had thought the copying would do it. But the penciled sheets did not seem like nor smell like the library book so she had given it up, **consoling** herself with the **vow** that when she grew up, she would work hard, save money and buy every single book that she liked.

As she read, at peace with the world and happy as only a little girl could be with a fine book and a little bowl of candy, and all alone in the house, the leaf shadows **shifted** and the afternoon passed.

---

temptation, desire to do something, usually unwise or wrong
stoop, small porch up the steps of a building
consoling, comforting
vow, a promise
shifted, moved a short distance

✓ **LITERARY CHECK**

How does the **flashback** give the reader more insight into the main character?

Before You Go On

1. Where is Francie's favorite place to be at home? Why?

2. What do Francie's fear and her wishes tell you about the kind of person she is? Explain.

 On Your Own

What do you admire about Francie? Explain.

About the Author

Betty Smith was an American author who grew up in Brooklyn, New York, U.S.A., as a German immigrant. The character of Francie was loosely based on herself. She is best known for this novel, which is one of the most well-known novels of the 20th century.

Review and Practice

Reader's Theater

Act out the following scene between Francie and the librarian.

Francie: Hello, excuse me. [*looking over the library desk for the librarian, who is reaching for something below the counter*]

Librarian: [*standing up*] Yes?

Francie: Could you recommend a good book for a girl?

Librarian: How old?

Francie: She is eleven.

Librarian: [*reaching down for a book and laying it down, saying what she always said without thinking or looking at Francie*] It's due back in a week.

Francie: [*peering up to look at the book and then politely, but discouraged*] If I Were King by McCarthy? Oh, thank you, but you gave me that one already.

Librarian: [*still not looking at Francie*] Excuse me. Would you like the book again?

Francie: [*with some sense of urgency*] Yes, please, yes. I can read it again.

Comprehension
109

Recall

1. Where does Francie live?

2. What place in her neighborhood does she like to visit most?

Comprehend

3. Why does Francie think the librarian keeps recommending the same books?

4. Why do you think Francie doesn't seem to mind too much that the librarian does this?

Analyze

5. Considering the setting where Francie read, why do you think the author chose the title *A Tree Grows in Brooklyn*? Explain.

6. What do her plans for the future **indicate** to you about Francie and the kind of person she is? Can you identify with any of her plans? Explain.

Connect

7. What book would you recommend that Francie read? Explain.

8. What would you like to talk with Francie about? The library and the librarian? The books she's read? Explain.

Discussion

Discuss with a partner or in a small group.

1. From what you read, besides reading, what does Francie value in life? Explain.

2. The story is set in Brooklyn, New York, U.S.A., in 1912. Could it **occur** anywhere or at a more recent time in history? Explain.

 What does home mean? What do you think "home" means to Francie? Use details and examples from the excerpt to explain.

Listening Skill

Listen carefully to your classmates. Identify the most important ideas. Retell or summarize these ideas in your own words.

Response to Literature

[W][B] 109

Work with a partner. Write a dialogue between Francie and the librarian. Imagine that Francie confronts the librarian about some of her observations. Use details from the story, as well as inferences about the two characters, to help you write the dialogue. Consider beginning with:

Francie: May I ask you why you never seem to remember me?

Librarian: Well, I am very busy, you know. There are so many books and so many children with so many questions. I just don't have time to remember every one.

Francie: But I come here every day of the week and even on Saturday.

Once you have finished writing the dialogue, role-play the two talking to each other. Practice, using tone of voice and gestures you think each might use. When you are ready, present your dialogue to the class.

Grammar

Adjectives and Adjectival Phrases

An adjective modifies or describes a noun or pronoun. An adjective may be a single word or a phrase. Adjectives often appear before the noun they modify but may come after it.

> The **pink-and-white peppermint** <u>wafers</u> bought that morning . . . [modifies *wafers*]
> A **lazy warm** <u>wind</u> carried a **warm sea** <u>smell</u>. [modifies *wind*; modifies *smell*]

A prepositional phrase can also act as an adjective to describe a noun. A prepositional phrase begins with a preposition such as *of, to, in,* or *at.*

> She looked at the row **of freshly-sharpened pencils**. [modifies *row*]

Practice A

110

Work with a partner. Underline the noun or pronoun that the adjectives modify. The first one is done for you.

1. My mother has a **white cotton** <u>cloth</u>.
2. She's going to use that round hoop.
3. He's going to embroider a beautiful design.
4. Francie looked past the **little, round** leaves.
5. Then she saw them: they were red, yellow, gold, and ivory-white.
6. It was a **wonderful** sight.

Practice B

Underline the prepositional phrases that function as adjectives in the sentences below. The first one is done for you.

1. He entered a room <u>of anxious students</u>.
2. The baby rabbit looked like a ball of fluffy white cotton.
3. She closed her eyes while relaxing in the shade of the tree.
4. After the rain, the tent was heavy with moisture.
5. These exotic, fragrant flowers are a decoration of the restaurant.
6. The glare of the sun on the water blinded the fishers.

Adverbs and Adverbial Phrases

An adverb describes a verb, but it can also describe an adjective or another adverb. An adverbial phrase is a group of words that collectively modifies a verb, adjective, or another adverb.

Notice three adverbs or adverbial phrases that modify the verb *moved* in the sentence below.

> She <u>moved</u> her eyes **slowly up the jug past the thin green stems**.

- *Slowly* is an adverb that tells how her eyes moved.
- *Up* and *past* are adverbs that tell where her eyes moved.
- *Slowly up the jug* and *past the thin green stems* are adverbial phrases.

Practice A

111

Work with a partner. Circle the adverb or adverbial phrase in each sentence. The first one is done for you.

1. (Quickly and quietly), he opened the door.
2. Lilly opened her presents with extreme care.
3. The wind blew through the trees.
4. We walked without saying a word to anyone.
5. Sally will probably take notes in class.
6. Gene tapped his fingers nervously on the table.

Practice B

Complete the paragraph with adverbs from the box. More than one correct answer is sometimes possible. The first one is done for you.

extremely	dangerously	immediately	totally	quickly	perfectly

When he entered his bedroom he felt (1) ___immediately___ at ease. He (2) _____ closed the shades to block the sunlight. Even though his homework assignment was (3) _____ difficult, he didn't mind working on it in this (4) _____ comforting atmosphere. If he couldn't understand the assignment this time, he might be (5) _____ close to failing the unit test on Friday. In the comfort of his room, however, he felt (6) _____ positive about it all.

Grammar Skill

A *phrase* is a group of words that go together, but do not make a complete sentence.

Grammar Check

✓ What does an **adverb** describe?

Apply

Work with a partner. Write three sentences each with an adverb and an adverbial phrase. Ask your partner to underline the adverbial phrase and circle the adverb in your sentence.

Writing

Write a Plot Summary

A plot summary is a kind of expository writing. To identify the plot of a story, look for events that develop a conflict or problem that gets resolved by the story's end. Be sure to include important details such as the main characters and the setting. In your plot summary, briefly describe the conflict or problem the character(s) face and explain how the conflict is resolved.

Writing Prompt

Think about a story you know well. It may be a story presented in a book, film, or television show. Write a summary of the plot. Be sure to use adjectives and adverbs correctly.

(1) Prewrite Begin by choosing a story with a plot that you can summarize.

- Choose a book, film, story, or television show with a plot.

- What was the conflict and how was it resolved?

- Write the details that you'll need for your summary in a graphic organizer.

112

Here's a graphic organizer created by a student named Andrew for the excerpt from the novel *A Tree Grows in Brooklyn*.

Characters: Francie and the librarian
Setting: a library and apartment building in Brooklyn, New York, in 1912
Conflict: Francie feels intimidated by the librarian, but approaches her anyway.
Main events: Francie asks the librarian for a recommendation and checks out the book.
Resolution: She reads on her fire escape where she feels at peace with the world—with her book under the tree.

(2) Draft Use your graphic organizer to help you write a first draft.

- Remember to briefly describe the conflict and its resolution.

- Make sure your summary is brief but includes enough details that your reader can follow it.

- Be sure to use adjectives and adverbs correctly.

(3) Revise Read over your draft. Look for places where the writing is unclear or needs improvement. Complete (√) the Writing Checklist to help you identify problems. Then revise your draft, using the editing and proofreading marks listed on page 401.

(4) Edit and Proofread Check your work for errors in grammar, usage, mechanics, and spelling. Trade papers with a partner to obtain feedback. Use the Peer Review Checklist on Workbook page 112. Edit your final draft in response to feedback from your partner and your teacher.

(5) Publish Prepare a clean copy of your final draft. Share your plot summary with your class. Save your work. You'll need to refer to it in the Writing Workshop at the end of the unit.

Here is Andrew's plot summary of the excerpt from *A Tree Grows in Brooklyn*. Notice how he describes the main character, the setting, and the most important events, as well as the conflict and its resolution.

> Andrew Denkus
>
> <u>A Tree Grows in Brooklyn</u>: Plot Summary
>
> <u>A Tree Grows in Brooklyn</u> is about a girl named Francie, whose family lives in Brooklyn, New York, in 1912. Her parents are immigrants, and the family's life is difficult. But Francie finds a way to make her life exciting by reading everything she finds. In the excerpt, it's a Saturday so Francie goes to the library to ask the librarian for a book recommendation. She loves the sights and smells of the library. At home, she has a special place to read: out on her fire escape where a tree grows through the cement and shades her. There, where no one can see her and where she feels as though she can see everything, she sits and reads her books.

Writing Checklist

Organization:
- [ ] I included only the main conflict of the story and its resolution in my summary.

Word Choice:
- [ ] I included adjectives and adverbs in my summary.

Conventions:
- [ ] I used adjectives and adverbs correctly.

Prepare to Read

What You Will Learn

Reading

- Vocabulary building: *Literary terms, word study*

- Reading strategy: *Analyze text structure*

- Text type: *Literature (poetry)*

Grammar

- Adverbial clauses of time

- Adverbial clauses of purpose, reason, and contrast

Writing

- Write a response to literature

THE BIG QUESTION

What does home mean? Imagine being forced to leave your homeland in a hurry—when a war begins and bombs are falling all around. If you could take one possession with you, what would it be? Why is this item important to you? Discuss with a partner.

Build Background

In this section, you will read a narrative poem called **The Lotus Seed**. A narrative poem, like a short story, has a plot and characters. However, the structure of a narrative poem looks different. It tells a story in verse.

The Lotus Seed is about a woman who was forced to leave her home country, Vietnam. For hundreds of years, emperors ruled Vietnam. The Vietnamese believed the emperor was wise about all things. The emperors lived in a magnificent palace that had beautiful gardens filled with lotus plants.

The last emperor was Nguyen Vinh Thuy, who became emperor at the age of twelve in 1926. He took the name Bao Dai, meaning "Keeper of Greatness." Because the French had conquered Vietnam in the late 1800s, he had little power, but was a symbol of Vietnam's heritage.

By 1945, many Vietnamese wanted to be independent from France. Bao Dai resigned as emperor in support of Ho Chi Minh, the leader of the independence movement. After a long war, the Vietnamese defeated the French in 1954.

Soon after, a civil war began between the northern and southern parts of the country. The United States helped the southerners. The war ended in 1975, when the south was defeated. As the northern armies began to move south, many Vietnamese left the country by boat. Most of them came to live in the United States.

◀ Refugees flee Vietnam in 1975.

Vocabulary

Learn Literary Words

In the narrative poem you're going to read, the **speaker** of the poem is identified right away. Knowing this helps you realize that you will experience the events of the story through the speaker's eyes, or from her point of view. Read the opening lines from the poem. Who is the speaker? Who do you think might be the main character?

> My grandmother saw
> the emperor cry
> the day he lost
> his golden dragon throne.

A poet often uses a poetic device like a **symbol** to make the poem rich and more dramatic. For example, a flag is a decorated piece of cloth that stands for a country and often for people's strong feelings about their country. A symbol may, as in this poem, be an object that stands for something else. Read these lines from the poem that tell about the grandmother and identify what the seed is a symbol of for her:

> . . . she carried the seed
> inside her pocket
> for good luck, long life,
> and many children.

What does the seed represent to the grandmother?

Practice
113

With a partner, read the definition and example above. Then look at the ideas in the chart below. Work with a partner to think of a symbol for each idea. Draw or write your ideas for the symbol in the chart or on a separate sheet of paper. Share your symbols with the class.

Idea	Symbol
happiness	
sadness	
Earth-friendly	
freedom	
victory	

▲ The Vietnamese flag

Listening and Speaking: Academic Words

Study the **purple** words and their meanings. You will find these words useful when talking and writing about poetry. Write each word and its meaning in your notebook, then say the words aloud with a partner. After you read *The Lotus Seed*, try to use these words to respond to the poem.

Academic Words

attached
examined
significant
symbolize

attached = emotionally connected to		I am very **attached** to that vase. It belonged to my grandmother.
examined = observed carefully		We **examined** the shells carefully before removing them from the sand.
significant = important		It is hard to tell if the rains will bring a **significant** amount of rain to the garden.
symbolize = represent a quality or a feeling		To many people, yellow roses **symbolize** friendship.

Practice 114

Work with a partner. Use the **purple** words to help you complete the sentences.

1. One family keepsake that I'm **attached** to is _____.

2. When we **examined** the family photo album, we saw _____.

3. The most **significant** sight on the journey to our new home was _____.

4. If I take my _____ with me when I travel, it will **symbolize** home to me.

A Chinese vase ▶

Word Study: Spelling Long *o*

Learning to identify sound-spelling relationships will help you read more fluently. The narrative poem you are going to read contains words with the long *o* sound. Here are a few different spellings: *o*, *oa*, *o_e*, and *ow*.

o	oa	o_e	ow
so	boat	home	own
lotus	soak	throne	show

Practice
115

Work with a partner. Copy the headings from the chart above into your notebook. Take turns saying four words from the chart for your partner to spell until all words have been spelled correctly. Then write each word from the box below in the correct column. Finally, write a sentence using each word.

alone	below	close	coast	golden	old	road	window

Reading Skill

Make sure you understand sequence words commonly found in instructions, such as *first*, *next*, *then*, and *finally*. These words help you to understand how to complete a task.

Reading Strategy   Analyze Text Structure

Recognizing the structure of a work of literature will help you appreciate it better. A narrative poem tells a story, much like a short story does. Take a look at the poem on pages 224–227. Does it look like a story? While a narrative poem relates a conflict and its resolution, it uses verse or lines of poetry, arranged in stanzas, to do this. It does not use paragraphs though it may include some direct quotations, or spoken language.

To help you use text structure to understand a narrative poem, follow these steps and think about the questions:

- Determine who the speaker is. Who is telling the story?
- Notice the characters. Who are they and what are they like?
- Like a story, notice the setting. Where does it take place?
- Look for a conflict. How is it resolved?
- Notice where there is a direct quotation. Is it important?
- Notice how the sentences are broken up into lines. What is the effect?
- Be aware of poetic devices like symbols and repetition.

As you read the narrative poem, notice how it is like and unlike a short story. Use the ways it is like a story to help you understand it. Use the poetic elements to help you enjoy it!

116

Set a purpose for reading As you read, think about why Bà chose the lotus seed as a memory of home. What aspect(s) of home does the seed represent?

The Lotus Seed

Sherry Garland

My grandmother saw
the emperor cry
the day he lost
his golden dragon throne.
She wanted something
to remember him by,
so she snuck down
to the silent palace,
near the River of Perfumes,
and plucked a seed
from a **lotus pod**
that rattled
in the Imperial garden.
She hid the seed
in a special place
under the family altar,
wrapped in a piece of **silk**
from the **ao dai**
she wore that day.
Whenever she felt sad
or lonely,
she took out the seed
and thought of the
brave young emperor.
And when she married
a young man
chosen by her parents,
she carried the seed
inside her pocket
for good luck, long life,
and many children.

When her husband
marched off to war,
she raised her
children alone.
One day bombs fell
all around,
and soldiers
clamored door to door.
She took the time
to grab the seed,
but left her **mother-of-pearl**
hair combs lying
on the floor.
One terrible day
her family scrambled
into a crowded boat
and set out
on a stormy sea.
Bà watched the mountains
and the waving **palms**
slowly fade away.
She held the seed
in her shaking fingers
and silently said good-bye.
She arrived in a
strange new land
with blinking lights
and speeding cars
and towering buildings
that scraped the sky
and a language
she didn't understand.

---

lotus pod, hard, natural pouch that holds the seeds of the lotus plant
silk, soft, delicate material
ao dai, long dress
clamored, shouted loudly
mother-of-pearl, shiny substance found inside some seashells
palms, trees with broad, flat leaves that grow only at the top

✓ **LITERARY CHECK**

What is the seed a **symbol** of? What does it represent to Bà?

Reading Skill

Take turns reading each stanza of the poem. Listen to the way your partner reads. If you don't understand an idea or word, discuss with a partner. Take turns putting the sentences from the poem into your own words to help you. Then read the stanza aloud again to better appreciate it.

Before You Go On

1. What caused the emperor to cry?

2. How can you tell that Bà is attached to the young emperor?

 **On Your Own**

What happened on the day "bombs fell all around"? How did the day affect Bà?

She worked many years,
day and night,
and so did her children
and her sisters
and her cousins, too,
living together
in one big house.
Last summer
my little brother
found the special seed
and asked questions
again and again.
He'd never seen a lotus **bloom**
or an emperor
on a golden dragon throne.
So one night
he stole the seed
from beneath the family altar
and planted it
in a pool of mud
somewhere near Bà's
onion patch.
Bà cried and cried
when she found out
the seed was gone.
She didn't eat,
she didn't sleep,
and my silly brother
forgot what spot of earth
held the seed.
Then one day in spring
my grandmother shouted,
and we all ran
to the garden

and saw
a beautiful pink lotus
unfurling its petals,
so creamy and soft.
"It is the flower
of life and hope,"
my grandmother said.
"No matter how ugly the mud
or how long the seed lies **dormant**,
the bloom will be beautiful.
It is the flower
of my country."
When the lotus blossom
faded and turned
into a pod,
Bà gave each of
her grandchildren
a seed
to remember her by,
and she kept one
for herself
to remember the emperor by.
I wrapped my
seed
in a piece of silk
and hid it
in a secret place.
Someday I will plant it
and give the seeds
to my own children
and tell them about the day
my grandmother saw
the emperor cry.

✓ **LITERARY CHECK**

What can you tell about the **speaker** by reading the poem?

---

bloom, open up its flowers
unfurling, unrolling and opening
dormant, inactive

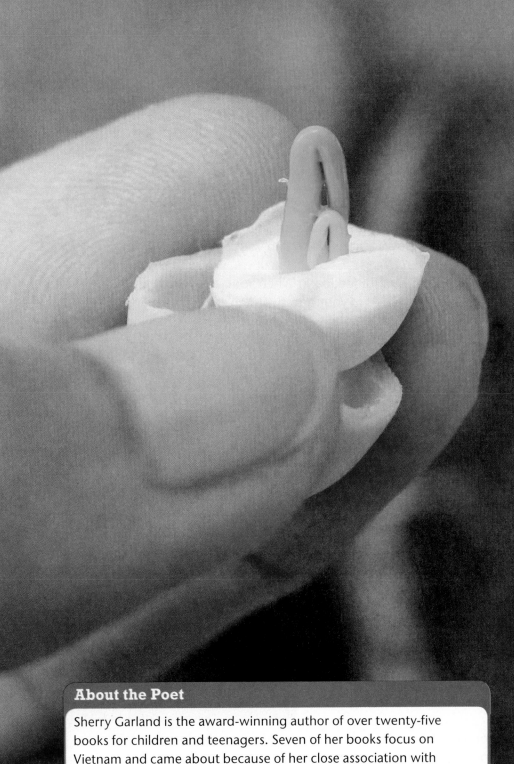

About the Poet

Sherry Garland is the award-winning author of over twenty-five books for children and teenagers. Seven of her books focus on Vietnam and came about because of her close association with Vietnamese families in the Houston, Texas, U.S.A., area. She also traveled to Vietnam for research purposes. As a fifth-generation Texan, she sets many of her books in the Lone Star State. Ms. Garland currently lives in Central Texas.

Before You Go On

1. Why does Bà get so upset when she discovers her lotus seed is gone? How do they "find" it?

2. What does the speaker plan to do with the seed Bà gave her?

👤 **On Your Own**

Why do you think Bà says what she does about the bloom of the flower? Explain.

Review and Practice

Dramatic Reading

One of the best ways to appreciate a poem is to read it aloud, with feeling. Work in small groups to read aloud the stanzas from the poem on pages 224–227. Be sure each stanza is read aloud and that everyone participates.

Read your stanza(s) with your group and talk about it. What feelings does it create? Underline words you want your listeners to notice. How will you say the words to show feelings? How can you use facial expressions and gestures?

Practice reading the poem. Ask your group for feedback. When you are ready, take turns reading your stanzas aloud in your group. Then, take turns, in your groups, reading the stanzas aloud to the class.

> ### Learning Strategy
>
> Be sure to use non-verbal cues. How do you think Bà held, carried, or hid the seed? Did she clutch it tightly? Decide how you will show this.

Comprehension
117

Recall

1. Whom did Bà want to remember?
2. Where did Bà get the lotus seed?

Comprehend

3. Why did Bà hide and carry the lotus seed on the occasions she did? What did it remind her of? How did it make her feel?
4. Why did Bà's grandson steal the lotus seed? What is it that he cannot understand?

Analyze

5. Why do you think the author wrote the poem *The Lotus Seed*? What did she want to share with her readers?
6. Why was the lotus seed so important to Bà? Why is it so effective as a symbol in the poem?

Connect

7. What one thing would you take if you had to leave your homeland? What does it **symbolize** to you?
8. Which character in the poem did you identify with the most? Why?

▲ Mekong Delta, Vietnam

Discussion

Discuss with a partner or in a small group.

1. Do you think the lotus flower was more **significant** to Bà before she left her country or after she left her country? Explain.

2. Do you think the lotus seed will ever mean as much to the speaker as it did to Bà? Explain.

 What does home mean? The speaker says she plans to tell her children about the day her grandmother saw the emperor cry. Is there a story that is told over and over again in your family? How does passing stories along to family members keep a sense of home alive?

Response to Literature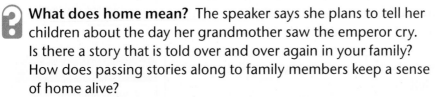
117

Work with a partner. Discuss what the poem would be like if there were a different speaker: Bà or her grandson or the emperor. Take notes about how the character of your choice feels about Bà and the lotus seed. Rewrite part of the poem or write a stanza of your own from that character's point of view. Take turns reading your work for the class.

Grammar

Adverbial Clauses of Time

An adverbial clause of time answers the question *When?* An adverbial clause is a subordinate clause. It must be used with a main clause. Sentences with main and subordinate clauses are called complex sentences. Adverbial clauses begin with subordinate conjunctions. An adverbial clause can come at the beginning or end of a sentence. When it comes at the beginning, use a comma after the clause.

> **After Bà arrived in a new land,** she lived in one big house with her family.
> Bà took the seed **before she left**.
> **When her husband marched off to war,** she raised her children alone.
> My brother stole the seed **while we weren't looking.**

Practice A
118

Underline the adverbial clause of time in the sentences below. The first one is done for you.

1. <u>Whenever it rains</u>, our street floods.
2. We ate dinner as soon as she arrived.
3. You can borrow my bicycle until I get back from vacation.
4. By the time you finish, it'll be too late!
5. While we were swimming, a huge wave crashed on us.
6. We can have chocolate cake after we finish dinner.

Practice B

Work with a partner. Correctly combine two clauses below to make complex sentences. The first one is done for you.

Whenever I eat shellfish,	I eat breakfast.
After she washed the car,	until she's finished studying.
Before I brush my teeth,	after I get up.
She isn't coming	the store was closed.
I always make my bed	it rained.
By the time we got there,	I get sick.

Adverbial Clauses of Purpose, Reason, and Contrast

Some adverbial clauses answer the questions *How?* and *Why?* Adverbial clauses can also contrast two ideas. Use the following subordinating conjunctions to show purpose, reason, and contrast. Remember that when an adverbial clause begins a sentence, it is followed by a comma.

Purpose	**In order that she would have good luck,** she carried a seed. She carried the seed **so that she would have good luck.**
Reason	I'll hide my seeds **because I want to give some to my children.** **Since I want to give my children seeds,** I'll hide mine in a secret place.
Contrast	**Although Bà was sad to leave her home,** the lotus seed gave her hope. The lotus seed gave Bà hope **even though she was sad to leave her home.**

Practice A
119

Underline the adverbial clause of purpose, reason, or contrast in the sentences below.

1. <u>Since we don't have enough money</u>, we can't go to the movies.
2. The teacher usually stands so that everyone can see and hear her.
3. In order that we could win the game, we needed to practice more.
4. He came to class today even though he had a cold.
5. As I don't want to spoil the surprise, I'm not going to tell you.

Practice B

Work with a partner. Circle the subordinating conjunction in parentheses that best completes each sentence. The first one has been done for you.

1. ((Although,) Since, So that) I was tired, I stayed up late.
2. Sara didn't want to see him (because, so that, in order that) she was upset.
3. (As, So that, Although) I hate shopping, I love new clothes.
4. (Since, In order that, Though) she's a flight attendant, she travels a lot.
5. We got up early (since, in order that, because) we could catch our train.

Writing

Write a Response to Literature

In this unit, you have written two types of exposition. You are going to write another type: a response to literature. A response to literature is a type of expository writing in which you explain, interpret, or respond to some aspect of a work of literature. You should organize your response around a clear idea and support the idea with details and examples from the text.

Writing Prompt

Write a response to a story or another piece of literature. Think about how the story or work affected you. Decide on a main idea you can use for your paragraph. Be sure to use adverbial clauses of time, purpose, reason, or contrast correctly.

① **Prewrite** Begin by choosing a story, poem, or other work of literature to write about.
120

- Think about your reaction to the work.

- Write a clearly stated main-idea sentence.

- Think about some specific examples to support your main idea.

- List your ideas in a graphic organizer.

Here's a word web created by a student named Madeline in response to the poem *The Lotus Seed*.

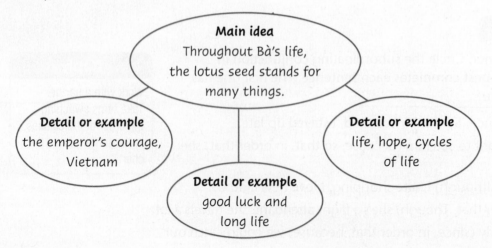

Main idea
Throughout Bà's life, the lotus seed stands for many things.

Detail or example
the emperor's courage, Vietnam

Detail or example
good luck and long life

Detail or example
life, hope, cycles of life

② **Draft** Use your word web to help you write a first draft.

- State your reaction to the piece of literature.

- Support your main idea with details and examples.

- Use adverbial clauses of time, purpose, reason, or contrast correctly.

③ **Revise** Read over your draft. Look for places where the writing is unclear or needs improvement. Complete (√) the Writing Checklist to help you identify problems. Then revise your draft, using the editing and proofreading marks listed on page 401.

④ **Edit and Proofread** Check your work for errors in grammar, usage, mechanics, and spelling. Trade papers with a partner to obtain feedback. Use the Peer Review Checklist on Workbook page 120. Edit your final draft in response to feedback from your partner and your teacher.

⑤ **Publish** Prepare a clean copy of your final draft. Share your response to literature with the class. Save your work. You'll need to refer to it in the Writing Workshop at the end of the unit.

Here is Madeline's paragraph. Notice how she uses adverbial clauses of time to describe the symbolic significance of the lotus seed.

> **Writing Checklist**
>
> **Organization:**
>
> ☐ I organized my response around a clear main idea.
>
> **Ideas:**
>
> ☐ I supported my main idea with details and examples.
>
> **Sentence Fluency:**
>
> ☐ I used adverbial clauses of time, purpose, reason, or contrast correctly.

Madeline Shaw

<u>The Lotus Seed</u>

   <u>The Lotus Seed</u> tells the story of Bà, a woman who flees her home in Vietnam to go to the U.S.A. Bà takes only one thing with her: a lotus seed. She had taken the lotus seed from the emperor's garden on the day he lost his throne. It reminded her of his bravery and gave her courage. She carried the seed for luck when she got married. And she clutched it in her hand as she sailed away from home. One night her grandson steals the seed and plants it, breaking her heart. But in the spring Bà discovers that her seed has grown into a beautiful lotus blossom. She calls it "the flower of life and hope." Throughout Bà 's life, the seed stands for many things. First it reminds her of the emperor's courage. When she weds, it represents good luck and long life. When she first comes to the U.S.A., it represents Vietnam. When the lotus flower blooms, it represents life and hope. Finally, when the lotus flower produces seeds, it represents the continuing cycles of life.

Link the Readings

Critical Thinking

Look back at the readings in this unit. Think about what they have in common. They all tell about home. Yet they do not all have the same purpose. The purpose of one reading might be to inform, while the purpose of another might be to entertain. In addition, the content of each reading relates differently to what home means. Now complete the chart below.

Title of Reading	Purpose	Big Question Link
"97 Orchard Street" "The Pros and Cons of Tenement Life"		
from *A Tree Grows in Brooklyn*	to entertain	
The Lotus Seed		A young mother must leave her home country.

Discussion

Discuss with a partner or in a small group.

- How do you think the immigrants mentioned in "97 Orchard Street" and the grandmother in *The Lotus Seed* felt about moving to a new country? What was similar and what was different?

What does home mean? What ideas do the readings in this unit share? Which reading do you relate to the most? Why?

Media Literacy & Projects

Work with a partner or in a small group. Choose one of these projects.

(**1**) Create a brochure or poster that describes the Lower East Side Tenement Museum, its exhibits, and its tours. You can visit the library for more information or use the internet to find images. Remember to include the museum's location, operating hours, and telephone number. Share your brochure or poster with the class.

(**2**) Make a menu of foods you enjoy from your family heritage. Include foods from as many areas as you consider to be your ethnic or geographic background. Decorate the menu and share it with classmates.

(**3**) The lotus plant is important in many cultures and religions. Research a legend or myth about a lotus flower and narrate, or tell, it to a partner.

(**4**) Make a collage about what happened in *The Lotus Seed*. Include a picture of the Imperial Garden, the boat crowded with immigrants, "the strange new land with blinking lights and speeding cars and towering buildings that scraped the sky," and other details from the poem.

Further Reading

Choose from these reading suggestions. Practice reading silently for longer periods with increased comprehension.

Grey Owl, Vicky Shipton
This book tells the amazing story of Grey Owl, a Native American who wanted to save his land and its forests and animals.

Homesick: My Own Story, Jean Fritz
In this blend of fact and fiction, the author describes the many things she loved about her childhood in China during the 1920s.

Making It Home: Real Life Stories from Children Forced to Flee, Beverly Naidoo
Displaced from their homes by war, children, ages six to seventeen, from Kosovo, Bosnia, Afghanistan, Iraq, the Congo, Liberia, Sudan, and Burundi talk about their experiences as refugees.

The House on Mango Street, Sandra Cisneros
A young woman growing up in a tough environment in Chicago Illinois, U.S.A. expresses her emotions through poems and stories.

Listening & Speaking Workshop

TV News Show

With a team, you will present a TV news show about events in your community.

① Think About It

You have probably watched the news on TV—but do you know what reporters do before the cameras roll? They interview people, conduct research, and write a script. Their reports focus on the 5Ws of a story: *who, what, where, when,* and *why.*

Work in small groups. Make a list of recent or upcoming events in your community. For example:

- An election for mayor or city council
- The school board's decision to build a new school
- A concert by a local band
- The opening of a new skate park

Have each group member choose a different idea from the list.

② Gather and Organize Information

Discuss and plan the overall structure of your show. If possible, watch a TV news show to get ideas. Choose one person to be your news anchor (the main person who presents the news on TV). The anchor will introduce each segment and its reporter.

Research Check local newspapers or interview community members to find information for your show. Take notes and get answers to the 5Ws.

Order Your Notes Think about the best order in which to tell your news story. Then make an outline showing your main points in this order.

Use Visuals Look for photos, maps, and other visuals to use during your news show. Think about how and when you will show each visual.

Prepare a Script As a group, write a short opening and closing for your news show. For example, the anchor might say: "Welcome to the Channel 6 Evening News. I'm Stanley Stevens. Tonight's top story will be of special interest to young people. Here's Julia Jenkins reporting live from Springfield's new skate park." Then use your outline and notes to write a script for your individual report. Start your news story in a way that will get people's interest. Remember to focus on the 5Ws.

③ Practice and Present

Read your script over and over again until you know it well. To make your script richer and more interesting, use a variety of grammatical structures, sentence lengths, sentence types, and connecting words. Be sure to look "into the camera." Make smooth transitions between news stories. Help each other with visuals as needed. Listen to your team members as they provide you with directions about how to better your performance. Be sure to follow these suggestions as they are given to you.

Deliver Your TV News Show Although this is a formal presentation, you should appear relaxed and comfortable as you present it. Be sure your scripts and visuals are ready before you begin. Do not rush or mumble! Speak clearly, and pronounce names and numbers carefully. Emphasize key ideas by pausing, slowing down, speaking more loudly, or repeating them at the end of your story.

④ Evaluate the Presentation

You will improve your skills as a speaker and a listener by evaluating each presentation you give and hear. Complete (√) this checklist to help you judge your team's TV news show and the news shows of your classmates.

- ☐ Was the news show presented in a professional and interesting way?
- ☐ Did the speakers look "into the camera" most of the time?
- ☐ Was each story about an event in your community?
- ☐ Did the speaker use formal or informal language? Was it appropriate?
- ☐ Could the show be improved?

Speaking Skills

Always face the audience (or imaginary TV camera) when you speak. Don't hide behind your script or visuals!

Use specific verbs and descriptive adjectives to help the audience visualize the event.

Listening Skills

When presenting your show, listen carefully to your fellow team members, and learn your cues—words or actions that signal it is your turn to speak.

When listening to another's show, listen for answers to the 5Ws. Does each story include these important details? If not, request more information.

Strengthen Your Social Language

In social contexts as well as in some of your content-area classes, you will need to ask for and give information. Go to your Digital Resources for this unit. This activity will help you acquire key structures, expressions, and words needed for extended speaking assignments and in everyday academic and social contexts.

Writing Workshop

Expository Essay

Write an Expository Essay

Now that you know how to develop one, you are going to write a five-paragraph expository essay, using one of the paragraphs you wrote in this unit. You may choose from: a magazine article, a plot summary, or a response to a work of literature.

Writing Prompt

Choose one of the paragraphs you wrote for this unit and expand it into a five-paragraph essay. Be sure to use adjectival clauses correctly.

① **Prewrite** Review your previous work in this unit. Choose the paragraph you want to expand. Then think about your readers and answer these questions:

W B
121

• What do your readers already know about your topic?

• What questions do you think they will have?

List your questions and answers in a graphic organizer such as a question-and-answer outline. Also think about interesting details you want to add when you expand your paragraph into an essay.

A student named Blaise decided to expand her paragraph about a Boston museum. Here is the outline she prepared.

> I.   What is the Museum of Science?
>   A. An exciting science museum
>   B. Located in Boston
> II. What is its mission?
>   A. Stimulate interest in science
>   B. Show importance of science
> III. What can a visitor do there?
>   A. Planetarium and movie theater
>   B. Courses and exhibits
> IV. What is my favorite exhibit?
>   A. Lecture on lightning
>   B. Demonstration of lightning
> V.   What makes the museum special?
>   A. One of the foremost science
>   museums
>   B. Educational, interactive, and fun

(2) Draft Use your graphic organizer and the model on page 242 to help you write a first draft.

- Remember to introduce your topic in the first paragraph.

- Develop the topic by adding ideas, details, and examples.

- Sum up the important information in your concluding paragraph.

(3) Revise Read over your draft. Think about how well you have addressed purpose, audience, and genre. Your purpose is to inform. Is your essay clearly organized? Is it appropriate in content and tone for the intended audience?

Keep these points in mind as you revise your draft. Complete (√) the Writing Checklist below to help you identify additional issues that may need revision. Mark your changes on your draft, using the editing and proofreading marks listed on page 401.

> **Learning Strategy**
>
> Monitor your written language production. Using a writing checklist will help you assess your work. Evaluate your essay to make sure that your message is clear and easy to understand.

Six Traits of Writing Checklist

- ☐ **Ideas:** Does my essay present interesting information about the topic?
- ☐ **Organization:** Do I present information in a way that suits my topic?
- ☐ **Voice:** Does my writing show my interest in the topic?
- ☐ **Word Choice:** Do I use transitions accurately?
- ☐ **Sentence Fluency:** Do I use a variety of sentences: simple, compound, and complex?
- ☐ **Conventions:** Do I use adjectival clauses correctly?

Here are the revisions Blaise plans to make to her first draft.

A Great Place to Visit

The Museum of Science in Boston, Massachusetts, is an exciting museum. ~~It~~ *that* can be visited many times without losing its appeal. The museum was founded in the 1830s but opened at its present ~~sight~~ *site* along the Charles River in 1951. It offer exhibits and activities. ~~They~~ *that* are both educational and fun.

The museum's mission is "to stimulate interest in and further understanding of science and technology and their importance for individuals and for society." *In fact,* The Museum of Science was the first all-inclusive science museum in the United States. It has also been ~~important~~ *a pioneer* in introducing interactive exhibits.

The museum has a planetarium where laser light shows are set to popular music. The museum also has a theater. ~~It~~ *that* presents movies about dinosaurs, sea life, the Grand Canyon, and other topics. One series of classes for high school kids are called "Mini Med-School." Each class focus on a different health issue and is taught by a doctor ~~They~~ *who* specialize*s* in that field. Courses for kids and adults are held at the museum throughout the year. Examples of the museum's many exhibits include *Butterfly Garden, Making Models, Natural Mysteries,* and *New England Habitats.*

> Edited to include adjectival clauses and to correct an error in the spelling of a homophone.

> Revised to correct use of possessives, correct spelling, added a transition word, and improved word choice.

> Edited to improve logical sequence of ideas and to use adjectival clauses.

My favorite exhibit at the museum is about lightning. After visitors are seated, one of the staff members talk about how lightning is made. The lecture is fascinating, but the demonstration that follows is even better! A machine actually produces bolts of lightning. Lightning right there in front of you! This exhibit is both dramatic and informative.

Boston's Museum of Science is one of the foremost science museums in the nation. If you visit this museum, you will learn about science and technology, while at the same time have fun. It is a wonderful museum to explore, whether you are a resident of Boston or a tourist from far away.

(4) **Edit and Proofread** Check your work for errors in grammar, usage, mechanics, and spelling. Then trade essays with a partner and Complete (√) the Peer Review Checklist below to give each other constructive feedback. Edit your final draft in response to feedback from your partner and your teacher.

121

Peer Review Checklist

- ☐ Was the essay clearly organized?
- ☐ Was the information interesting?
- ☐ Did I understand the topic better after reading it?
- ☐ Did the first paragraph introduce the topic?
- ☐ Did the concluding paragraph sum up the main points?
- ☐ Could changes be made to improve the essay?

Look at the next page to see the changes Blaise decided to make to her final draft as a result of her peer review.

Blaise Yafcak

A Great Place to Visit

The Museum of Science in Boston, Massachusetts, is an exciting museum that can be visited many times without losing its appeal. The museum was founded in the 1830s but opened at its present site along the Charles River in 1951. It offer[s] exhibits and activities that are both educational and fun.

> *Revised to correct an error in subject-verb agreement.*

The museum's mission is "to stimulate interest in and further understanding of science and technology and their importance for individuals and for society." In fact, the Museum of Science was the first all-inclusive science museum in the United States. It has also been a pioneer in introducing interactive exhibits.

The museum has a planetarium where laser light shows are set to popular music. The museum also has a theater that presents movies about dinosaurs, sea life, the Grand Canyon, and other topics. Courses for kids and adults are held at the museum throughout the year. One series of classes for high school kids [is] called "Mini Med-School." Each class focus[es] on a different health issue and is taught by a doctor who specializes in that field. Examples of the museum's many exhibits include *Butterfly Garden*, *Making Models*, *Natural Mysteries*, and *New England Habitats*.

> *Revised to correct errors in subject-verb agreement.*

My favorite exhibit at the museum is about lightning. After visitors are seated, one of the staff members talk[s] about how lightning is made. The lecture is fascinating, but the demonstration that follows is even better! A machine actually produces bolts of lightning. Lightning right there in front of you! This exhibit is both dramatic and informative.

> *Revised to correct an error in subject-verb agreement.*

[B]oston's Museum of Science is one of the foremost science museums in the nation. If you visit this museum, you will learn about science and technology, while at the same time have fun. It is a wonderful museum to explore, whether you are a resident of Boston or a tourist from far away.

> *Revised to correct an error in capitalization.*

(5) **Publish** Prepare a clean copy of your final draft. Share your essay with the class.

WB
122

Test Preparation

Practice

Read the following test sample. Study the tips in the boxes. Work with a partner to respond to each item.

Coming Home

1   Natalia and her family had a terrific vacation. Visiting family in Colombia is always fun. Natalia played with cousins she had not seen in years.

2   The long plane ride home made Natalia tired. Her little sister Anna whined and cried. Mother tried to quiet her. Father gave Anna candy. Nothing worked.

3   Anna curled up against Natalia's shoulder. Natalia talked softly to the girl. She told Anna that she should fall asleep. If she did, she could dream about home. Anna could play with her friends. She could play with her toys. Anna could dream of lying in bed with Natalia in their own bedroom.

4   All the talking made Natalia very sleepy. She <u>drifted off</u>, still holding Anna's hand. She had sweet dreams. Soon she heard Anna calling her name. They were finally home.

1 According to the passage, Natalia visited—.
- **A**   her parents and sister
- **B**   cousins at the airport
- **C**   family in Colombia
- **D**   friends back home

2 In the selection, what does <u>drifted off</u> mean?
- **A**   floated away
- **B**   landed softly
- **C**   flew away
- **D**   fell asleep

Taking Tests
You will often take tests that help show what you know. Study the tips below to help you improve your test-taking skills.

Tip
If you think an answer is only partly true, the answer is probably not correct. Look for the answer that is completely true.

Tip
Do not worry if other students finish the test quickly. How fast or how slowly someone else takes a test does not mean you are too slow or not doing well answering the questions.

WB
123–126

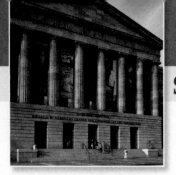

Smithsonian American Art Museum

Acknowledging the Past Reaching for the Future

The United States is a country made up of millions of people who are far away from their homelands. American artists often explore the emotions that this situation can bring about. Sometimes they show hope and excitement, other times loneliness and grief.

Carmen Lomas Garza, *Camas para Sueños* (1985)

In *Camas para Sueños* (Spanish for "Beds for Dreams"), two girls sit on the roof of their home looking at the full moon. Inside the house their mother stretches out a bright pink blanket to make the bed. Mexican-American artist Carmen Lomas Garza painted this scene of herself and her sister as young girls. They wear almost matching outfits—spotted shirts, pants, and similar shoes—which highlight their closeness. Below, their mother works hard to make their home a clean, safe place to have pleasant dreams. This painting celebrates Garza's sense of place as a girl within her family. As a Mexican American she sometimes felt less than welcomed by the locals in her town in south Texas, but in her own home she felt safe.

▲ Carmen Lomas Garza, "Camas Para Sueños (Beds for Dreams)" ©1985 Carmen Lomas Garza Gouache painting 28⅛ x 20½ inches Collection of the Smithsonian American Art Museum

Hung Liu,
The Ocean Is the Dragon's World,
1995, mixed media, 96 x 82½ in.,
Smithsonian American Art Museum ▶

Hung Liu, *The Ocean Is the Dragon's World* (1995)

Artist Hung Liu grew up in China in the 1950s when there was great political unrest. Liu did her artwork in the United States, but she uses her art to recreate a world that was lost in China. In *The Ocean Is the Dragon's World*, she painted a portrait of the great aunt of the last Emperor of China, who sits in the center of the canvas looking out at the viewer.

The decorated robes of the Empress fill the painting. You can also see peacock feathers (upper left) and flowers. Liu hung an actual empty metal birdcage onto the canvas! She also added a piece of bamboo painted with Chinese letters on the far right border. This added touch makes the painting look like the cover of a bound book (the Chinese read from right to left). Who knows what stories this grand courtly woman might have to tell?

Both of these artists either came from another country or were the first generation in their family to live in the United States. They use their art to explore the distance between the world their families left behind and the world they discovered in the United States.

Discuss What You Learned

1. Why do you think Carmen Lomas Garza called her painting "Beds for Dreams"?

2. In what way is the subject matter of *The Ocean Is the Dragon's World* different from *Camas para Sueños*?

BIG QUESTION
If you were an artist creating an artwork that explored the idea of "home," would you concentrate on the past or would you look toward the future? Explain your answer.

127–128

What is the human spirit?

THE BiG QUESTION

This unit is about the human spirit. You will read an informational text that describes someone who conquers life's obstacles with determination. You will also read literature about individuals who demonstrate the human spirit in the face of adversity. Reading, writing, and talking about these topics will help you practice using academic language and will help you become a better student.

Reading 1
Social Studies

"Alone on a Raft"

_____

Reading Strategy
Main idea and details

Reading 2
Play

"Three Letters: A Play in One Act" by Fran Hodgkins

_____

Reading Strategy
Read aloud

Reading 3
Short Story

"A Place in the World"

_____

Reading Strategy
Make inferences

Listening and Speaking—Radio Commercial

At the end of this unit, you will choose a topic and create and present a **radio commercial**.

Writing—Persuasive Speech

At the end of this unit you will write a **persuasive speech**. To help you do this, you will write a letter to the editor, a persuasive paragraph, and a review.

Quick Write

Write a few sentences about a time when you or someone you know had to face something difficult. How did you or that person deal with it?

View and Respond

Go to your Digital Resources. Watch the video and answer the questions.

Prepare to Read

What You Will Learn

Reading

- Vocabulary building: *Context, dictionary skills, word study*

- Reading strategy: *Main idea and details*

- Text type: *Informational text (social studies)*

Grammar

- Inseparable phrasal verbs

- Separable phrasal verbs

Writing

- Write a letter to the editor

THE BIG QUESTION

What is the human spirit? Sometimes we read stories about ordinary people who find themselves in incredibly challenging or dangerous situations. It might be someone fighting a disease or a person in a plane crash who is lost in the wilderness. Where do they find the courage to survive these experiences? What is it about the human spirit that sometimes lets us become more than we ever thought possible? Do we all have this kind of strength or spirit within us? And where exactly does it come from? Share your ideas with your peers and teacher. Ask for their feedback and support in order to develop background knowledge about this topic.

Build Background

You will read an informational text called **"Alone on a Raft."** It tells the story of a young Chinese man named Poon Lim who was the only survivor of a British boat that sank off the coast of South Africa in 1942. He was forced to live alone on a small wooden raft for more than four months at sea. His raft slowly drifted across the Atlantic Ocean until he was finally rescued off the coast of Brazil. After he recovered in a Brazilian hospital, he went to England and was given an award by King George VI.

▲ A torpedo similar to this one sank Poon Lim's ship.

Vocabulary

Listening and Speaking: Key Words

Read and listen to these sentences. Use the context to figure out the meanings of the highlighted words. Use a dictionary to check your answers. Then write each word and its meaning in your notebook.

Key Words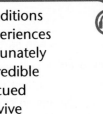

conditions
experiences
fortunately
incredible
rescued
survive

1. A young man lost at sea managed to survive by catching fish and birds.

2. Poon Lim's story of survival is incredible because it's so hard to believe he survived so long at sea.

3. The conditions on the raft were difficult but became even worse after the storm.

4. Brazilian fishermen rescued the young man ten miles off the coast.

5. Fortunately, Poon Lim was very resourceful and managed to live.

6. A variety of experiences, like traveling and learning new things, are important in life.

Practice
129

Write the sentences in your notebook. Choose a key word from the box above to complete each sentence. Then take turns reading the sentences aloud with a partner.

1. The fire department came and _____ the cat from the top of the tree.

2. Extremely challenging _____, like being in an earthquake, can sometimes bring out the best in human spirit.

3. The man was lost in the desert but managed to _____ by drinking water he found inside cactuses.

4. The weather _____ on the mountain were life-threatening and the climbers had to descend.

5. Human beings are sometimes capable of _____ strength and courage.

▲ Conditions at sea can be very difficult to survive.

6. _____, her house was not affected by the nearby forest fire.

Listening and Speaking: Academic Words

Study the **purple** words and their meanings. You will find these words useful when talking and writing about informational texts. Write each word and its meaning in your notebook. After you read "Alone on a Raft," try to use these words to respond to the text.

aspect = one part of something that has many parts		She finds dealing with people to be the most rewarding **aspect** of her work.
impact = effect that an event or a situation has on someone or something		One **impact** of World War II was a demand for more workers on merchant ships.
persistence = determination to do something even though it is difficult or other people oppose it		It takes great **persistence** to survive more than four months lost at sea.
remarkable = amazing or worthy of attention		The young man had a **remarkable** journey at sea.

Practice 130

Work with a partner to answer these questions. Try to include the **purple** word in your answer. Write the sentences in your notebook.

1. Which **aspect** of your life is the most challenging right now? Why?

2. What one event has had the greatest **impact** on your life? Why?

3. Has there ever been a time when you showed great **persistence**? Explain.

4. What is the most **remarkable** book you have ever read?

◀ A forest fire can have a terrible impact on wildlife.

Word Study: Capitalization

There are rules for using capital letters.

Use Capital Letters for . . .	Examples
The pronoun *I*	Sometimes **I** study at night.
The first letter of the first word in every sentence	**T**he wooden raft was two-and-a-half meters square.
Proper nouns and Roman numerals: • The names/titles of people • Geographical terms • Historical events, eras, calendar items • Streets, cities, states, countries, continents • Ethnic groups, national groups, languages	**P**oon **L**im, **K**ing **G**eorge **VI** **A**tlantic **O**cean **W**orld **W**ar **II** **H**ainan, **C**hina **C**hinese, **B**ritish

Practice 131

Work with a partner. Copy the sentences below into your notebook. Capitalize each proper noun.

1. luis is from bogotá, colombia.
2. We don't have to go to school on independence day.
3. In the summer, we like to spend time near the pacific ocean.
4. My aunt, lisa velarde, speaks both spanish and italian.

Reading Strategy · Identify Main Idea and Details

The main idea of a passage is the most important idea. The paragraphs of a text all relate to it. Within each paragraph is a main idea as well, which may be at the beginning, in the middle, or at the end of the paragraph. The details of a paragraph relate to the main idea. To identify the main idea of a text and the details that support it, follow these steps:

- Skim the text. Look at headings and visuals. What is the most important idea?
- Read the whole text. Look for examples, facts, dates, and sentences that tell more about the main idea of the text. These are the details.
- Pay attention to headings, charts, and other visuals as these also provide supporting details.

As you read "Alone on a Raft," identify the main idea of each paragraph and of the whole article. Then find details that support those main ideas.

 132

Alone
on a
Raft

What would it be like to be lost at sea? How long could one person survive without help from others? Could someone live for days or even months all alone on the ocean? One man did just that. In 1942, Poon Lim began an incredible journey with only a small raft, a few supplies, smart thinking, and a strong will to stay alive.

Disaster

On November 10, 1942, a British ship named the *Ben Lomond* set sail from the city of Cape Town in South Africa. It was headed for **Suriname**, then, on to New York City in the United States. Thirteen days later, disaster struck. A German submarine attacked. At 11:30 in the morning, it fired two **torpedoes** at the British ship.

The *Ben Lomond* sank in just two minutes. Among the **crew** members were 24 British sailors and 23 Chinese sailors. Most of the men died that day. Some people believe that a sailor named Poon Lim was the only survivor.

By some accounts, the crew of the German submarine saw Lim floating away, but decided not to go after him. They probably thought he would not survive on the open water. But he did. Who was Poon Lim, and how did he manage to stay alive after disaster struck?

Suriname, a small country on the northeastern coast of South America
torpedoes, underwater weapons fired from a ship
crew, the people who work on board a ship

▲ Poon Lim used skill and intelligence to survive after his ship was sunk in the South Atlantic.

▲ The *SS Benlomond* weighed about 6,000 metric tons, but was no match for German torpedoes.

Life as a Cabin Boy

Poon Lim was a sailor from the island of Hainan, China. When he was 16 years old, he signed up to work as a **cabin boy**. He joined the crew of a British passenger ship.

Sadly for Lim, Chinese workers were treated poorly at that time. They were paid low wages and given the worst jobs. They also were forced to sleep in cramped, crowded rooms. These conditions caused Poon Lim to hate life at sea. After a while, he decided to quit. He moved to Hong Kong to study **mechanics** instead.

Six months later, Poon Lim heard from a cousin who was working on another British ship. He told Lim that conditions were improving for Chinese workers. World War II had broken out in Europe, and many young British men had signed up to fight. This meant that **merchant** ships, which carried supplies, desperately needed sailors. Many ships were offering better pay and living spaces to workers from China.

The war had reached Hong Kong, too. The city was in danger of an attack by Japan. So, Poon Lim decided to return to sea. He took a job working under his cousin on a British merchant ship called the *SS Ben Lomond* (also known as the *Benlomond*).

---

cabin boy, a young man who works on a ship, doing small jobs for the captain or crew
mechanics, the study of machines
merchant, selling goods to governments or other companies

Listening Skill

Follow along in your book as you listen to the audio. Notice the words in bold type. To understand them, read the definitions at the bottom of the page. Knowing the meanings of these words will help to enhance and confirm your comprehension of the story.

Before You Go On

1. What were conditions like for Poon Lim on the British passenger ship?

2. Where was the ship *the Ben Lomond* traveling to and from?

 **On Your Own**

How do you think Poon Lim manages to survive?

A Little Luck

In 1942, as the *Ben Lomond* was sinking, Poon Lim managed to grab a **life jacket**. He needed it to survive. Even though he had worked on ships for years, he was a poor swimmer.

Poon Lim floated for about two hours until he got lucky. He spotted one of the ship's life rafts, which was a small wooden platform about two-and-a-half meters from one side to the other. A **canvas** roof covered part of the raft. On board, he found some food and supplies. He realized there was enough to help him stay alive.

Reading Skill

Look at the chart. What items in the life raft do you think were most helpful in keeping Poon Lim alive? Why do you think so?

What Poon Lim Found on the Life Raft

- 40 liters of water
- some lime juice
- several tins of biscuits and hard crackers
- pemmican, a dried meat similar to jerky
- malted milk tablets
- lumps of sugar
- chocolate
- a flashlight
- two flares

---

life jacket, a vest that can float to help a person stay above water
canvas, a strong, heavy cloth

New York

Suriname

Cape Town

◀ Poon Lim was aboard a ship that left Cape Town, South Africa, and was heading for Suriname, South America.

Life on the Raft

The raft was equipped with a flashlight, flares, and a few other items. For food and drink, he had a jug of water, tins of biscuits, lumps of sugar, hard crackers, and even some chocolate. Thinking he would be rescued soon, Lim decided to make the food last for 30 days. He counted the days by tying knots in a rope. However, a month came and went, and he was still lost at sea.

Poon Lim realized it would be hard for anyone to find him. The seas were dangerous because of the war. It would have been a risk to search for any survivors from the *Ben Lomond*. Lim knew he needed to find a way to survive on his own and hope that the raft would follow ocean **currents** to land.

First, he had to deal with the fact that he wasn't a good swimmer. He was worried that he could fall off the raft and drown. So, he tied a rope from his wrist to the raft. He also began to practice swimming twice a day. It not only helped him improve, it also was great exercise and kept him strong.

To stay alive, Poon Lim also needed food to eat and water to drink. To get fresh water, he used the canvas roof and his life jacket to build a rain-catcher.

---

currents, bodies of water moving in one direction

▲ A U-boat crew watches a British merchant ship sink. A similar scene took place when the Ben Lomond sank.

Before You Go On

1. How much food did Poon Lim have with him on the raft?

2. How did Poon Lim get fresh water after his supplies ran out?

On Your Own

How do you think his experience affected Poon Lim's spirit? Explain.

Reading 1   **255**

From Bad to Worse

For food, there were plenty of fish in the waters all around him. Poon Lim just had to find a way to catch them. So, he used wire from the flashlight and sharp pieces of metal from the biscuit tins to make a fishing line with hooks. For **bait**, he used some of the hard crackers.

He also discovered a way to catch birds. He made a nest out of seaweed that was stuck to the bottom of the raft. Then he left a dead fish beside it. When a seagull landed on the nest to eat the fish, Lim snatched the bird.

After two months, Poon Lim was getting used to life on the raft. His smart inventions and strong spirit were keeping him alive. But he had more to worry about than hunger and thirst. There were also sharks and storms!

Sharks swam all around him. They smelled blood from the fish he caught, and often circled the small raft. But instead of being afraid, Poon Lim knew they could be another source of food.

He pulled a nail from one of the wooden boards and turned it into a hook. When a small shark tried to ram the raft, he shoved the hook into the animal and pulled it out of the water. Soon, he was eating shark meat and dried shark fins.

Poon Lim also faced storms at sea. One day, a big one hit. Wind and rain pounded the raft. They ruined his supply of food and water. Fortunately, he later caught a bird. It helped him live a little longer.

---

bait, food used to catch fish or other animals

▼ Poon Lim found surprising ways to catch animals from the ocean.

▲ Modern survival rafts like this owe a great debt to Poon Lim's experience.

133 Days Later

Poon Lim survived on that tiny raft on the ocean for an amazing 133 days. No one has lived on a raft for a longer period of time. He later remarked, "I hope no one will ever have to break that record."

Lim thought that if he kept floating, he would reach land or be rescued eventually. But some days, it was hard to keep hoping. Once a ship passed nearby. The crew saw him, but did not stop. Lim believed they ignored him because he was Chinese.

At last, on April 15, 1943, Brazilian **fishers** spotted the raft about 10 miles from the shore of their country. Lim had traveled all the way across the Atlantic Ocean. The fishers took him on board their boat and brought him to the city of Belém.

Poon Lim was in remarkable health for someone who had been at sea for so long. He could walk on his own and had lost only 20 pounds. He spent four weeks recovering at a Brazilian hospital. Then he went to England, and eventually moved to the United States.

Poom Lim's incredible story inspired people in Britain and across the globe. King George VI awarded him a British Empire Medal. The British Royal Navy added survival tips based on his experiences into official manuals for sailors. Lim showed the world that with some smart thinking, determination, and some luck, you could survive almost anything!

---

fishers, people who catch fish for a living

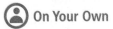

Before You Go On

1. What was the impact of the big storm on Poon Lim and his raft?

2. What was Poon Lim awarded after he was rescued?

🔵 **On Your Own**

What lessons can you learn from Poon Lim's experiences?

Review and Practice

Comprehension 133

Recall

1. What was the name of the ship that sank?
2. When did the ship sink?

Comprehend

3. Why did the merchant ship that Poon Lim was on sink?
4. How did Poon Lim make the supplies on the raft last?

Analyze

5. Why did the crew on the German boat let Poon Lim live?
6. Why do you think it is unknown if Poom Lim was the only survivor of the sinking ship?

Connect

7. What do you think was most **remarkable** about what Poon Lim did to survive? Explain.
8. How do you think this survival experience changed Poon Lim? Explain.

▲ British flag

In Your Own Words

Use the vocabulary below to summarize each section of the reading for a partner.

Disaster	➡	Suriname, torpedoes, crew, survivor, impact
Life as a Cabin Boy	➡	cabin boy, mechanics, conditions, merchant
A Little Luck	➡	life jacket, canvas
Life on the Raft	➡	rescued, currents, persistence
From Bad to Worse	➡	bait, inventions, spirit, sharks, storms
133 Days Later	➡	fishers, remarkable, experiences

Discussion

Discuss with a partner or in a small group.

1. Which **aspect** of Poon Lim's story do you find most interesting, and why?

2. Why is it important to be persistent? Can you give other examples of persistence, either your own or those of people you've read or heard about?

What is the human spirit? Do you think that challenges, such as those faced by Poon Lim, make a person stronger? How? Explain.

Read for Fluency

It is often easier to read a text if you understand the difficult words and phrases. Work with a partner. Choose a paragraph from the reading. Identify the words and phrases you do not know or have trouble pronouncing. Look up the difficult words in a dictionary.

Take turns pronouncing the words and phrases with your partner. If necessary, ask your teacher to model the correct pronunciation. Then take turns reading the paragraph aloud. Give each other feedback on your reading.

Extension
133

Poon Lim may hold the world record for a single person staying alive at sea on a raft, but there are many other stories of people lost at sea on rafts or boats, or even stranded on a deserted island. Work with a partner to find another story that you think shows great persistence and courage. When your research is complete, share your information with the class. Explain why you chose that particular story.

◀ This survivor on a deserted island is signaling for help.

Grammar

Inseparable Phrasal Verbs

A phrasal verb is created by combining a verb and a preposition. A phrasal verb has its own special meaning, different from the meanings of the words that make it up.

Many phrasal verbs are inseparable, which means that the object cannot be inserted into the middle of the phrase. As its name suggests, the phrase is inseparable. A negative phrasal verb is formed the same as a one-word verb, with a form of *do + not* or a form of *be + not*.

> **Grammar Skill**
>
> A phrasal verb can be in any form (past, present, future, etc.). It can also be used with modals.

> World War II had **broken out** in Europe, [means *started*] and many young British men had **signed up** to fight. [means *decided officially to join an effort or a cause*]

Practice A
134

Work with a partner. Choose the correct meaning of each underlined phrasal verb from the box. The first one has been done for you.

> **Grammar Check**
>
> ✓ What is a **phrasal verb**?

| asked to answer a question | deal with | met by chance | originate |

1. I raised my hand, and the teacher <u>called on</u> me.
   <u>asked to answer a question</u>

2. Where do those grapes <u>come from</u>? _____

3. I <u>ran into</u> Philip the other day. _____

4. <u>Get over</u> it! Your haircut looks just fine. _____

Practice B

Choose the correct preposition from the box to complete the phrasal verb in the sentences below. The firt one has been done for you.

| into | off | on | through |

1. My best friend and I always carry __*on*__ about movies we like.

2. I have a lot of reading to get _____ before Monday.

3. Hello! I didn't expect to bump _____ you here.

4. Excuse me. Can you tell me where to get _____ the train for the library?

> **Apply**
>
> Work with a partner. Use these phrasal verbs to talk about the reading
>
> *go after*
> *run out (of)*
> *stay up*
> *sign up*
> *look out (for)*

Separable Phrasal Verbs

Many phrasal verbs are separable. The object can either follow the preposition or can come between the verb and preposition.

> He **thought over** the problem.
> He **thought** the problem **over**. [means *considered*]

Here is a list of some common separable phrasal verbs and their meanings.

bring back [means *return*]	cheer up [means *make happier*]	find out [means *discover*]
work out [means *solve*]	look over [means *examine*]	make up [means *invent*]
help out [means *assist*]	talk over [means *discuss*]	

Practice A
135

Work with a partner. Copy the sentences into your notebook. Then complete each sentence with one of the phrasal verbs from the box above. The first one has been done for you.

1. When I'm sad, my friends always <u>cheer</u> me <u>up</u>.
2. Even if it takes hours, she will _____ the crossword puzzle.
3. Let's _____ this _____. We should chat so we aren't upset with each other.
4. I have to _____ my gift _____ to the store. It doesn't fit.
5. My two-year-old sister loves to _____ stories.
6. If I have any problems, my brother always _____ me _____.

Practice B

Rewrite the sentences in your notebook, separating the phrasal verb in bold. The first one has been done for you.

1. I'm sorry, but I need some time to **think over** your idea.
   I'm sorry, but I need some time to think your idea over.
2. I wasn't able to **figure out** a solution.
3. I'm not going to **bring up** the issue again.
4. Is that true, or did you **make up** the story?
5. Maybe we can **talk over** our differences.
6. I need to **look over** my report before I hand it in.

Grammar Skill

When a pronoun is the object of a separable phrasal verb, it always comes before the preposition. *We will help her out.*

Grammar Check

✓ In a **separable phrasal verb**, where can the object be placed?

Apply

Work with a partner. Restate each sentence in Practice A, changing the position of the object. If it's not possible, say why.

Writing

Write a Letter to the Editor

People write letters to editors of newspapers or magazines to express their opinions about a topic. Sometimes a letter to the editor includes an idea for solving a problem or improving something within the community. Now you will write a letter to the editor. Begin your letter by stating the issue that concerns you. Then give your opinion on the issue. Provide facts and/or examples to support your opinion. Conclude by restating your opinion in a strong and persuasive way.

Writing Prompt

Write a letter to the editor of your school or local newspaper about an issue you feel strongly about in your school or community. Express your opinion clearly. Support your point of view with facts and/or examples. Be sure to use phrasal verbs correctly.

① Prewrite Begin by choosing an issue in your school or local community. Why are you writing to the editor?

W B
136

• Write the issue at the top of the page in your notebook.

• Think about why you feel strongly about it. What do you want to happen?

• Think of reasons to support your opinion.

• Write your ideas in a graphic organizer like the one here.

Here's a word web created by a student named Ari. He is writing about why he thinks there should be a movie made about Poon Lim's journey.

Fact
His experience is unique. He survived longer at sea than anyone else.

Opinion
A movie should be made about Poon Lim's journey.

Example
His survival story would be inspirational to many people.

Example
People could learn about survival at sea if they saw a movie about his experience.

(2) **Draft** Use your word web to help you write a first draft.

- Explain the issue and then present your opinion of it.
- Provide facts and examples to support your opinion.
- Use phrasal verbs correctly.

(3) **Revise** Read over your draft. Look for places where the writing is unclear or needs improvement. Complete (√) the Writing Checklist to help you identify problems. Then revise your draft, using the editing and proofreading marks listed on page 401.

(4) **Edit and Proofread** Check your work for errors in grammar, usage, mechanics, and spelling. Trade papers with a partner to obtain feedback. Use the Peer Review Checklist on Workbook page 136. Edit your final draft in response to feedback from your partner and your teacher.

(5) **Publish** Prepare a clean copy of your final draft. Share your letter to the editor with the class. Save your work. You'll need to refer to it in the Writing Workshop at the end of the unit.

Writing Checklist
Ideas:
☐ I stated the issue clearly.
Organization:
☐ I supported my opinion with facts and/or examples.
Conventions:
☐ I used phrasal verbs correctly.

Here is Ari's letter. Notice how he clearly states his opinion and supports it with facts and examples.

October 8, 2019

To the Editor,

   I am writing about an extraordinary story of survival that I recently read about, and I think the story would make a great movie. During World War II, Chinese sailor Poon Lim survived for 133 days alone on a raft at sea. Lim was the only survivor when the British merchant ship he was on sank—destroyed by German torpedoes. I think the story would make a great film for several reasons. First, Lim's accomplishment was remarkable. Historians say that no one has ever survived as long as he did at sea. People should find out about this incredible record. Also, his story would likely be inspirational to any movie audience. I also think it might teach people a few things about survival and facing difficult challenges. I'm sure many people would enjoy seeing a film about Poon Lim's experiences.

Sincerely,

Ari Janoff

Prepare to Read

What You Will Learn

Reading
- Vocabulary building:
  Literary terms, word study
- Reading strategy:
  Read aloud
- Text type:
  Literature (play)

Grammar
- Present and past perfect
- Factual and unreal conditionals

Writing
- Write a persuasive paragraph

❓ THE BIG QUESTION

What is the human spirit? Imagine that you have to live with your family in a camp like the one shown below. This internment camp was set up during World War II for Japanese Americans to live in while the United States was at war with Japan. You have food to eat and a place to sleep, but you cannot leave the camp and you have to follow many rules. How would you feel? What would you miss most about the outside world? Would this experience break your spirit? Discuss with a partner.

Build Background

You will read a play called **"Three Letters: A Play in One Act."** It is about a young Japanese-American girl and her parents living in an internment camp during World War II. The camp is in California in the United States.

The Ito family tries to stay busy, but they can never forget that they are not free and that they had to leave their life and farm behind to live under the guard of soldiers who do not trust them. The daughter is more accepting of the situation and wants to not think too much about the family's problems. The parents seem to be more affected by the situation and are especially concerned about their son, who is a soldier in the war.

▲ A Japanese internment camp during World War II

Vocabulary

Learn Literary Words

Literary Words

drama
stage directions

You will read a **drama** that is based on what is known about what families experienced living at Japanese internment camps during World War II. A drama is a play that is written and performed by actors. The sections of a play are called "acts." This play is in just one act, so it's referred to as a "one-act play." The written version of a drama is called a script. It is made up of dialogue and stage directions. Characters' names precede the dialogue they speak. **Stage directions** tell the actors how to speak and act; stage directions can also describe the setting, sound effects, and lighting. They are often printed in italics and set within brackets [ ]. The actors do not read stage directions aloud. For example, read the script excerpt below from "Three Letters: A Play in One Act."

Learning Strategy

Use words that you already know to learn new and essential language, or words that you must know in order to understand your schoolwork.

> **Yoshiko:** That's *not* funny. *[YOSHIKO resumes sweeping, in an area she has already swept.]*
> **Masuo:** I was only trying to cheer you up.
> *[YOSHIKO stops sweeping and sighs.]*

Practice WB 137

Read the script excerpt below with a partner. Then answer these questions: Who are the characters? What are the stage directions? How do they help you understand what is going on and how the characters feel? Which lines are spoken?

Yoshiko: You cannot go alone.

Louise: I'm older than George when he first went out by himself.

Yoshiko: That was different.

Louise: *[getting angry]* Because he's a boy.

Yoshiko: *[trying hard to be patient]* It's different with you.

Louise: Because I'm a *girl*.

Yoshiko: *[losing her temper]* Because we are HERE!

[The outburst embarrasses everyone, especially YOSHIKO.]

Yoshiko: *[softly, but sternly]* You are not going alone, and that's final.

[YOSHIKO exits, going inside with the broom. LOUISE sits down on one of the rocks, facing her father, who is still on the stoop.]

Listening and Speaking: Academic Words

Study the **purple** words and their meanings. You will find these words useful when talking and writing about literature. Write each word and its meaning in your notebook, then say the words aloud with a partner. After you read the excerpt from "Three Letters: A Play in One Act," try to use these words to respond to the text.

Academic Words

assisted
correspond
occupants
regulations

assisted = helped someone		The girl **assisted** her mother with the housework.
correspond = communicate by letter		The soldier likes to **correspond** with his family every week.
occupants = people who live in a building, room, etc.		The **occupants** of the camp had to follow many rules.
regulations = official rules or orders		The soldier arrested the woman because she did not obey the **regulations**.

Practice

W B
138

Choose a **purple** word from the box above to complete each sentence. Then take turns reading the sentences aloud with a partner.

1. Over three hundred _____ lived in the building last year.

2. A theater employee _____ the elderly woman in finding a seat.

3. Some people think there are too many _____ limiting what people can do at the facility.

4. When the pen pals _____ with each other, they sometimes make plans to get together.

◄ During World War II, between 110,000 and 120,000 Japanese Americans were relocated to internment camps.

Word Study: Antonyms

Antonyms are words that have the opposite or nearly opposite meanings from each other. For example, the antonym for the word *above* is *below*, and the antonym for *fast* is *slow*. Knowing antonyms can help build your vocabulary, and it also helps you to figure out the meanings of unfamiliar words.

Miwa **found** a fan that someone else **lost**.
The soldier was peering **inside** the door as the family was looking **outside**.

Practice
139

Copy the chart below in your notebook and complete it by yourself. Then share your answers with a partner. Did you find the same antonyms? Check a thesaurus to see if there are other antonyms for each word.

Word	Antonym
forward	
doubt	
failure	
divide	
beginning	
strength	

Reading Strategy   **Read Aloud**

Reading aloud brings a story and characters to life. It can make reading more fun, especially when you're reading a play, a poem, or a story. To read a play aloud, follow these steps:

- Read the list of characters and choose one person to be each character.
- Read your lines to yourself. Read the stage directions. Notice details for how your character feels and about what the character is doing. These will help you know how to say your lines and how to act as you say them.
- Read the play aloud as a group. Listen carefully to the other actors so that you know when to say your lines.

   As you read "Three Letters: A Play in One Act," pay attention to your lines and the stage directions. When you perform the play in a group, speak clearly and listen carefully to the other actors.

140

Set a purpose for reading As you read, think about Masuo and Yoshiko's feelings about being in the internment camp. How does Louise feel? Would you feel any differently?

Three Letters
A Play in One Act

Fran Hodgkins

CHARACTERS
MASUO ITO, a man in his late 40s, formerly a farmer
YOSHIKO ITO, a woman in her mid-40s, Masuo's wife
LOUISE ITO, their daughter, 15

Scene: *Manzanar War Relocation Center in California, U.S.A.*

Time: *July 1943*

Setting: *Outside the Itos' in Manzanar. The wall of the **barracks** where the Itos and other families live is visible; it is covered in a slapdash coat of white paint. There is a small makeshift porch made of **salvaged** wood, with one step, that leads to a door into the barracks. A large desert rock sits next to the steps; a few plants grow at its base, astonishingly healthy despite the heat and dust, a tribute to Masuo's skill with growing things.*

At rise: *YOSHIKO is energetically sweeping the dust off the porch.*

[MASUO enters from offstage, left, carrying a small paper parcel and a letter. YOSHIKO looks up.]

MASUO: *[holds up the parcel]* The tea you sent for came in the mail.

YOSHIKO: That's good news. Now we won't have to wait in line at the mess hall first thing in the morning. It seems like no matter how early we get there, every other occupant of Manzanar gets there first.

[YOSHIKO continues sweeping, and MASUO can tell there is something on her mind.]

---

barracks, buildings where soldiers live
salvaged, saved instead of thrown away

> ✔ **LITERARY CHECK**
>
> What is the setting of the **drama**? Who are the characters?

> **Reading Skill**
>
> Identify the words you don't understand as you read and ask your teachers or peers for help with those words.

MASUO: What is it?

YOSHIKO: I can never get anything clean here. The green wood they built things out of has shrunken in the heat, and the tarpaper might as well not even be there! Dust blows in through the cracks. Even with the newspaper I stuff into them . . . .

MASUO: And then the wind blows the newspapers in, along with more dust. Why don't you sit down for a moment? It's much too hot to work so hard.

YOSHIKO: I would be working harder at home, in our own strawberry fields. *[pauses]* Do you think our plants are all right?

MASUO: *[sits on the step]* I wish I knew for sure. *[begins to open the letter]*

YOSHIKO: *[resumes sweeping with an energy born of anger]* The dust! The heat! I can sweep the dust, but I can't get rid of this heat. Then it's freezing at night. Louise went to the showers this morning and the pipes were all frozen.

MASUO: At least the day's heat thaws them out.

YOSHIKO: And this barracks! It's not a proper home. There's no privacy. We hear all of our neighbors' conversations and they hear all of ours. What kind of home is this for a girl like Louise? What kind of home is this for a family? What kind of place is this they've brought us to? This is no place for good people.

MASUO: I know, my dear. I know.
[YOSHIKO continues to sweep.]

✓ **LITERARY CHECK**

What do the **stage directions** in this scene describe?

Before You Go On

1. What are the conditions like at the barracks?

2. Why does Yoshiko keep sweeping the floor?

👤 **On Your Own**

Who do you think is coping better at the camp: Masuo or Yoshiko? Explain.

MASUO: Joe at the post office said it'll be cooler tomorrow. Only 95 degrees Fahrenheit. Much better than the 100-degree heat we had last week.

[YOSHIKO stops abruptly and glares at him.]

YOSHIKO: That's *not* funny. *[YOSHIKO resumes sweeping, in an area she has already swept.]*

MASUO: I was only trying to cheer you up.

[YOSHIKO stops sweeping and sighs.]

YOSHIKO: I know. But it's not just the heat and the dust. *[YOSHIKO looks left and right, to see if anyone is within earshot.]* You know the Toshis?

MASUO: *[pauses to think]* Toshi? Toshi. Oh, yes, the family from San Francisco.

YOSHIKO: Their son Harold was taken away by the **MPs** last night. They said he was a troublemaker, that he had been stealing from other people!

MASUO: *[sadly]* So many young people are acting out now that we're trapped here.

[YOSHIKO grunts.]

MASUO: Oh, dear. What has Louise done now?

YOSHIKO: She's becoming impossible.

[MASUO reaches up and gently takes his wife's hand.]

MASUO: She is a Nisei, an American, my beloved. And she is a young woman. Combine the two and you have someone with a mind of her own.

YOSHIKO: I would never have dared act the way she does! I would never have dreamed to ask my parents to go to a public musical performance alone.

MASUO: I know. Things are very different now.

YOSHIKO: She thinks I am being—what did she say? A **"fuddy-duddy."**

[MASUO laughs.]

YOSHIKO: I don't think being a fuddy-duddy is cause for amusement.

[With effort, MASUO controls himself.]

MASUO: No, of course it isn't. I'm sorry. I can tell you are upset.

YOSHIKO: If only George were here. He could talk sense into her.

[The amusement vanishes from MASUO's face, replaced by worry.]

MPs, military police
fuddy-duddy, a person who is fussy and old-fashioned

Yoshiko: You should not have let him go.

Masuo: What choice did I have? He was old enough to enlist.

Yoshiko: What will we do?

Masuo: We will wait. He will serve his country with honor, and then he will come back to us. And then, when the war is over, we'll all go back home. *[turns back to the letters]* Ah, here is one from Barb Costley, our favorite neighbor.

Yoshiko: She's very nice.

Masuo: *[opens the letter and reads]* Oh, no.

Yoshiko: What is it? *[He does not respond, so she takes the letter and reads it herself.]* What?! The other neighbors have divided up our farm?

Masuo: *[softly]* Barb saved the house. Her mother is living there. But the fields are all gone, seized by other neighbors.

Yoshiko: Masuo! Now, we have no home to go home to!

Masuo: Shh! Louise does not need to know that.

Before You Go On

1. What does Yoshiko say happened to Harold Toshi?

2. Why doesn't Yoshiko and Masuo's son live with them?

👤 **On Your Own**

Why do you think Louise's father doesn't want her to hear the latest news from their neighbor Barb's letter? Explain.

[LOUISE enters from stage right. She runs to her father and hugs him.]

Louise: Papa! May I go to the mess hall tonight? There is going to be music! A jazz **quartet**!

Masuo: I think you and your mother have talked about this already.

Yoshiko: You cannot go alone.

Louise: I'm older than George when he first went out by himself.

Yoshiko: That was different.

Louise: *[getting angry]* Because he's a boy.

Yoshiko: *[trying hard to be patient]* It's different with you.

Louise: Because I'm a *girl*.

Yoshiko: *[losing her temper]* Because we are HERE!

[The outburst embarrasses everyone, especially YOSHIKO.]

Yoshiko: *[softly, but sternly]* You are not going alone, and that's final.

[YOSHIKO exits, going inside with the broom. LOUISE sits down on one of the rocks, facing her father, who is still on the stoop.]

Louise: I just don't understand. She's not usually like this when I ask to do something. I *always* ask. I obey all the camp regulations. I go to classes, and help with camp activities. And I've never once broken a **curfew**. Not like some of the other kids.

---

quartet, group of four musicians
curfew, a rule requiring people to be indoors during a specified time

MASUO: *[scoots across the stoop to be closer to LOUISE and pats her arm]* Yes, you always ask. You are a good, respectful daughter. You are the one bright spot we have in this . . . this prison!

LOUISE: Papa! I've never heard you talk like that.

MASUO: There are watchtowers. Guards with guns. Barbed wire. They call this a "relocation camp," but we know what it is. That's why your mother tries so hard to keep things normal, with the tea.

LOUISE: And the sweeping.

MASUO: Yes, and the sweeping. And why she insists I garden. The plants and the soil, they heal my heart.

LOUISE: I wish George were here. He could talk some sense into her.

MASUO: Your mother's very upset about George enlisting.

LOUISE: Why? *[takes a letter from pocket]* He wrote to me last week, and it sounds like he's doing great. Speaking Japanese has made him a standout among the new **recruits**. *[takes letter from envelope and scans it]* Here, right here, he says he's probably going to be a translator. That's a good thing, right? I mean, translators—they don't go to the front.

MASUO: *[looking a little uncomfortable]* No, translators probably don't go to the front.

LOUISE: You don't know this. One time, in the vegetable garden when we were working with some of the older **Issei**, he told me he had to enlist. He said he was afraid of what would happen to the family if he didn't.

MASUO: I was afraid of something like that. Our George is not a fighter. He's not a man meant for war.

LOUISE: No, he's better with a clarinet than a rifle.

MASUO: But he is an honorable son. He **volunteered** to prevent the rest of us from being—what is the word, Louise?

LOUISE: *[grins]* I think you mean "bugged" Papa.

MASUO: Yes, that's the word. Bugged. Bothered. But your mother is angry that he signed up.

LOUISE: In his letter, George said he's proud to be in the army. He's proud to protect this country. To protect us.

MASUO: I am so worried about him. I am so afraid that he will not come home.

LOUISE: But he's going to be a translator! He'll be fine.

---

recruits, new soldiers
Issei, first generation of Japanese Americans
volunteered, worked willingly without pay to help

Before You Go On

1. Why do Louise's parents not want her to go to see the jazz quartet?

2. What does Louise reveal to her father about George's motivation to go into the army?

On Your Own

Why do you think Louise feels better about George? Explain.

Masuo: *[takes a letter from his pocket and holds it up]* This letter from George came yesterday. He says he has asked for a transfer. He has asked to join the 100th.

Louise: The—wait, what? No! *[takes the letter from MASUO and reads it quickly]*

Masuo: He says he wants to be part of the Japanese-American force in Europe.

Louise: *[looking shocked]* Oh, Papa! They are great fighters, but so many get wounded. Their men have received so many **purple hearts**.

[MASUO and LOUISE are silent for a moment.]

Louise: Now I understand why Mama is upset.

Masuo: She is afraid your brother will not return. She is afraid that we will have no one to take care of us when we are old.

Louise: *[determined]* If anything happens to George, I will take care of you, Papa.

[MASUO looks benevolently amused.]

Masuo: I appreciate your **optimism**, Louise.

---

purple hearts, American military medals for someone wounded or killed in war

optimism, positive thinking

LOUISE: I'm serious. With the war, women are doing many more things than they did before. My friends at school and I are already talking about college. At school, Mrs. Hirisaki says I am so good at math, I could be a mathematician. I could be an engineer or a scientist. She says I could go to college back east.

MASUO: Let's not get ahead of ourselves, Louise. It is very, very difficult for a girl to be a scientist.

LOUISE: But not impossible.

MASUO: No, not impossible. I remember my mother telling me about someone she went to school with. Kono Yasui. She is a great scientist in Japan. And there are others, too. If you work hard, perhaps you have a chance.

[YOSHIKO comes out the door.]

YOSHIKO: I forgot the tea.

LOUISE: *[blurts]* Don't worry, Mama, I'm sure George will be okay in Europe!

YOSHIKO: *[to MASUO]* You told her! I didn't want her to worry about her brother. Did you tell her about the farm, too?

LOUISE: What about the farm?

YOSHIKO: *[angrily]* Stolen! Right from under our noses. *[LOUISE and MASUO stare at her, open mouthed; YOSHIKO pauses, takes a deep breath, and collects herself.]* I am sorry. I don't know what has come over me. Please forgive me.

LOUISE: *[crosses to YOSHIKO and gives her a brief hug]* Mama, I will worry about George no matter what. But my worrying about him will not keep him any safer. *[turns to MASUO]* I'm sorry about the farm, Papa.

MASUO: There's nothing we can do about it right now. We need to think about the future.

YOSHIKO: You are both right. *[takes the tea from MASUO]* Let's have some tea.

LOUISE: *[brightly and impulsively]* I know! Let's all go tonight to hear the quartet. George's friend Ted Kashino is going to play the clarinet.

MASUO: Ah. George taught Ted well. He's quite good. Not as good as George, but . . . .

YOSHIKO: *[is silent for a moment, her face showing her internal conflict about all that has happened. Then she gives her daughter a small smile]* Let's wash up. It will be nice to escape for a little while. *[opens the door and walks through it; LOUISE follows, as does MASUO]*

LOUISE: *[from inside the house]* And when the clarinet plays, we can think about George.

[Curtain]

✓ **LITERARY CHECK**

What character in this **drama** would you like to play?

Before You Go On

1. How does the information in the latest letter from her brother affect Louise?

2. What causes Yoshiko to tell her daughter about their farm? Explain.

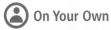 On Your Own

Are you surprised about the change in Yoshiko at the end of the play? Explain.

Review and Practice

Dramatic Reading

One of the best ways to understand and appreciate a play is to perform it. Work in small groups to act out a scene from "Three Letters: A Play in One Act."

Choose from these scenes:

- Masuo tells Yoshiko about the letter from Barb.
- Louise asks her parents if she can go to hear the jazz quartet.
- Louise and her father talk about George.
- Yoshiko is upset and ends up telling Louise about the farm.

Each group should choose a director. The director will assign parts to other group members. He or she will also direct the actors, using the description of the scene and the stage directions. As a team, discuss each character in the play and how he or she should be portrayed.

Evaluate your progress as you practice the scene. How can you improve your presentation? Can you add props, costumes, or music? Keep practicing until you feel comfortable. Then act out your scene for the rest of the class.

Comprehension
141

Recall

1. Where does the Ito family live now?
2. Where is their son and brother George?

Comprehend

3. What are some of the **regulations** that Louise must obey?
4. Louise's brother **corresponded** with the family about the war. What did he tell them?

Analyze

5. Why is the play called "Three Letters"?
6. How do Louise's parents change at the end of the play?

Connect

7. Do you think Louise has a good relationship with her parents? Is she closer to one parent than the other? Explain.
8. The family members cope differently with their situation. Which one do you think copes the best? Explain.

Discussion

Discuss with a partner or in a small group.

1. What do you think are some of the differences between the Nisei generation, which Louise is part of, and the Issei generation, her parents? Explain.

2. Do you think it was fair of Louise's parents to not want her to go to hear the jazz quartet? Explain.

 What is the human spirit? How does the Ito family show the human spirit? How do people like the family in the play deal with unfairness? What can readers learn from this family? Explain.

Response to Literature W B 141

You have learned a little bit about life in internment camps in the United States during World War II. Now do more research with a partner. Find out more about what life was like for Japanese Americans in these camps. Why did the government say the policy was necessary? How long did the policy last? What happened to these Americans when they were released? Share your findings with the class.

Reading Skill

Make sure you recognize the difference between information questions and *yes/no* questions so you can answer questions appropriately. *Yes/no* questions often begin with words *does/do, is/are, was/were,* or *has/have.*

Listening Skill

Listen for implicit ideas, or ideas that are not stated directly. Pay attention to the speakers' tone of voice, gestures, and expressions.

▲ Most Japanese internment camps were located in the American West.

Grammar

Present and Past Perfect

You can use the present perfect to show that an action began at a specific time in the past and continues into the present. Form the present perfect with *has* or *have* and the past participle.

> We **have lived** here **for over ten years**. We've lived here **since 2005**.

You can use the past perfect to tell about events that happened before other events in the past. Form the past perfect with *had* + the past participle. To show the completed action, *already* is often used.

> By the time Masuo received George's letter, George **had** *already* **signed** up to transfer.

You can use the past perfect with the simple past to tell about two events. The clause in the past perfect tells about an earlier event. The clause in the simple past tells about the event that came later.

They **had lived** in the camps   before the war **ended**.   **NOW**

Grammar Skill

Use *for* to talk about a period of time starting in the past and continuing up to the present. Use *since* to show a time or date in the past when something began.

Practice A
142

Work with a partner. Use the words below to write sentences in your notebooks. Use the present perfect. The first one has been done for you.

1. she / finish / the book / yet? *Has she finished the book yet?*
2. The snow / start / just.
3. you / see / this movie / already?
4. We / be / to the museum / never.

Grammar Check

✔ When do you use the **present perfect** and when do you use the **past perfect**?

Practice B

Complete each sentence with the simple past or the past perfect of the verbs in parentheses.

1. By the time she _____ (be) twenty, she _____ (live) in four countries.
2. Juan _____ (live) in Puebla before he _____ (move) to Oaxaca.
3. The game _____ already _____ (start) when we _____ (arrive).

Apply

In your notebook, write three statements about yourself using the present perfect, and three using the past perfect. Share them with a partner.

Factual and Unreal Conditionals

A conditional sentence consists of an *if*-clause that presents a condition and a result clause that tells what may or may not happen if the condition is met. A factual conditional can tell about a condition that is *true* in the present or *may be true* in the future. An unreal conditional presents a condition that is untrue or not possible.

Type of Conditionals	Examples
Present Factual: The condition may be true in the present.	**If** a disease spreads, people get sick. **If** a storm hits, we stay indoors.
Future Factual: The condition may be true in the future.	**If** your house floods, where will you go?

The present unreal conditional tells about a condition that is *untrue* in the present. Use the simple past in the *if*-clause, and *would*, *could*, *should*, or *might* + the base form of the verb in the result clause.

A past unreal conditional tells about a condition that was *untrue* in the past. For the past unreal conditional, use the past perfect in the *if*-clause, and *would have*, *could have*, *should have*, or *might have* + the past participle form of the verb in the result clause.

Type of Conditionals	Examples
Present Unreal: The condition is not true in the present.	If he were there, he would be allowed to go to the dance.
Past Unreal: The condition was not true in the past.	If he had been there, he would have been allowed to go to the dance.

Practice A

143

Work with a partner. Circle the factual conditional that best completes the sentence.

1. If it (were to rain / rains) tomorrow, we (stay / should stay) home.
2. If we (were to eat / eat) out, my parents (will pay / paid) for the check.

Practice B

Work with a partner. Circle the unreal conditional that best completes the sentence.

1. If I (were / had been) you, I (put / would put) that money away.
2. They (did miss / would have missed) the bus if it (had come / came) on time.

Grammar Skill

You can also use *were* when talking about yourself in the present unreal conditional. *If I were older, I would go to New York.*

Grammar Check

 What verb form do you use in the *if*-clause with **factual conditionals**?

Apply

Work with a partner. Discuss your answers to the following questions. What would you do if . . .
- you found someone's wallet?
- you learned your friend had cheated on a test?
- you were caught lying to your parents?

Writing

Write a Persuasive Paragraph

You have learned about different forms of persuasive writing. Now you will write a persuasive paragraph. Begin your paragraph by introducing a topic you feel strongly about and one that you want others to take the same position about. Clearly state your opinion on the issue. Use strong words that will convince your readers. Support your opinion with facts and details. Anticipate opposing opinions and tell why they should be rejected. Conclude your paragraph by restating your position about the issue in a new way.

Writing Prompt

Write a paragraph about an issue you feel strongly about. As with a letter to the editor, try to persuade your reader to adopt your position. Unlike a letter to the editor, when writing a persuasive paragraph, you are not speaking to anyone in particular. Be sure to use the present perfect and past perfect correctly.

(1) Prewrite Begin by choosing an issue that you feel strongly about.

W B
144

• Think about why you feel strongly about this topic.

• What reasons can you give to support your opinion?

• Why might others disagree with your opinion?

• List your ideas in a graphic organizer like the one below.

Here's a pros-and-cons chart created by a student named Julio, telling his opinion about whether Louise's family made the right decision about going to the jazz concert together.

Pros	Cons
Louise is excited about it.	Masuo and Yoshiko dislike the camp and don't want to do anything that will make it more acceptable.
There will be a jazz quartet.	
The family can enjoy life at the camp together for once.	The family could risk getting into trouble or missing curfew.

(2) Draft Use your pros-and-cons chart to help you write a first draft.

- First, explain your position about the issue.
- Then give supporting reasons.
- Be sure to present both sides of the argument.

(3) Revise Read over your draft. Look for places where the writing is unclear or needs improvement. Complete (√) the Writing Checklist to help you identify problems. Then revise your draft, using the editing and proofreading marks listed on page 401.

(4) Edit and Proofread Check your work for errors in grammar, usage, mechanics, and spelling. Trade papers with a partner to obtain feedback. Use the Peer Review Checklist on Workbook page 144. Edit your final draft in response to feedback from your partner and your teacher.

(5) Publish Prepare a clean copy of your final draft. Share your persuasive paragraph with the class. Save your work. You'll need to refer to it in the Writing Workshop at the end of the unit.

Writing Checklist

Organization:
- [ ] I presented both sides of the argument.

Voice:
- [ ] I clearly stated my opinion and gave supporting reasons for it.

Conventions:
- [ ] I used past perfect and present perfect with *for/since* correctly.

Here is Julio's paragraph. Notice how he clearly states his position, supports it, and presents both sides of the argument.

Julio Vasquez

The Right Decision

I think Louise's family made the right decision to go to the jazz quartet together. Even though Masuo and Yoshiko think the camp is a terrible place to be, they want Louise to grow up happy. And Louise has probably been wanting to go out since she got to the camp. Not only that, she's heard that her brother's friend Ted is going to be playing the clarinet. Even Masuo recalls that it was George who had taught Ted to play the clarinet. This means they should be able to do something fun to remind them of the days before they were at the internment camp. Even though they could face trouble if they miss curfew or run into a problem, they are responsible people and haven't broken any rules before. I think it presented a good opportunity for the family to forget their troubles and have fun for a little while. In my opinion, it was the right decision.

Prepare to Read

What You Will Learn

Reading

- Vocabulary building: *Literary terms, word study*

- Reading strategy: *Make inferences*

- Text type: *Literature (short story)*

Grammar

- Quoted speech and reported speech

- Present perfect progressive

Writing

- Write a review

? THE BIG QUESTION

What is the human spirit? Everyone experiences tragedies in their lives. Loved ones may get ill, man-made and natural disasters may occur; you just never know what life is going to throw at you. Maybe what's more important than the tragedy itself is how you deal with it. Do you pick yourself up and push forward, or does the tragedy break your spirit? What is it in some people that gets them through almost anything? Is there anything you can imagine that would break your spirit? Use your prior experiences to answer these questions with a partner.

Learning Strategy

Compare new information to your prior experiences. This will make the new information more meaningful to you, and it will be easier to understand.

Build Background

You are going to read a short story called **"A Place in the World."** It is the story of a town struggling to recover after a strong hurricane. The storm destroyed more than buildings—it threatened to destroy the spirit of many townspeople. Mrs. Moreno's small kiosk had served the community for as long as people could remember. When Miguel tries to organize help from the community, will things work out for Mrs. Moreno? Or will the destruction brought by the storm permanently break her spirit?

◀ A street kiosk

Vocabulary

Learn Literary Words

Literary Words

dialogue
theme

A **dialogue** is a conversation between characters. In poems, novels, and short stories, dialogue is usually enclosed in quotation marks (" ") to indicate a speaker's exact words. Punctuation marks (! . , ?) and adverbs like *politely* let the reader know how the speaker spoke. Read the dialogue from "A Place in the World" below.

> "Good morning," I said politely.
> Mrs. Moreno nodded. "You look just like your Papa, Miguel. Now, what can I get for you, Imelda?"

From what you read, how do the two individuals feel about each other?

The **theme** is a central message in a story. Sometimes a theme is directly stated in the text. More often, it is presented indirectly. The reader must decide what the theme is based on what the text reveals about people and life.

Practice
145

Work with a partner. Read the excerpt from "A Place in the World" below. Then answer the questions.

> "Who did this?" demanded Mrs. Moreno.
> "I—I . . .," I began. I had not planned for this!
> She halted in front of me, her dark eyes boring into mine; the intensity of her stare made me feel like a bug. I blurted, "We just want you to come back—we miss you."
> With that, Mrs. Moreno spun on her heels and began to walk away, but five paces later she stopped and buried her face in her palms. After a moment she turned back to us and asked, "You all did this, for me?"

1. What is the dialogue in the story excerpt? How can you tell?
2. Who is the conversation between?
3. From this passage and the title of the story, what do you think the theme might involve?

Listening and Speaking: Academic Words

Study the purple words and their meanings. You will find these words useful when talking and writing about literature. Write each word and its meaning in your notebook, then say the words aloud with a partner. After you read "A Place in the World," try to use these words to respond to the text.

Academic Words

alter
crucial
proceed
tradition

alter = to make or cause change	➡	We worried the storm would **alter** our town so much that we would barely recognize it.
crucial = critical or extremely important	➡	There is a **crucial** decision coming up about the new school.
proceed = move forward or continue	➡	We will **proceed** with our plans to rebuild the kiosk in the neighborhood.
tradition = a belief or custom that has existed for a long time	➡	Every year, the students at my school hold a bake sale to help raise money for charity. It is a **tradition**.

Practice 146

Work with a partner to answer these questions. Try to include the purple word in your answer. Write the sentences in your notebook.

1. What situations alter people's lives the most?
2. What do you think is the most crucial class in school?
3. How would you proceed to investigate storm damage, once it is safe to do so?
4. What is one tradition that your school celebrates every year?

◀ Summer barbeques are a **tradition** in this family.

Word Study: Words Ending with Consonant + -*le*, -*al*, -*el*

Words that end with a consonant + -*le*, -*al*, or -*el* can be difficult to spell because they stand for the same sound. Specific rules for when to use -*le*, -*al*, or -*el* do not exist. Therefore, it is best to memorize the spelling of each new word you learn. Read the examples below.

Word Ending	Example	Sentence
-*le*	rubb**le**	There were piles of **rubble** in front of the building.
-*al*	princip**al**	The **principal** called me into her office.
-*el*	trav**el**	They **travel** far on foot every day.

Practice
147

Work with a partner. Copy the words from the box below into your notebook. Circle the letters at the end that stand for the same sound. Then say one of the words. Ask your partner to spell it aloud. Check your partner's spelling. Then have your partner say the next word. Continue until you can spell all of the words correctly.

bagel	crumple	dental	handle	jewel	unable

Reading Strategy   Make Inferences

Sometimes, you need to make inferences about what is happening in a story or about other aspects of it. The author may not state everything directly. As you read, think about the story and ask yourself: *What's happening? What are the characters like?* Look for details to help you. If you don't find what you want to know, you may need to make inferences. Follow these steps:

- Look for any details the author does use about the action or characters.
- Think about your own experiences.
- Use the details and what you know to make inferences, or figure out what is going on or what a character is like.

As you read "A Place in the World," think about what the author means but does not say directly. What inferences can you make based on details in the story?

148

Set a purpose for reading As you read, notice how Mrs. Moreno deals with the aftermath of the storm. Is she able to retain her spirit in the face of all the devastation?

A Place in the World 🎧

Its name was Rose, which was a deceptively pretty name for something that roared through my island like a million freight trains, leaving us **battered** and bruised in its wake.

My family and I and most of our other neighbors were fortunate; the advance hurricane warning we'd received had given us enough time to cover our windows with sheets of plywood and gather enough supplies to survive if the power went out. Other than a few roof tiles missing, our house escaped the worst. After the storm, when my sister, Imelda, called from the mainland to check on us, my mother mourned the loss of all her tomato plants. But she acknowledged that things could have been much worse—and were for many.

Once we had cleared away the **debris** that littered our own property, my father suggested we walk around the neighborhood to see what had been damaged; my mother opted to stay and see what she could salvage from her garden.

We walked down the middle of the now deserted street—there were a few people out, but there was none of the traffic you would normally encounter on a weekday. As Papa and I walked, we saw all the damage: bricks, tree limbs, and chunks of roofing material littered the streets. One huge limb had landed on a car and nearly flattened it, causing my father to remark, "Somebody's going to be very, very unhappy about that."

As he spoke, I spied something bright white peeking out of a pile of dirt and paper. I looked a little closer. It was a power cable for a tablet. And not just any power cable.

******

Mrs. Moreno's kiosk had been part of this neighborhood as long as I could remember. When I was just starting school, Imelda had introduced me to Mrs. Moreno.

"Mrs. Moreno has everything."

"I bet she doesn't," said my six-year-old self.

"She does," insisted Imelda, who was

---

battered, damaged by repeated punishment
debris, remains, scrap, or litter

twelve and knew better. "She has all the school supplies you'd ever need and fruit and gum. And batteries, too: all kinds of them. One day Papa was walking me to school, and the batteries in his **hearing aids** weren't working. We stopped, and Mrs. Moreno not only had the batteries, but she even put them in for him! Yes, she has everything—you'll see."

"If we stop, we'll be late," I objected, though to be honest I was more worried about being proven wrong than about being late.

Despite my complaints, which were **half-hearted** at best, Imelda hustled me across Calle Central to a dilapidated wooden structure that seemed to be held together by the advertisements that papered its outside. "Mrs. Moreno!" Imelda called.

Tall and thin, Mrs. Moreno greeted Imelda cheerfully, and looked at me curiously, able to see me even though I was not tall enough to peer over the counter. "This is my brother, Miguel," Imelda said.

"Good morning," I said politely.

Mrs. Moreno nodded. "You look just like your Papa, Miguel. Now, what can I get for you, Imelda?"

After a moment's consideration, Imelda asked for a packet of graph paper, a binder clip, and a hexagon key.

The first two I recognized, but the last one had me stumped. "What's a hexagon key?" I whispered when Mrs. Moreno had turned away.

Before Imelda could reply, Mrs. Moreno said, "A hexagon key is a small tool used to tighten **fasteners** that have a hexagon-shaped hole in the top." Her voice got softer and louder as she moved around the kiosk, and when she turned back to us, she held a packet of paper and a clip, which

---

hearing aids, devices used to help people who have hearing problems
half-hearted, without enthusiasm
fastener, tool or device to hold something closed, such as a bolt or screw

✓ LITERARY CHECK

What does the **dialogue** reveal about Mrs. Moreno?

Before You Go On

1. What did Miguel find in the hurricane debris that made him think of Mrs. Moreno?

2. What does Miguel think about in his memory of Mrs. Moreno?

 On Your Own

Why do you think the story begins with the hurricane and then switches to Miguel's memory of Mrs. Moreno?

she handed to my sister. Then she held up a large ring, from which dangled dozens of thin bars of metal that ranged from an inch to four inches in length. "And what size hexagon key, chica?" she said.

My sister stammered, and the older woman's eyes sparkled with amusement. "You like to test me, don't you, Imelda? When you really need a hexagon key, you need to tell me the size. See, I have a whole ring of them. For now, you just need the paper and clip, yes?" Then she laughed, and her amusement was so genuine, so infectious, that we both joined in. Mrs. Moreno leaned over the counter and addressed me, saying, "Your sister is a clever one. You are, too?"

I nodded, even though I wasn't sure what *clever* meant.

"Here, just for clever ones today." She held out to me a yellow smiley-face sticker. Grinning, I stuck it on my shirt. That was back in first grade, when smiley-face stickers were in high demand.

******

After Imelda went away to college, I stopped by Mrs. Moreno's at least once a week. Sometimes I visited because I needed a notebook or a pen or something else for school, while other times I stopped on the way home for an orange or a pack of gum. One day, I had forgotten the charger for my tablet and there was no time to run back home; in a panic, I raced to the kiosk and asked Mrs. Moreno if she had a power cable, even though I knew it was a **long shot**. To my astonishment and delight, Mrs. Moreno held one out—just the kind I needed.

Then my heart sank—not only had I forgotten the power cable, but I'd also left my wallet on my dresser, which meant I had no money! Seeing the look on my face, Mrs. Moreno understood my situation instantly. "Here, *mijo*," she said, taking my hand and dropping the cable into it. "Bring it back after school. Now, get going, or you'll be late."

I stuffed the cable into my bag, thanking her profusely, and raced the last few

---

long shot, something that will not likely happen

mijo, in Spanish, affectionate phrase for "my dear"

blocks to school, where I slid into my seat just before the bell. When class began, I took out the tablet and the cable and only then noticed the smiley-face sticker on the end. Elena, who sat next to me, noticed it too and said, "Been to see Mrs. Moreno? I can tell from the sticker; she loaned me that same cable last Tuesday, even though it left her own tablet uncharged all day."

******

It was that very same cable, with a tattered smiley-face sticker still visible on one end, that I held now safely in my hands. My stomach clenched with fear, and I said, "Papa, we need to hurry!" before I broke out into a run for Calle Central.

"Miguel! Wait!" my father called. But I didn't stop; I raced around fallen limbs and skidded on mud, clutching the cable desperately in my hand until I reached the corner. I was glad there was no traffic; in my urgency, I felt I would have run right over the cars, from **trunk** to **hood**.

When I got to the **intersection**, that's when I saw what I had feared: Mrs. Moreno's kiosk was gone.

Winded, Papa panted up behind me. "Miguel, what's going on?"

I pointed and said, "Look, Papa. It's gone."

It took a moment, but then the light of recognition came into his eyes. "Oh, no."

I saw movement out of the corner of my eye, and I turned my head to the left to see Ms. Soto waving to us from the front porch of the hardware store; she and her family live in an apartment above their shop. We crossed the street to join her. "Terrible, yes?" she said. "Our **basement** flooded, and we're afraid everything will rust before it dries out. But still, it could be worse." She cast an eye toward the spot where the kiosk had stood.

---

trunk, part of a car that holds supplies, usually in the back
hood, part of a car that holds the car's mechanics, usually in the front
intersection, place where roads meet
basement, section of a building that is underground

Before You Go On

1. What does Miguel think about in his second memory of Mrs. Moreno?

2. What happened to Mrs. Moreno's kiosk?

On Your Own

What words would you use to describe Miguel at this point in the story?

"We saw it happen—a huge wave came racing down the street and hit the kiosk, which came apart like it was made of **matchsticks**. Poor Carmen."

Alarm made my heart thud; with great difficulty I managed to ask, "She wasn't—in there, was she?"

Ms. Soto shook her head and I felt myself relax a little. "Oh, no. She went to her daughter's house and waited out the storm there; I saw her at the end of the street a couple of hours ago—I recognized her because she is so tall, you know? But she didn't come near; she just looked at where the kiosk had been and then turned away, walking back the way she had come."

I held out the cable and said, "I knew there was something wrong when I found this."

Ms. Soto nodded gravely. "Before the storm hit, she tried to **shore up** the shack with some wood, but there was very little she could do. Her late husband was not much of a builder; and although she loved that shack, she always said a strong breeze would knock it down." With a sigh, Ms. Soto said, "We had more than a breeze yesterday."

We were all three of us silent for a moment, thinking about our neighborhood's loss. "You said she went to her daughter's house?" I asked finally.

"Oh yes, past the factory, on Calle Cruz. But be prepared, Miguel; I don't think she is going to rebuild, and we'll all need to find a new place to buy our newspapers and mints."

******

Half an hour later, we were standing in front of a small blue house where a woman in a red t-shirt swept storm-blown leaves and twigs off the front steps. "Excuse me," my father said. "We are looking for Mrs. Moreno. Do you know where she is?"

The woman eyed us a bit suspiciously. "Mama's in the house. Who are you?"

My father introduced us, and added, "We're just concerned about Mrs. Moreno, after seeing what happened . . . ." He allowed the sentence to hang, unfinished, in the air, while Mrs. Moreno's daughter looked both of us up and down, and decided, after an agonizing wait, that we **passed muster**. She set the broom aside, told us to wait, and went inside the little blue house. The still air carried voices out to where we stood in the street, but I couldn't make out any words. When she came out, she wore a sad expression and said softly, "I'm sorry. My mother does not want to see anyone."

---

matchsticks, wooden matches for lighting a flame
shore up, reinforce or strengthen
passed muster, viewed as being accepted

"But—" I began, but my father put a hand on my arm and shook his head.

"Please give her our best," he said to Mrs. Moreno's daughter, before we turned away and walked slowly home.

******

Over the next few weeks, everyone in the neighborhood worked together to clean up after the storm. We moved tree branches, repaired broken walls, patched roofs, and shoveled mud that, as the days passed, dried into dirt. The neighborhood looked almost back to normal, but I won't say that it looked like the hurricane never happened—partly because something was still missing.

As I helped Luis, the **mason**, repair one of the brick walls that had collapsed during the storm, I worried about Mrs. Moreno and her kiosk. It was bad enough that the neighborhood had lost the kiosk; I was worried that if she chose not to rebuild, she would give up in more ways than just one. I remembered a story my father had told me about a man who had lost his fishing boat, and how he had just **withered away**, sitting on the docks and looking out to sea. "Losing his boat made him lose his spirit, too," Papa had recalled, adding, "Everyone needs to have a purpose, a place in the world." The kiosk had been Mrs. Moreno's place in the world, I realized, and I was afraid that without it she, like the man without his boat, might fade away.

Then an idea struck me like a hammer on a nail, and I knew exactly what we could do. *Ka-chunk!* I set two more bricks on my pile and exclaimed to Luis,

---

mason, a person who works and builds with stone and brick
withered away, faded or wasted away; became weakened

Before You Go On

1. Why didn't Mrs. Moreno want to see anyone when Miguel and his father visited?

2. What does Miguel's father say that everyone needs in life so they don't lose their spirit?

👤 On Your Own

What idea do you think struck Miguel "like a hammer on a nail"? What do you think caused it? What is Miguel going to do?

Reading 3   **291**

who was **overseeing** the brick cleanup, "I have to go! I have to get home!"

I took off running and soon burst through the door of my house, finding my parents having coffee in the kitchen. "I know what to do!" They listened closely as I described what I had in mind, and when I finished, they were both quiet for a moment, **mulling it over**.

Eventually, my mother spoke. "It's going to be a great deal of work. It's a wonderful idea, but how can you possibly do it alone?"

Papa said, "Remember, Miguel—Carmen's husband built the original kiosk by himself, and it was never—how can I put this?"

"Very **sturdy**?" I suggested.

"Exactly. You have a great plan, but you're going to need help."

My parents exchanged glances, and then my mother smiled. "You know, I've been meaning to take down the plywood that's still covering the back windows upstairs. It would be perfect for Miguel to use."

"I'll get the ladder," said Papa.

"And I'll get the **crowbar**," said Mama.

Working together, we removed the sheets of plywood and carried them to the corner of Calle Central, where Ms. Soto came over to see what we were up to. When we explained our idea, she clapped her hands together and said, "I have lumber out back that you can use, and a power saw, and even a **pneumatic** power tool that will make the work go much faster. You can run a power cord from the shop, too."

As we worked, other people stopped by to watch. When they learned what we were doing, they went home and returned with their own contributions: Mr. Diaz brought a peg board and hooks; Elena and her brothers brought corrugated metal for the roof; another neighbor brought a door, explaining, "The hurricane took that room off my house, but the door is still good." Luis heard what we were doing and brought a truckload of bricks and bags of mortar. "This will make it hard to blow down," he said, "just like in the story of the big bad wolf!" The Ruiz kids brought yellow paint and started slapping it on with their hands before Ms. Soto got them to stop and use brushes.

We stood back and admired what we had built. I took a can of spray paint and made a big smiley face on the back wall of the new kiosk. Everyone laughed.

"What is going on here?" growled a familiar voice.

---

overseeing, manage or be in charge
mulling over, thinking about
sturdy, strong
crowbar, tool used as a strong lever pneumatic, operated by air or gas under pressure
pneumatic, operated by air or gas under pressure

I turned in surprise to see Mrs. Moreno. Her hair seemed grayer, and her mouth turned down at the corners. Mrs. Moreno circled the kiosk, looking it up and down and **scowling** as she walked. I glanced at my parents, who seemed to be holding their breath.

"Who did this?" demanded Mrs. Moreno.

"I—I . . . ," I began. I had not planned for this!

She halted in front of me, her dark eyes boring into mine; the intensity of her stare made me feel like a bug. I blurted, "We just want you to come back—we miss you."

With that, Mrs. Moreno spun on her heels and began to walk away, but five paces later she stopped and buried her face in her palms. After a moment she turned back to us and asked, "You all did this, for me?"

Everyone nodded. Murmurs of "*Sí, señora*," ran through the assembled neighbors.

"And you started this, Miguel?"

"Yes, ma'am."

She hugged me. "I . . . I can't tell you . . . ."

"So, you'll come back?"

Looking in her eyes, I caught a glimpse of that sparkle I knew so well. "What do you think, clever one?"

---

scowling, frowning angrily
Sí, señora, Spanish for "yes, m'am"

✓ **LITERARY CHECK**
What is the **theme** of this story?

Before You Go On

1. What was Miguel's idea to help Mrs. Moreno?

2. What two examples from the text show that Mrs. Moreno was pleased?

 **On Your Own**

How do you think Miguel felt about getting people to pitch in to help Mrs. Moreno? How do you feel when you do something for others?

Review and Practice

Reader's Theater

In groups of four, act out this scene at Mrs. Moreno's daughter's house.

Papa: [nodding respectfully to the woman] Excuse me. You must be Mrs. Moreno's daughter? Is she here?

Daughter: [stops sweeping] Yes, my mother's inside. [eying them up and down] I don't think I know you.

Papa: We visit her kiosk all the time—we have for years.

Daughter: [sadly and looking down] It's all gone.

Papa: We know. We'd just like to talk to her.

Daughter: Let me ask her. [puts broom down and goes inside]

Mrs. Moreno: [heard from inside] Tell them I can't talk now. It's just too hard. [sobbing] And I don't want them to see me like this.

Daughter: It's OK, Mama. I understand. I'll tell them. [goes back outside and looks at Papa and Miguel] I'm sorry. My mother just can't talk to anyone right now.

Miguel: But, we just want to . . . . [interrupted by Papa, who puts his hand gently on his son's shoulder]

Papa: We understand. Please tell her we are thinking of her. [to Miguel as they walk away] Now is not a good time, son.

Comprehension
149

Recall

1. What challenge is Miguel's town facing?

2. What does Mrs. Moreno sell at her kiosk?

Comprehend

3. What two flashbacks are part of the story?

4. How did the hurricane **alter** Mrs. Moreno's life?

Analyze

5. How is Mrs. Moreno's kiosk a **tradition** in the town?

6. Given that many people in the town have suffered losses, why does everyone react the way they do about Mrs. Moreno's loss?

Connect

7. If you were Mrs. Moreno, would you want to speak to the townspeople right away? Explain.

8. If you were Imelda, away on the mainland, how would you feel and what would you do about Mrs. Moreno's situation? Explain.

Discussion

1. What do you think ended up being the more **crucial** fixture of the community, the kiosk or Mrs. Moreno? Explain.

2. Which character in the story helped Mrs. Moreno the most? Why?

3. What motivates Miguel to do what he does? Do you think it was the story his father told him about the fisher? Do you agree with the message of that story? Why?

 What is the human spirit? Think about each story character. How do you think each one showed the human spirit? Which story character would you want to help you after a loss? Explain.

Response to Literature

▲ Helping others can be very rewarding.

First, choose several story characters. Work with a partner to write notes from each character to post on Mrs. Moreno's kiosk to welcome her back. In your notes, share your feelings about her or mention what you did to help her "get back on her feet." Display your notes on a classroom bulletin board. Then with your partner, discuss how the kiosk is Mrs. Moreno's "place in the world." Write a message from Mrs. Moreno to all the townspeople to thank them for helping her to keep her "place in the world." Post it, too, on the bulletin board. Share and compare your postings with the class.

Grammar

Quoted Speech and Reported Speech

Use quotation marks (" ") and a comma (,) to separate direct, or quoted, speech from the phrase that identifies the speaker.

> "Good morning," I said politely.
> "Please give her our best," he said to Mrs. Moreno's daughter.

Reported speech does not use quotation marks and may be a paraphrase of the person's exact words. The verb form usually changes. Use the reporting verb *said* when reporting statements. *That* often follows *said*.

> "I don't want to see anyone," she said. [quoted speech]
> She said (that) she didn't want to see anyone. [reported speech]

To report *Wh-* questions, use statement word order, not question word order. For *yes/no* questions, use *if* or *whether* and statement word order. Use the reporting verb *asked* when reporting questions.

> "What's happening?" asked Papa. [quoted speech]
> Papa asked what was happening. [reported speech]
> "Do you have a power cable?" she asked. [quoted speech]
> She asked if we had a power cable. [reported speech]

Practice A
150

Work with a partner. Correctly punctuate the quoted speech. Write your responses in your notebook. The first one has been done for you.

1. She said I'm going to the park. She said, "I'm going to the park."
2. I'm not hungry Kevin said.
3. The server asked Do you want anything else.
4. Are you coming Tina asked.

Practice B

Work with a partner. Change the quoted speech in Practice A into reported speech. Write the sentences in your notebook. The first one has been done for you.

1. She said that she was going to the park.

Present Perfect Progressive

The present perfect progressive shows the duration of an action that began in the past and continues into the present. Form the present perfect progressive with *has* or *have* + the past participle *been* + the present participle. The present participle is the *-ing* form of the verb.

You can also use the present perfect progressive without a specific mention of time to show a general activity that is in progress.

Examples	Meaning
We'**ve been living** here **for eight years**. We'**ve been living** here **since we left Madrid**.	The action began in the past (eight years ago, since they left Madrid) and continues into the present.
Mario **has been talking** about seeing that movie. I've **been doing yoga** a lot.	The action has been in progress recently or lately, without a specific mention of time.

Practice A
151

Work with a partner. Complete the sentences with the present perfect progressive of the verbs in parentheses.

1. It _____ all day, and it is still coming down. (snow)
2. I _____ all night, and I'm still not finished. (study)
3. Pam _____ baseball for three years now. (play)

Practice B

Work with a partner. Complete the sentences with either the present perfect or the present perfect progressive form of the verbs in parentheses. The first one has been done for you.

1. Many store owners _have been assessing_ their losses. (assess)
2. We _____ all morning. (walk)
3. It _____ since noon. (not, rain)
4. They _____ on this block for a long time. (live)

Writing

Write a Review

A review, or a writer's opinion about a book, movie, or other work, is a kind of persuasive writing. The purpose of a review is to evaluate a work and then recommend that others read or view it or avoid it. Begin a review with a summary or description of the work. Then state your opinion of it and give reasons and examples to support your viewpoint. Try to persuade others to adopt your position about the work.

Writing Prompt

Choose a book, album, film, or play to review. State your opinion clearly and support it with examples from the work. Use reported speech and quoted speech correctly.

1 **Prewrite** Begin by choosing a work to review.

W B
152

- Think of a book, an album, a film, or a play that you want to review.

- What was your opinion of it? Why did you like or dislike it? Think of some examples and details to support your reasons.

- Write your ideas in a graphic organizer.

Here's an idea web created by a student named Blaise for the story "A Place in the World."

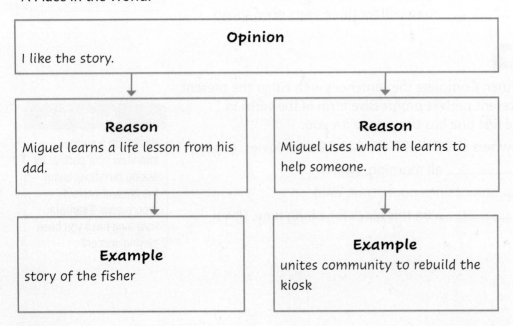

Opinion
I like the story.

Reason
Miguel learns a life lesson from his dad.

Reason
Miguel uses what he learns to help someone.

Example
story of the fisher

Example
unites community to rebuild the kiosk

② Draft Use your idea web to help you write a first draft.

- Remember to include a brief summary.

- State your opinion with reasons and examples to support it.

- Use quoted and reported speech correctly.

③ Revise Read over your draft. Look for places where the writing is unclear or needs improvement. Complete (√) the Writing Checklist to help you identify problems. Then revise your draft, using the editing and proofreading marks listed on page 401.

④ Edit and Proofread Check your work for errors in grammar, usage, mechanics, and spelling. Trade papers with a partner to obtain feedback. Use the Peer Review Checklist on Workbook page 152. Edit your final draft in response to feedback from your partner and your teacher.

⑤ Publish Prepare a clean copy of your final draft. Share your review with your class. Save your work. You'll need to refer to it in the Writing Workshop at the end of the unit.

> **Writing Checklist**
>
> **Ideas:**
> ☐ I stated my opinion clearly.
>
> **Word Choice:**
> ☐ I used examples to support my opinion.
>
> **Conventions:**
> ☐ I used reported speech and quoted speech correctly.

Here is Blaise's review of the story "A Place in the World." Notice how she includes her opinion and uses examples to support it.

Blaise Yafcak

"A Place in the World"

"A Place in the World" is about a boy named Miguel who decides to help an older woman from his community, Mrs. Moreno. She is a fixture in the community and everyone loves her. After she loses her kiosk in a hurricane, the woman's spirit is broken and she retreats from the world. Miguel is reminded of a story his father had told him about an old fisher who lost his boat and kept staring off, looking for it. His father told him that when the fisher lost his boat, he lost his spirit, too. Then his father added, "Everyone needs to have a purpose, a place in the world." At that point, Miguel decides that is what Mrs. Moreno's kiosk was to her. And he sets out to unite the community to help her. They all pitch in and build her a new kiosk, and she decides to return to her old livelihood there. It's a wonderful story about the strength of the human spirit and the power of helping others. I was very moved by the story and I highly recommend "A Place in the World." I hope the message of the story means as much to you as it did to me.

Link the Readings

Critical Thinking

Look back at the readings in this unit. Think about what they have in common. They all tell about the human spirit. Yet they do not all have the same purpose. The purpose of one reading might be to inform, while the purpose of another might be to entertain or persuade. In addition, the content of each reading relates to the human spirit differently. Complete the chart below.

Title of Reading	Purpose	Big Question Link
"Alone on a Raft"		One man shows a strong will to survive despite overwhelming odds.
"Three Letters: A Play in One Act"	to entertain	
"A Place in the World"		

Discussion

Discuss with a partner or in a small group.

• Which person or story character in the unit do you think best demonstrated the human spirit? Explain.

What is the human spirit? What character traits did the people in the stories share? How do these character traits reflect the strength of the human spirit?

Media Literacy & Projects

Work with a partner or in a small group. Choose one of these projects.

(1) Create a large "human spirit timeline" in your classroom. Use the internet to do research. Draw pictures of people or groups whose lives and work have reflected the human spirit throughout history. Write a short paragraph to explain each entry on the timeline. Hang your timeline up in the classroom for others to see.

(2) Present a "Human Spirit Award" to someone in your school. Write a persuasive argument telling why the person you chose deserves the award. Read your argument to the class, and take a vote.

(3) Interview someone in your community who has worked hard to help others. Before conducting your interview, prepare a list of questions. Share your interview with the class.

(4) In a small group, decide what you think happens next in the play "Three Letters: A Play in One Act," and write the next scene. Include another letter or two that the family receives. Then decide on roles and act out how the family reacts to the new letters. Create a script to help you. Perform your new scene for the class.

Further Reading

Choose from these reading suggestions. Practice reading silently for longer periods with increased comprehension.

The Last of the Mohicans, James Fenimore Cooper
This story is a classic tale of adventure and struggle on the North American frontier.

The River, Gary Paulsen
Two years before this story begins, teenager Brian Robeson survived in the wilderness for fifty-four days with only a hatchet. Now he agrees to go back into the wilderness to teach a government worker how to survive.

Who Was Harriet Tubman? Yona Zeldis McDonough
Born a slave in Maryland, Harriet Tubman knew firsthand what it meant to be someone's property. Tubman's life was proof of what just one person can do.

All the Light We Cannot See Anthony Doerr
When the paths of Marie-Laure, a blind French girl, and German spy Werner cross during World War II, the human spirit prevails.

Listening & Speaking Workshop

Radio Commercial

You and a partner will create and present a radio commercial.

① Think About It

When you listen to the radio, you hear commercials. The purpose of a commercial is to persuade listeners to buy a product, attend an event, or support a cause. Radio commercials are very short: They typically last just thirty seconds or a minute.

Work with a partner to develop a list of products, events, or causes you could advertise in a radio commercial. These may be real or imaginary. For example:

- A new type of cell phone
- A community theater production
- A local fundraiser

② Gather and Organize Information

With a partner, choose a topic from your list. Then make notes about what to include in your radio commercial. What persuasive words could you use? What details should you use to describe the product, the event, or the cause? What sound effects or music would make your commercial interesting and memorable?

Research / Reflect If your topic is a real product, event, or cause, go to the library, talk to an adult, or conduct research on the internet to get more information about it. Take notes on what you find. If your product, cause, or event is imaginary, make up the details that you will need to describe it. Use a dictionary or thesaurus to find persuasive language you can use.

Order Your Notes Study your notes. Decide which arguments, examples, and supporting details you will include in your commercial. Write each one on a separate note card. Choose the best order for presenting your ideas, and number your cards in that order.

Prepare a Script Use your note cards to write a script for your radio commercial. To make your script richer and more interesting, use a variety of grammatical structures, sentence lengths, sentence types, and connecting words. Also, be sure to start your commercial in a way that will get the audience's attention.

(3) Practice and Present

With your partner, choose which parts of the script each of you will each present. Remember, a radio audience can't see gestures or visuals, so you must convey your message with your words and tone of voice. Practice presenting to a friend or family member, or record each other and listen to the recording. If you are using recorded sound effects, check that your equipment works and that you can use it easily.

Deliver Your Radio Commercial Give your presentation from the back of the room so your classmates can hear but not see you—as if you were actual radio announcers. Emphasize persuasive words by changing the volume or tone of your voice. Slow down when you come to the most important points.

(4) Evaluate the Presentation

You will improve your skills as a speaker and a listener by evaluating each presentation you give and hear. Complete (√) this checklist to help you evaluate your commercial and those of your classmates.

- ☐ Was the purpose of the commercial clear?
- ☐ Did the speakers persuade you to buy the product, attend the event, or support the cause? Why or why not?
- ☐ Could you hear and understand the speakers easily?
- ☐ Did the speakers make effective use of tone of voice, music, and sound effects?
- ☐ Are there ways the radio commercial could be improved?

Speaking Skills

Use sound effects, music, and your tone of voice to get your listeners' attention.

Listening Skills

What is the speaker trying to persuade you to do? If you don't understand, ask questions at the end of the presentation.

Listen for information that would make you want to buy the product, attend the event, or support the cause. Tell the presenter what you found effective about the commercial.

Strengthen Your Social Language

Writing a script helps you learn basic vocabulary and language structures. Go to your Digital Resources and do the activity for this unit. This activity will require you to use and reuse basic language in other meaningful writing activities.

Writing Workshop | Persuasive Speech

Write a Persuasive Speech

In persuasive writing, the writer expresses an opinion and tries to convince others to agree with it. A speech is one form of persuasive writing. Speechwriters aim to persuade listeners to think or act a certain way. A strong persuasive speech begins with a paragraph that clearly states the writer's opinion. The speech gives reasons and evidence, including facts and examples, that support the writer's position. Speechwriters also explain why they think opposing arguments should be rejected. A persuasive speech concludes with a paragraph that restates the writer's opinion in a new and memorable way.

> **Writing Prompt**
>
> Choose an issue that concerns you. Then, write a five-paragraph speech. Persuade your audience to agree with your position about the issue. Be sure to use correct verb forms.

(1) **Prewrite** Review your previous work in this unit. Brainstorm a list of possible topics in your notebook. Choose the issue that most interests you. In your notebook, answer these questions:

• What do you think is an important issue in your community?

• What is your opinion and how can you convince others to agree with you?

• What action would you like your listeners to take after hearing your speech?

Use a pros-and-cons chart to organize your ideas. In the *Pros* column, list arguments that support your opinion. In the *Cons* column, list opposing arguments so that you can respond to them in your speech.

153

A student named Julio decided to write a persuasive speech about the importance of volunteering. Here is the pros-and-cons chart he created:

Pros	Cons
Important to volunteer A way to help other individuals and the community Can meet new people and learn a lot	Not enough time to volunteer No local places to volunteer

(2) **Draft** Use your pros-and-cons chart and the model on page 308 to help you write a first draft.

- Remember to introduce your topic in the first paragraph. Say why it is important.

- State your opinion and give convincing reasons with details and examples.

- Explain why others might disagree with you and say why your position is the best one to take.

- Write a concluding paragraph that restates your opinion in a memorable way.

(3) **Revise** Read over your draft. Think about how well you have addressed questions of purpose, audience, and genre. Your purpose is to persuade. Is your speech clearly organized? Is it appropriate in content and tone for the intended audience? Did you include details that will persuade your audience to agree with you? Read your speech aloud to hear how it sounds.

Keep these questions in mind as you revise your draft. Complete (√) the Writing Checklist below to help you identify additional issues that may need revision. Mark your changes on your draft using the editing and proofreading marks listed on page 401.

Six Traits of Writing Checklist

☐ **Ideas:** Do I present both sides of the issue?

☐ **Organization:** Do I support my opinion with reasons, facts, and examples in an order that makes sense?

☐ **Voice:** Does my writing show my feelings about the issue?

☐ **Word Choice:** Do I use persuasive words that will appeal to listeners?

☐ **Sentence Fluency:** Do my sentences flow well when read aloud?

☐ **Conventions:** Does my writing follow the rules of grammar, usage, and mechanics?

Here are the revisions Julio plans to make to his first draft.

The Importance of Volunteering

After disasters such as major hurricanes, people often join together
to assist the victims, who have suffered losses Whether through food drives, clothing drives, or
soup kitchens, the efforts of volunteers have helped individuals and
communities recover from times of darkness. By volunteering and
taking time out of <u>your</u> day to do something beneficial for others, <u>you</u>
can be that one person who changes someone's life, for the better

Revised to make the tone more persuasive.

Many people I know volunteer out of "the goodness of their
hearts. Some also volunteer at more than one place. A few of the
organizations that welcome volunteers to work for them include the
Salvation Army, People to People, and meals on Wheels, as well as
some hospitals, libraries, soup kitchens, and thrift shops

Revised to add a missing preposition.

For example You might choose to visit the elderly or to assist at a daycare
center. As a volunteer you might find yourself aiding families who are
coping with everyday problems. Volunteers can also be called upon
to provide support to a community in a time of crisis. For example,
emergency situations can require immediate action by a large number
of volunteers to assist in running shelters or delivering food.

Edited to improve logical sequence of ideas and to introduce a transition word.

Many people don't volunteer because they "can't find the time," or because they "do not [don't] have any local organizations to contact[.]" I believe that if they really wanted to help out, they could probably make the time in their schedules or travel a small distance out of their way. Volunteering is important! It not only helps others but also benefits the person who volunteers! As a volunteer, <u>you</u> can meet new people and learn new things. I been a volunteer [for] several years, and it is a very rewarding experience.

¶ [Why don't you explore volunteer opportunities in your community today?] Volunteering is a way to show the good inside of you. When you harness this good, it can be used to change your life and the life of others.

Edited to correct an error in mechanics, add a missing preposition, and to use contraction appropriate to spoken language.

Revised to make the ending more dynamic and memorable.

(4) **Edit and Proofread** Check your work for errors in grammar, usage, mechanics, and spelling. Then trade papers with a partner and complete (√) the Peer Review Checklist below to give each other constructive feedback. Edit your final draft in response to feedback from your partner and your teacher.

153

Peer Review Checklist

☐ Was the writer's opinion clearly presented?
☐ Was the opinion supported with details and facts?
☐ Did the writer present both sides of the argument?
☐ Did the writer give reasons for not adopting the opposing opinion?
☐ Did the concluding paragraph sum up the main points in a memorable way?
☐ Could changes be made to improve the speech?

Look at the next page to see the additional changes Julio plans to make when he prepares his final draft.

Julio Vasquez

The Importance of Volunteering

After disasters such as major hurricanes, people often join together to assist the victims who have suffered losses. Whether through food drives, clothing drives, or soup kitchens, the efforts of volunteers have helped individuals and communities recover from times of darkness. By volunteering and taking time out of <u>your</u> day to do something beneficial for others, <u>you</u> can be that one person who changes someone's life for the better.

Many people I know volunteer out of "the goodness of their hearts." Some also volunteer at more than one place. A few of the organizations that welcome volunteers to work for them include the Salvation Army, People to People, and <u>meals on Wheels</u>, as well as some hospitals, libraries, soup kitchens, and thrift shops.

As a volunteer, you might find yourself aiding families who are coping with everyday problems. For example, you might choose to visit the elderly or to assist at a daycare center. Volunteers can also be called upon to provide support to a community in a time of crisis. For example, emergency situations can require immediate action by a large number of volunteers to assist in running shelters or delivering food.

Many people don't volunteer because they "can't find the time," or because they "don't have any local organizations to contact." I believe that if they really wanted to help out, they could probably make the time in their schedules or travel a small distance out of their way. Volunteering is important! It not only helps others but also benefits the person who volunteers! As a volunteer, <u>you</u> can meet new people and learn new things. I _{have} been a volunteer for several years, and it is a very rewarding experience.

Why don't you explore volunteer opportunities in your community today? Volunteering is a way to show the good inside of you. When you harness this good, it can be used to change your life and the life of others.

Revised to correct errors in mechanics.

Revised to correct an error in punctuation.

Revised to use the present perfect correctly.

---

5 **Publish** Prepare a clean copy of your final draft. Share your speech with the class.

154

Test Preparation

Practice

Read the following test sample. Study the tips in the boxes. Work with a partner to choose the best words to complete the sentences.

Taking Tests
You will often take tests that help show what you know. Study the tips below to help you improve your test-taking skills.

History Report

Today students are reading about what they will need to do to complete a report for a history class. The selection below is about preparing to present the report.

1   After you have finished your research, you are ready to create note cards. You will use the note cards to remind you of the information you found. This lets you talk about your __**1**__, instead of reading the entire report. This makes your presentation more interesting to listen to.

2   The note cards should each give an important fact about this __**2**__ in history. Add details about the fact on the card. Do not write in complete sentences. Just write phrases that will remind you of what to say.

3   After you write all of your note cards, put them in order. You can group your cards by __**3**__ ideas, or you can put them in time order. Make sure that the grouping of the ideas will make sense to your audience.

Tip
As you read the passage, think of a word that would make sense in each blank.

4   Practice giving your report more than once. You should speak for five minutes. If you cannot speak that long, you need more information in your report. If you do not know what to say about a fact, add more details to your note cards. Ask friends or adults to listen to your presentation. Then let them tell you if anything was __**4**__.

1 A person
 B project
 C present
 D public

2 A group
 B alarm
 C watch
 D period

3 A similar
 B interesting
 C faithful
 D concerned

4 A undone
 B unclear
 C unopened
 D untied

Tip
Reread each sentence with each of the four choices. Select the word that makes the most sense in the passage.

155–158

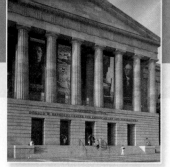

Everyday Obstacles, Everyday Courage

The media often shows dramatic images that celebrate the human spirit, for example, a photograph of a space shuttle blasting off. But the power of the human spirit plays out in everyday actions as well. Many American artists have celebrated these less obvious examples of courage.

Residents of Bourbon County, Kentucky, *Fan Quilt, Mt. Carmel (1893)*

Splendid fans of many colors parade across this quilt. A group of women from Paris, Kentucky, made it more than 100 years ago. They pieced together different types of brightly colored fabric into forty-two separate squares. Then they sewed in the names of 110 men and women who lived in their county. The fan shapes are certainly fun, but not unusual for a quilt from this time period. The fact that so many people worked together to create this one quilt is wonderful proof of the community spirit they shared.

Residents of Bourbon County, Kentucky, *Fan Quilt, Mt. Carmel,* 1893, mixed media, 85 x 72¼ in., Smithsonian American Art Museum ▶

Daniel Chester French, *Spirit of Life (1914)*

In *Spirit of Life*, a young woman with wings raises a basin in her left hand and a pine branch in her right. Daniel Chester French, one of America's most famous sculptors, made this small sculpture in bronze as a model for a larger work. He planned to have water flow from the basin. French made the sculpture as a memorial for a businessman who had built health resorts in Saratoga Springs, New York. *Spirit of Life* marks a death by celebrating life.

Michael Olszewski, *Speaking to Hear (1989)*

In *Speaking to Hear*, artist Michael Olszewski places two small panels side by side. He wants to show how difficult it can be to tell two sides of a story from two different points of view. The panels are made from silk, a delicate fabric. Olszewski then used complicated stitching and embroidery to represent the words of a conversation.

In the left panel, Olszewski painted alternating orange and black stripes like a flag across the center of the silk. Then he added a solid red band down the middle. He reverses these images in the panel on the right. The two pieces seem to represent people coming from two different directions. But there's a feeling that the two "sides" are working toward some kind of understanding.

▲ Daniel Chester French, *Spirit of Life*, 1914, bronze, 30 x 34⅞ in., Smithsonian American Art Museum

▲ Michael Olszewski, *Speaking to Hear*, 1989, silk, parts A and B: both 22½ x 21¼ in., Smithsonian American Art Museum

These artworks offer wonderful examples of artists working in all sorts of ways to capture and honor the spirit and courage that people show in their everyday lives.

Discuss What You Learned

1. How does each artwork relate to the idea of courage?

2. What kind of artwork would you create to illustrate how people face everyday obstacles with courage?

 BIG QUESTION
Why do you think an artist might be interested in courage and the human spirit?

159–160

How does the sky influence us?

This unit is about the sky. In it, you will read both literary and informational texts about humans' relationship with the sky. Reading about this topic will give you practice using academic language and will help you become a better student.

Reading 1
Myth

"The Girl Who Married the Moon" retold by Joseph Bruchac and Gayle Ross

Reading Strategy
Read for enjoyment

Reading 2
Poems/Social Studies

- "Stars" by Sara Teasdale
- "Escape at Bedtime" by Robert Louis Stevenson
- "Starry Nights"

Reading Strategy
Analyze text structure and elements of poetry

Reading 3
Science

- "The Moon"
- "No Need to Establish a Moon Base" by Matt Kachur

Reading Strategy
Take notes

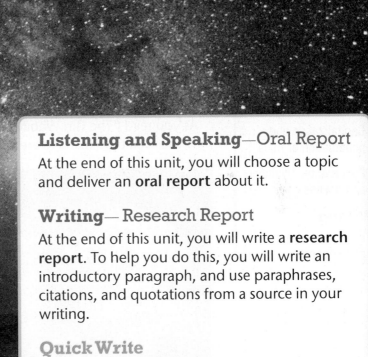

Listening and Speaking—Oral Report

At the end of this unit, you will choose a topic and deliver an **oral report** about it.

Writing— Research Report

At the end of this unit, you will write a **research report**. To help you do this, you will write an introductory paragraph, and use paraphrases, citations, and quotations from a source in your writing.

Quick Write

In your notebook, write a few sentences about the ways in which you think the sky influences us.

View and Respond

▶ Go to your <u>Digital Resources</u>. Watch the video
🔊 and answer the questions.

Prepare to Read

What You Will Learn

Reading

- Vocabulary building: *Literary terms, word study*

- Reading strategy: *Read for enjoyment*

- Text type: *Literature (myth)*

Grammar

- Prepositions

- More about antecedent/pronoun agreement

- Capitalization and punctuation of titles

- Punctuation: Hyphens and dashes

Writing

- Include paraphrases and citations

THE BIG QUESTION

How does the sky influence us? What would life be like for humans without the sun? How do both the sun and the Moon influence life on Earth? What do you know about the moon and its phases? Use your prior knowledge to discuss these questions with a partner.

Build Background

Talk with a partner about what you know about myths. This one is called **"The Girl Who Married the Moon."**

"The Girl Who Married the Moon" is about a group of people called the Alutiq, also known as Eskimo people. The early Alutiq lived in large villages on Kodiak Island, near Alaska. The women of these villages were responsible for gathering food and sewing clothes. Women were therefore thought to be important to their group's survival.

The Alutiq were also known for masking, or carving likenesses of ancestors, animals, and mythological beings into wood or bark.

As you read "The Girl Who Married the Moon," pay attention to how these cultural features are reflected in the story.

◀ The moon has four main phases.

Vocabulary

Learn Literary Words

A **myth** is a story from long ago that has been passed on by word of mouth. Myths reflect the cultures they're from. Myths often offer explanations about the natural world that were difficult for people who lived long ago to understand, such as the different appearances of the moon in the night sky.

> Once there was a Mexican people who loved the sun. The sun liked to be near them, and every day he slowly moved closer to Earth. Soon, Earth became too hot for the people to bear. They begged the sun to move higher into the sky, but he did not want to leave them.
>
> Then, one day, a boy offered to travel high into the sky with the sun, so that he would not be lonely. Soon, the pair were traveling higher and higher into the sky together, and that is where they have been ever since.

Sometimes, **personification** is used in myths. Personification gives human qualities to nonhuman animals or things. What is personified in the myth above? How is this done?

Practice 161

Work with a partner. Take turns reading the examples of personification below. Identify what is being personified and its human qualities.

1. The sunflowers nodded their yellow heads in the summer breeze.

2. Throughout the night, thunder grumbled and growled.

3. The trees shivered in the winter cold.

4. I can hear raindrops dancing on the rooftop.

5. The moon peeked over the treetops.

6. I saw the lamp as it winked at me through the window.

Listening and Speaking: Academic Words

Study the **purple** words and their meanings. You will find these words useful when talking and writing about literature. Write each word and its meaning in your notebook, then say the words aloud with a partner. After you read "The Girl Who Married the Moon," try to use these words to respond to the text.

compatible = able to exist together without problems	➡	It is always good when two close family members can be **compatible** and get along.
instructed = taught or showed someone how to do something	➡	Our coach **instructed** us not to take equipment from the locker room without her permission.
job = a particular duty or responsibility	➡	My **job** is to research the origins of the myth online. My partner will write the report.
phase = one stage of a process of change	➡	The moon was not quite in its final **phase**.

Practice
162

Write the sentences in your notebook. Choose a **purple** word from the box above to complete each sentence. Then take turns reading the sentences aloud with a partner.

1. Her _____ was to collect the books after class and return them to the library.

2. The librarian _____ us not to take out any reference books.

3. Our favorite _____ of the moon is when it's full.

4. My mother and father knew that they were _____ the first time they met.

▲ The librarian instructed the students on how to use the library.

Word Study: Spelling Long *i*

In "The Girl Who Married the Moon," you will read many words that have the long *i* sound. There are several ways to spell this sound. Read the information in the chart below for some examples.

Spelling Long *i*			
i_e	-igh	-y	i
like	brightly	sky	island
wife	might	cycle	climb
admire	high	rely	final

Practice
163

Work with a partner. Complete the last row of the chart with words that have the long *i* sound. Begin by taking turns saying a word from the chart and spelling it. Continue until you can spell each of the words correctly. Then, take turns saying and spelling these words: *side, blind, fry, fright*. Add them to the chart under the correct headings.

Reading Strategy   Read for Enjoyment

Reading for enjoyment is fun. Reading a myth for enjoyment is especially fun. To read a myth for enjoyment, follow these steps:

- To start out, think about what you know about myths. What culture does the myth you're going to read reflect? Think about the title of the myth. What do you think it might explain? Ask yourself what you'd like to find out.

- As you read, ask yourself what might happen next. Stop from time to time, to confirm or revise your predictions. Are you finding out what you thought you would?

- If you enjoyed a particular part of the myth, jot down some details you might want to remember.

Before you read "The Girl Who Married the Moon," ask yourself, "Why would a girl marry the Moon?" Then, read to find out . . . and enjoy!

W B
164

Set a purpose for reading As you read the myth, think about the title and these questions: What two characters are you finding out about? What is the myth mainly about? How does the myth explain something about the natural world?

The Girl Who Married the MOON

Retold by Joseph Bruchac and Gayle Ross

Long ago, in the village of Chiniak, on the island of Kodiak, there were two **cousins**.

They had reached the age when they could choose a husband. Both of them were strong and good-looking, and they were so well liked that almost any young man would have agreed to marry them. In fact, some **elders** said that these girls might easily choose—as did some of the women—to each have two husbands. Yet none of the young men in the village of Chiniak or any of the other villages on the island or even the nearby mainland interested those cousins.

---

cousins, relatives whose parents are siblings
elders, rulers of a village or tribe

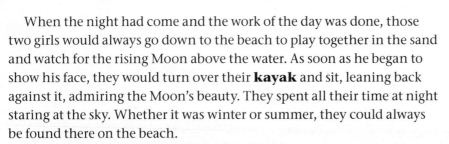

When the night had come and the work of the day was done, those two girls would always go down to the beach to play together in the sand and watch for the rising Moon above the water. As soon as he began to show his face, they would turn over their **kayak** and sit, leaning back against it, admiring the Moon's beauty. They spent all their time at night staring at the sky. Whether it was winter or summer, they could always be found there on the beach.

One night, one of the girls said, "I have fallen in love with the Moon."

"I have fallen in love with the Moon, too," said the other girl. "If he ever comes down to Earth, I will marry him."

Their parents worried about them when they heard that the two girls wished to marry the Moon. But no one told them to stop going to the beach at night.

---

kayak, canoe

Before You Go On

1. Describe the cousins. Why do they go to the beach every night?

2. How do the girls feel about the Moon?

On Your Own

From the title and what you've read, what do you think will happen, considering that the two cousins both feel the same way about the Moon? Explain.

Reading 1 **319**

As they watched the Moon crossing the sky one night, it disappeared behind some heavy clouds.

"Why does the Moon have to hide his face so early in the night?" one cousin complained.

"Yes," said the other cousin, "I wish he would show himself again. I wish he would come here and choose one of us to marry him."

Suddenly they heard the sounds of footsteps on the gravel of the beach and the voice of a young man.

"You have been saying that you love me," the voice said. "I have come to marry you."

The two girls leapt to their feet. A tall, handsome man wearing a beautiful mask on his face stood before them. That mask shone brightly, and they knew they were looking at the Moon.

"Yes," said the girls. "We will marry you."

"My work is hard," Moon said, "and I can take only one wife. I will take the one who is the most **patient**."

"We have always done everything together," said the girls. "You must take us both."

"Then you must close your eyes," Moon said. "Do not open them until I tell you."

The girls closed their eyes and waited. Moon reached down and held each of them by the long hair on their head, lifting them up into the air. The two cousins felt their feet leave the ground and they felt the wind whistling by them. They kept their eyes closed as they had been told, but when a long time passed, one of the girls became impatient.

---

patient, willing to wait for something

I must see where we are going, she thought. I will just open one eye a little.

But as soon as she opened her eye, she found herself falling down and landing back on the beach alone. Her long hair was gone from her head, and her cousin was gone from her forever.

The other girl, though, did not open her eyes. All through the night, she kept her eyes closed as Moon crossed the sky. When he told her to open her eyes at last, she found herself standing in Moon's house on the other side of the sky.

At first, she was happy to be the wife of Moon.

"Go wherever you wish," her husband told her. "Only do not look behind the blanket and go into my storehouse."

Moon's wife agreed. She would do as her husband said. She settled down to her new life in the land on the other side of the sky, but it was not always easy. Sometimes her husband would spend a long time with her. Sometimes he would be gone all night and then sleep all day after he came home. She never knew when he was going to go or how long he would be gone. Soon she became **bored**.

---

bored, tired and impatient

Before You Go On

1. Why did Moon drop one of the cousins?

2. Moon's wife is patient. Why is she bored? Explain.

 **On Your Own**

What do you think will happen next? Why do you think so?

Reading 1 **321**

"Why must you always leave me?" She said to her husband. "Why is it that you come and go in such a strange way?"

"It is the work I must do," said Moon. "That is why I cannot always be with you."

"Can I go with you when you do your work?"

"No," said Moon, "my work is too hard. You must stay home and be happy when I am with you."

Moon's wife listened, but she was not happy. That night when her husband left, she began to **wander** about the land on the other side of the sky. She walked farther and farther and came to a place where she saw many trails, and she began to follow one. At the end of that trail, she saw a person lying facedown.

"What are you doing?" she asked. But the person would not answer her or look her way.

She tried more trails and found the same thing at the end—a person lying facedown. And each time she asked what the person was doing, she received no answer. At last she could stand it no longer. At the end of the next trail she took, when she found a person lying down, she began to **poke** the person with her foot.

"Answer me," she said. "Answer me, answer me. What are you doing?"

Finally the person turned and looked at her. She saw he had only one bright eye, sparkling in the middle of his face. "I am working," the person said. "Do not bother me."

When Moon's wife returned home, her husband had not come back. She sat down to wait, but she was still bored. She looked around and saw his **storeroom,** with a dark woven blanket covering the door.

---

wander, walk slowly without having a clear direction or purpose
poke, quickly push someone or something
storeroom, room where goods are kept

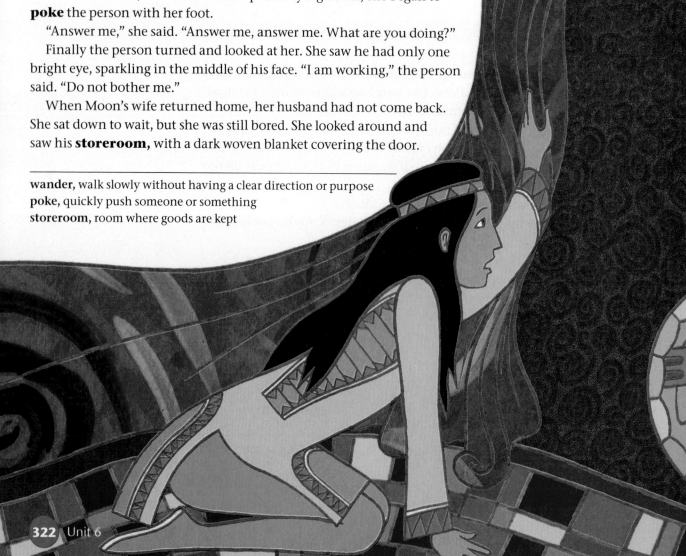

"It will not hurt to take one small look," she said. "Moon is my husband, and I should be able to go wherever I want in our house."

Then she went to the floor and pulled aside the blanket. There in the storeroom were the pieces of light her husband wore when he crossed the sky. There was a half-moon, a **quarter** moon, and all the other phases. The only one missing was the full moon, which her husband had worn when he left that evening. The pieces of light were so beautiful that Moon's wife could not resist.

---

quarter, one-fourth

Before You Go On

1. Why does Moon's wife become impatient?

2. What does Moon's wife find in the forbidden room?

 On Your Own

If you were Moon's wife, would you disobey his orders? Explain.

"I must try on one of them," she said, "to see how my husband feels when he is carrying them across the sky."

She reached down and picked up the one that was almost full and placed it on her face. As soon as she did so, it stuck there. She tried to remove it, but it would not budge. Although she wept and cried, the piece of moon would not come off. Then she heard her husband's steps coming across the sky.

She climbed into their bed and covered her head with a blanket.

"What is wrong?" Moon asked.

"I have a pain on my face," said his wife. "I do not feel well. Leave me alone."

But Moon became **suspicious**. He went to his storeroom and saw that one of the pieces of light was gone. He went back to his wife and pulled the covers from her head.

"Husband," Moon's wife said, "I became bored while you were gone. I tried on this piece of moon and now it is stuck."

Then Moon laughed. He laughed and laughed. And with careful hands, he pulled that piece of moon from her face.

"What else have you done today?" Moon said, still laughing.

His wife told him about following the many trails that led to people lying with their faces down and with a single bright eye in each of their heads.

"Those people are the stars," Moon said. "They should not be bothered while they are doing their work. It is clear to me that you need work to do also, my wife. Since you have shown that you are able to carry the moon you can help me. From now on, I will carry the pieces of moon each **cycle** until it is full, and then you can carry the pieces of moon until it is dark. That way, we will both have time to rest and neither of us will grow bored."

So it is to this day. The man of the moon carries the pieces of light from the time of the moon's first quarter until it is full, and the woman of the moon carries them from the time it is full until the moon grows dark. So they share the **duty** of carrying light across the sky.

> ✔ **LITERARY CHECK**
>
> How is **personification** used? What is personified?

> ✔ **LITERARY CHECK**
>
> What event in nature does this **myth** explain?

---

suspicious, doubtful
cycle, series of the moon's phases
duty, task

About the Authors

Joseph Bruchac grew up in Upstate New York with his Native American grandparents, from whom he learned traditional stories and the art of storytelling. Today, in addition to writing and storytelling, he works to preserve the culture of his people, the Abenaki.

Gayle Ross learned the art of storytelling from her grandmother. Today Ross writes about those myths and legends and shares them at schools and colleges across the country. Most often, she tells the stories of her father's people, the Cherokee. Ross is directly related to John Ross, who was chief of the Cherokee nation during the Trail of Tears.

Before You Go On

1. How does Moon react when he learns his wife entered the storeroom?

2. Who were the people Moon's wife spoke to during her walk? What were they doing?

👤 On Your Own

Did you like this myth? Why or why not?

Review and Practice

Reader's Theater

Act out the following scene with a partner.

Moon: What's wrong?

Wife: My face hurts. I don't feel good.

Moon: Hmm. What happened while I was gone?

Wife: [*covering her face with her hands*] I was bored while you were away, so I tried on this piece of moon and now it won't come off.

Moon: [*laughing as he pulls the piece of moon off his wife's face*] What else did you do today?

Wife: I took a walk, and I saw the strangest thing—there were people with only one eye that sparkled in the middle of their faces.

Moon: Those people are the stars—you shouldn't bother them when they're working. It seems like you need some work to do. From now on, you'll help me carry the moon across the sky.

> ### Speaking Skill
>
> Think about how the characters are feeling. For example, how do you think Moon feels when he asks his wife the first question? How do you think his wife is feeling? Say your lines to show the characters' feelings. Use the stage directions, where they appear [in brackets], to help you.

Comprehension

165

Did you understand the myth? If not, reread it with a partner. Then answer the questions below.

Recall

1. Where do the two cousins live?
2. What does Moon tell his wife the first time she asks to go with him when he does his work?

Comprehend

3. Which two pieces of light are not in the storeroom when Moon returns home?
4. What does the myth explain?

Analyze

5. What about the myth do you think made people keep retelling it?
6. Do you think Moon and his wife are good for each other? Why?

Connect

7. How about you? How do you feel about myths that explain natural occurrences? Explain.
8. From what you read in the myth, do you think Moon and his wife will continue to be happy together? Are they **compatible**? Explain.

Discussion

Discuss with a partner or in a small group.

1. From what you read about the myth, how did women contribute to their village? Were women valued and respected? Explain.

2. Based on the myth, what do you think the villagers value in a marriage? Explain.

 How does the sky influence us? Why do you think the night sky has inspired so many writers and artists? Which fascinates you more: the day or night sky? Why?

Listening Skill

Listen to your classmates' ideas. Before you contribute, summarize what you heard and then explain your viewpoint. Doing this will help you recall the discussion so far, and you might even end up changing your viewpoint.

Response to Literature
165

Work with a partner. Imagine that Moon has a new **job**, so his current position needs to be advertised. Find sample job descriptions or classified ads for jobs on university sites or ones your teacher provides. Write a description for Moon's job. In job descriptions or ads for jobs, phrases are often used. Use words and phrases such as *ability to lift heavy objects, patient, night, phase,* and *star.* You can use this as a model:

Must be _____ and available to work at _____. Knowing about the _____s of the moon required. _____ desired but not required. Previous night work as a _____ considered.

Share your job descriptions for Moon with the class.

◀ The moon and stars in the night sky.

Grammar

Prepositions

Prepositions are used to provide details or to show time, place, or direction. Common prepositions include *at, in, to, from, by, with, for,* and *of*. A preposition is always followed by a noun or noun phrase. Most prepositional phrases modify a noun or a verb.

SHOW TIME: ANSWER "WHEN?" The Moon looked full **from Monday to Wednesday**. We will stay **until it gets dark**.
SHOW PLACE OR DIRECTION: ANSWER "WHERE?" Her cousin was born **in Holland**. Do not go **into my storehouse**.
PROVIDE DETAILS: ANSWER "WHO?," "HOW?," OR "WHAT?" My grandmother was fond **of writing letters**. He tells how his painting **of the store** differs **from those by other painters**. We read a poem **by my teacher**.

> **Grammar Skill**
>
> A prepositional phrase can appear at the beginning or at the end of a sentence. When at the beginning, use a comma after a prepositional phrase.

Practice A
166

Work with a partner. Circle the correct preposition to complete each sentence.

1. Jake wrote letters (to / at / by) his sister, Leah.
2. The poem "Canis Major" is (until / about / above) the constellation of the same name.
3. It's an image taken (to / by / at) the Hubble telescope.
4. I went to the museum (with / from / over) my family.
5. The family moved (at / on /to) France in January.

> **Grammar Check**
>
> ✓ What always follows a **preposition?**

Practice B

Underline the prepositional phrase in each sentence.

1. The poem was written <u>by two students.</u>
2. The baby was born in July.
3. The plane is flying to London.
4. I memorized the poem with my classmates.
5. He lives at 69 Pine Street.

> **Apply**
>
> Work with a partner. Read the sentences in the chart above. Then find other examples in the reading of prepositions that show time, show place or direction, or provide details.

More about Antecedent / Pronoun Agreement

A pronoun takes the place of a noun. A pronoun agrees in number (singular or plural) and gender (masculine, feminine, or neutral) with its antecedent, or the noun it takes the place of.

> If **the stars** are behind the clouds, **they** are not visible.
> **The boy** was often sick. **He** was sometimes confined to bed.

When the gender of a noun is not known, it is called a "generic noun." It does not refer to a specific person or thing, but rather a whole group. With a singular generic noun, a singular pronoun is used. With a plural generic noun, use a plural pronoun.

> **The Hubble telescope** is famous for **its** beautiful images.
> Without telescopes, **astronomers** would not be able to do **their** jobs.

Grammar Skill

When a singular generic noun refers to a person, you may use *he* or *she* when referring to the antecedent.

Practice A
167

Work with a partner. Circle the antecedent in each sentence and underline all pronouns that refer to it.

1. (The boys) left <u>their</u> coats at my house.
2. When Ann's brother got home, he went straight to his bed.
3. Manny discussed his ideas about his paper with us.
4. Pat doesn't know what time she'll be finished with her appointment.
5. The young girl made her parents very upset with her.

Apply

Write two sentences describing myths about the Moon and two others describing facts about the Moon. Use pronouns that refer to the antecedent.

Example: Moon and his wife are happy. They ...

Practice B

Complete each sentence with the correct pronoun or pronouns that refer to the antecedent. Underline the antecedent.

1. <u>The artist</u> only sold one of <u>his</u> paintings in <u>his</u> lifetime.
2. My mother was not happy. _____ had wanted me to do well on the test.
3. The sun is the closest star to Earth. _____ is necessary for life on Earth.
4. The scientists were exhausted and _____ decided to take a break.
5. My brother thinks that _____ wants _____ career to be in astronomy.

Grammar Check

✓ What should **pronouns** always agree with?

Capitalization and Punctuation of Titles

Capitalize all words in a title, except for articles (*a, an, the*), prepositions of three letters or fewer (*of, in, for,* etc.), and the word *to* in an infinitive. Always capitalize the first word of a title and any proper nouns.

> "**T**he **G**irl **W**ho **M**arried the **M**oon"
> "**N**o **N**eed to **E**stablish a **M**oon **B**ase"

Grammar Skill

If you are handwriting a title, underline it with one continuous line. If you are using a computer, use the italics font or button.

Use punctuation rules for titles you refer to in your writing. Some titles are enclosed in quotation marks; others are italicized. A colon is used between the title and subtitle, which is usually capitalized.

Use quotation marks	Italicize
Short stories "A Place in the World" **Short poems** "Quilt" **Myths** "The Girl Who Married the Moon" **Legends** "Blue Willow" **Songs** "Workin' on the Railroad" **Interviews** "An Interview with Gary Paulsen" **Informational texts** "Deep Mapping"	**Novels** *The World I Live In* **Collections** *Salsa Stories* **Long poems** *The Lotus Seed* **Plays** *The Diary of Anne Frank: The Play* **Paintings** *Starry Night* **Movies** *A Woman Called Moses* **Magazines** *Time* **Newspapers** *The New York Times*

Grammar Check

✔ What **punctuation** do you use with **titles** of short stories?

Practice A 168

Work with a partner. Correct the punctuation and capitalization in the boldfaced titles. Write the sentences in your notebook.

1. My favorite novel is <u>Hatchet.</u>
2. I've just finished reading the novel **war and peace**.
3. Have you ever read the poem **stars** by Sara Teasdale?
4. We saw Miller's play **the crucible** last night.
5. T.S. Eliot's poem **the wasteland** was long and difficult.

Practice B

Circle the letters in the titles that need to be capitalized.

1. ⓟride and ⓟrejudice
2. "counting stars"
3. *black panther*
4. *back to the future*
5. *the times of india*

Apply

Work with a partner. Name five of your favorite novels, poems, plays, songs, magazines, or movies. Write each other's titles down with the proper punctuation and capitalization. Check each other's work.

Punctuation: Hyphens and Dashes

Use a hyphen with a two-word adjective before a noun, but usually not after the noun. Use a hyphen with some compound words and with numbers.

> Moon disappeared behind a **heavy-clouded** sky.
> The sky was **heavy clouded**.
> The technology is **state-of-the-art**.
> She married her husband when she was **twenty-one**.

Use a dash to signal an interruption of thought. You can also use a dash with an appositive. An appositive can be a noun, noun phrase, or clause.

> Some elders said that these girls might easily choose—as did some of the women—to each have two husbands.
> She tried more trails and found the same thing at the end—a person lying facedown.

Practice A
169

Complete the sentences below by adding hyphens where appropriate.

1. My brother is twenty-one years old.
2. She is wearing low heeled shoes.
3. "The Girl Who Married the Moon" is a well written story.
4. That new phone is state of the art.
5. My bicycle is high performance.
6. We were looking for a bicycle friendly path.

Practice B

Complete the sentences below by adding dashes where appropriate.

1. We read the story—a myth—and then answered questions.
2. Most of the students had the same problem not enough time.
3. He received a bicycle from his parents for his birthday.
4. A bright moon and shining stars this is what we saw in the night sky.
5. Some kids missed the bus my brother, for example and had to walk.
6. It's a beautiful place a place where lots of plants and animals live.

Include Paraphrases and Citations

At the end of this unit, you will write a research report. Each body paragraph has a main idea that is supported by details. A paraphrase, or a restatement of someone else's idea in your own words, can be used to support a main idea. You should highlight paraphrased text by providing an "in-text citation," or the source of the information you are using (the author or title of the piece, and the page number, if known, in parentheses). The citation should also be included in an alphabetized "Works Consulted List." (See the Writing Handbook on the Pearson English Portal for how to cite various sources.)

Writing Prompt

Write a paragraph about another myth. Be sure to include the main idea and supporting details. Paraphrase information you have found in other sources and provide an in-text citation. Use correct capitalization in titles. Be sure to use hyphens and dashes correctly.

(1) Prewrite Begin by choosing a myth that you know.

- Use the library or internet to research information.
- Identify a main idea for your paragraph.
- Select information to support your main idea.
- Paraphrase the information in your own words.
- Provide an in-text citation and a "Works Consulted List."
- Use a source chart like the one below to manage your citations.

Here's a source chart created by a student named Madeline for a paragraph about a Choctaw Myth.

170

Paraphrase	Source
According to the myth, the reason for a solar eclipse is that a black squirrel is eating the sun. Therefore, whenever the Choctaw saw a black squirrel, they would try to frighten it away, hoping to protect the sun.	"Eclipse of the Sun Blamed on Black Squirrel." <u>Choctaw Legends and Stories</u>. 13 September 2007. http://www.tc.umn.edu/~ mboucher/mikebouchweb/ Choctaw/legends2.htm.

② **Draft** Use your source chart to help you write a first draft.
- Support your main idea with details.
- Paraphrase information from sources.
- Provide in-text citations.
- Make a "Works Consulted List" (see below).

③ **Revise** Read over your draft. Look for places where the writing is unclear or needs improvement. Complete (√) the Writing Checklist to help you identify problems. Then revise your draft, using the editing and proofreading marks listed on page 401.

④ **Edit and Proofread** Check your work for errors in grammar, usage, mechanics, and spelling. Trade papers with a partner to obtain feedback. Use the Peer Review Checklist on Workbook page 170. Edit your final draft in response to feedback from your partner and your teacher.

⑤ **Publish** Prepare a clean copy of your final draft. Share your paragraph with your class. Save your work. You'll need to refer to it in the Writing Workshop at the end of the unit.

Here is Madeline's paragraph about a Choctaw Myth. Notice how she uses details to support the main idea.

> Madeline Shaw
> ### A Choctaw Myth
> To Native Americans, the natural world is very important and must be treated with respect. In the past, Native Americans also believed that most natural occurrences did not have simple explanations. They used myths to explain how and why things occurred. One Choctaw myth tries to explain the reason for solar eclipses—times when the Moon passes between the earth and the sun, briefly blocking the sun's light. According to the myth, when a solar eclipse occurs, the reason is that a black squirrel is eating the sun. Therefore, whenever the Choctaw saw a black squirrel, they tried to frighten it away, hoping to protect the sun (Choctaw Legends and Stories).
> #### Works Consulted List
> "Eclipse of the Sun Blamed on Black Squirrel." Choctaw Legends and Stories. 13 September 2007 <http://www.tc.umn.edu/~mboucher/mikebouchweb/Choctaw/legends2.htm>.

What You Will Learn

Reading

- Vocabulary building: *Literary terms, word study*

- Reading strategy: *Analyze text structure and elements of poetry*

- Text type: *Literature (poems); Informational text (social studies article)*

Grammar

- Expressions of quantity: *both, either, neither*

- Parallel structure

- Punctuation: Semicolons

- Punctuation: Colons

Writing

- Write an introductory paragraph

❓ THE BIG QUESTION

How does the sky influence us? For centuries, the night sky has been a subject explored in both science and art. Why do you think people are so fascinated by the night sky? Work with a partner to answer this question. Then, use your own impressions of the night sky. What do you like looking at up there? Do you have any favorite constellations? Make a list of what you like to view in the night sky and discuss with your partner. Then share with the class and make a class list of what all of you enjoy looking up at in the night sky.

Learning Strategy

Using what you already know about a topic and sharing what you know will help you as you discover more about it. Listen to your classmates as they share. What they share may help you, too.

Build Background

You are going to read two poems: **"Stars"** by Sara Teasdale and **"Escape at Bedtime"** by Robert Louis Stevenson. Both poems describe the stars in the night sky, but do so in different ways.

You will also read an article called **"Starry Nights."** It is about Vincent van Gogh, an emotionally-troubled artist who lived from 1853 to 1890. Van Gogh was fond of writing letters. You will read an excerpt from one of the letters that he wrote to his sister, Wilhelmina. In it, van Gogh describes how his painting of a starry night differs from those of other painters.

▲ A self-portrait by Vincent van Gogh

Vocabulary

Learn Literary Words

A **stanza** is a group of lines in a poem that are usually similar in length and pattern. Stanzas are separated by spaces. A stanza is like a paragraph in a story. A stanza may center on a thought or image. Read the stanza below from the poem "Stars."

> And a heaven full of stars
> Over my head.
> White and topaz
> and misty red.

Some poems have lines that rhyme with rhyming words at the end. **Rhyme** is the repetition of sounds at the ends of words. Rhyming gives the words and phrases in a poem a song-like quality.

The **rhyme scheme** in a poem is the regular pattern of words that end with the same sounds. To find the rhyme scheme, look at the end of every line in a poem. Then, begin by using the letter *a* and continue labeling the lines alphabetically, using the same letter for a line ending with the same rhyme. The stanza from "Stars" has the rhyme scheme *abab*. Use the letters *a/b* to label the rhyme scheme.

Learning Strategy

Use words that you already know to learn new and essential language, or words that you must know in order to understand your schoolwork.

Practice
171

Work with a partner. Take turns reading stanzas from the poem "Canis Major" about the constellation of the same name. What is the main thought or image in each stanza? Circle the rhyming words. What is the rhyme scheme?

> The great Overdog
> That heavenly beast
> With a star in one eye
> Gives a leap in the east.
> He dances upright
> All the way to the west
> And never once drops
> On his forefeet to rest.
> I'm a poor underdog,
> But to-night I will bark
> With the great Overdog
> That romps through the dark.
> —*Robert Frost*

Listening and Speaking: Academic Words

Study the **purple** words and their meanings. You will find these words useful when talking and writing about literature. Write each word and its meaning in your notebook, then say the words aloud with a partner. After you read "Stars," "Escape at Bedtime," and "Starry Nights," try to use these words to respond to the texts.

analyze = examine or think about something carefully in order to understand it	➡	Most artists **analyze** their subjects before painting them.
devices = how words are used in literature to achieve an effect	➡	Notice how a poet uses poetic **devices** like personification to give human qualities to objects.
elements = important parts of a whole system that work together to tell a story or create a feeling	➡	Recognizing **elements** of poetry, such as the speaker and the imagery, will help you understand a poem.
image = a picture that you can see on a camera, on a television, in a mirror, etc.	➡	The **image** of the child in the painting is very lifelike.

Practice 172

Work with a partner to answer these questions. Try to include the **purple** word in your answer. Write the sentences in your notebook.

1. How would you **analyze** the painting on the right?
2. What poetic **devices** can be used to describe the painting?
3. How do artistic **elements**, such as color and shape, impact the mood of the painting?
4. What does the **image** represent?

City in Shards of Light by Carolyn Hubbard-Ford ▶

Word Study: Lexical Sets

Lexical sets are sets of words that describe a central idea. For example, a lexical set for the word *light* includes the following words: *bright, brilliant, dazzling, illuminated, radiant, sparkling,* and *starry.* Read the lexical sets below.

dark	dim, gloomy, murky, shadowy
fast	fleeting, quick, rapid, speedy, swift
loud	deafening, ear-splitting, harsh, noisy, shrill, strident

Practice
173

Work with a partner. Take turns reading the words in the chart. Create a lexical set for each word. Write at least three words in each set.

beautiful	
slow	
strong	
sweet	

Reading Strategy   Analyze Text Structure and Elements of Poetry

Analyzing text structure can help you understand what kind of text you're reading. It can also help you to set a purpose for reading. To use the text structure and elements of a poem to help you interpret it, follow these steps:

- Use what you already know about poetry: look for words and phrases that form images and appeal to the senses. Look for comparisons with *like* or *as* (similes) and other devices like personification.

- Look for lines that rhyme and for groups of lines, or stanzas: these will help you with meaning. Notice the rhyme scheme.

- Look for punctuation and the ways that lines break to let you know when to pause: commas, semicolons, and periods. These, as well as stanzas, will help you follow the main thoughts in a poem.

- Notice the speaker's perspective at the beginning of each poem. Look for clues about their perspectives: where and how each looks at the night sky.

Review the text structures of "Stars" and "Escape at Bedtime." Discuss them with a partner.

174

Set a purpose for reading As you read the poems, think about how each poet feels about the night sky. What feelings do the poets express about it?

Stars

Sara Teasdale

Alone in the night
On a dark hill
With **pines** around me
Spicy and still,

And a heaven full of stars
Over my head,
White and **topaz**
And misty red;

Myriads with beating
Hearts of fire
That **aeons**
Cannot **vex** or tire;

Up the dome of heaven
Like a great hill,
I watch them marching
Stately and still,
And I know that I
Am honored to be
Witness
Of so much **majesty**.

> ✓ **LITERARY CHECK**
> How many **stanzas** are in this poem?

---

pines, tall trees common in North America
topaz, yellow-brown
myriads, uncountable numbers
aeons, very long periods of time
vex, bother
majesty, impressive or beautiful quality

About the Author

Sara Teasdale (1884–1933) most often composed poetry about love, the beauty of nature, and death. Her poems became especially popular during the early twentieth century. In 1918, Teasdale's work was recognized, and she was awarded the Columbia University Poetry Society Prize, later known as the Pulitzer Prize for Poetry.

Escape at Bedtime

Robert Louis Stevenson

The lights from the **parlour** and kitchen shone out
Through the **blinds** and the windows and bars;
And high overhead and all moving about,
There were thousands of millions of stars.
There **ne'er** were such thousands of leaves on a tree,
Nor of people in church or the Park,
As the crowds of the stars that looked down upon me,
And that **glittered** and winked in the dark.
The Dog, and the **Plough**, and the Hunter, and all,
And the star of the **sailor**, and Mars,
These shown in the sky, and the pail by the wall
Would be half full of water and stars.
They saw me at last, and they chased me with cries,
And they soon had me packed into bed;
But the glory kept shining and bright in my eyes,
And the stars going round in my head.

---

parlour, living room
blinds, objects that cover windows
ne'er, never
glittered, were very shiny
plough, farmer's tool
sailor, person who works on a ship

About the Author

Robert Louis Stevenson (1850–1894) was a
Scottish poet, novelist, and essayist. Some of
his best-known works are *Treasure Island* and
Kidnapped (novels) and *A Child's Garden of
Verses* (a collection of poetry).

✓ **LITERARY CHECK**

Which words in the
poem **rhyme**? Do
you notice a pattern?
How does noticing the
rhyme scheme help
you better understand
the poem?

Before You Go On

1. How are the stars
   personified, or given
   human qualities, in
   "Stars"?

2. How does the poet
   make the stars come
   alive in "Escape at
   Bedtime"? Explain
   what the Dog, the
   Plough, and the
   Hunter are.

👤 **On Your Own**

Which poem or poet do
you identify with more?
Explain.

Set a purpose for reading As you read the letter and study the painting, think about how van Gogh's thoughts influenced his art and his view about the night sky.

Starry Nights

Vincent van Gogh was born in 1853 in Holland. He became a painter when he was in his twenties and moved to France in 1886. Van Gogh spent the last years of his life in the south of France, painting landscapes and people. He suffered from **mental illness** and was confined at various times to mental hospitals, where he continued to paint until his death in 1890. Van Gogh sold only one painting during his lifetime. Today a van Gogh painting is worth millions of dollars. One of van Gogh's most famous paintings is called *Starry Night*.

Vincent van Gogh often wrote letters to his siblings. Some of these letters have been preserved in museums and are available for viewing. Following is an excerpt of a letter Vincent sent to his sister Wilhelmina. In it, he describes painting the picture *Café Terrace on the Place du Forum, Arles, at Night*.

---

mental illness, a sickness relating to the mind

◀ *Starry Night* by Vincent van Gogh.

Arles, 9 and 16 September 1888

My dear sister,

Your letter gave me a great deal of pleasure, and today I have the leisure to calmly reply. . . .

At present I absolutely want to paint a starry sky. It often seems to me that night is still more richly colored than the day; having **hues** of the most intense violets, blues, and greens. If only you pay attention to it you will see that certain stars are lemon-yellow, others pink or a green, blue and forget-me-not brilliance. And without my **expatiating** on this theme it is obvious that putting little white dots on the blue-black is not enough to paint a starry sky. . . .

▲ *Café Terrace on the Place du Forum, Arles, at Night* by Vincent van Gogh

In point of fact I was interrupted these days by my **toiling** on a new picture representing the outside of a café at night. On the **terrace** there are the tiny figures of drinkers. An immense yellow lantern illuminates the terrace, the **façade** and the sidewalk, and even casts its light on the pavement of the streets, which takes a pinkish violet tone. The **gables** of the houses in the street stretching away under a blue sky spangled with stars are dark blue or violet with a green tree. Here you have a night picture without black in it, done with nothing but beautiful blue and violet and green, and lemon-yellow. It amuses me enormously to paint the night right on the spot. They used to draw and paint the picture in the daytime after the **sketch**. But I find satisfaction in painting the thing immediately. . . .

Vincent

---

hues, colors
expatiating, speaking or writing in detail about a particular subject
toiling, working hard
terrace, patio
façade, front or outside of a building
gables, top, triangular parts of walls
sketch, drawing

Before You Go On

1. How many paintings did van Gogh sell in his lifetime? How is this different from how they sell today?

2. How does the image of stars in van Gogh's work differ from the traditional representation of stars as white dots in a black sky?

 On Your Own

Do you agree with van Gogh that the night is "more richly colored" than the day? Explain.

Review and Practice

Dramatic Reading

One of the best ways to appreciate a poem is to read it aloud, with feeling. Work in small groups of four and decide who will read each of the four stanzas of the poem "Stars."

Read your stanza to your group and talk about it. What **elements**, like rhyme and rhyme scheme, does the poet use? Does the poet use other literary **devices**, such as alliteration? What feelings does it create? Underline words you want your listeners to notice. How will you say the words to show feelings about the stars and the night sky?

Practice reading your stanza. Ask your group for feedback. When you are ready, take turns reading your stanzas aloud in your group.

Then, take turns, in your groups, reading the poem aloud to the class. Follow a similar procedure for "Escape at Bedtime" with each of you, in your groups, reading four lines from the poem.

Speaking Skill

Communicate your enthusiasm in what you are saying, so your classmates will be enthusiastic about it, too.

Comprehension 175

Recall

1. From where does the speaker in "Stars" look at the night sky?
2. From where does the speaker in "Escape at Bedtime" look at the night sky?

Comprehend

3. How do the poets and the artist feel about the night sky? Explain.
4. From their work, what kind of people do you think the poets and the artist were? Explain.

Analyze

5. What images do you think are most effective in "Stars"? What poetic devices does the poet use in the last stanza of "Stars" to describe the stars? What is the effect?
6. How does the poet personify, or give human qualities to, the stars toward the end of "Escape at Bedtime"? What is the effect?

Connect

7. Think about the two poets' perspectives and feelings about the night sky. Which poem did you enjoy more? Why?
8. Do you think van Gogh's paintings reflect the strong feelings about the night sky that he conveys in his letter? Explain.

Discussion

Discuss with a partner or in a small group.

1. Which "picture" of the night sky was more powerful to you: the artist's letter and work, the poem "Stars," or the poem "Escape at Bedtime"? Explain.

2. Which title did you think was the most effective for the subject? Why?

How does the sky influence us? Would you rather talk to a scientist who studies the stars or a poet who writes about them? Why?

Response to Literature W B 175

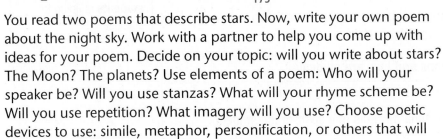

You read two poems that describe stars. Now, write your own poem about the night sky. Work with a partner to help you come up with ideas for your poem. Decide on your topic: will you write about stars? The Moon? The planets? Use elements of a poem: Who will your speaker be? Will you use stanzas? What will your rhyme scheme be? Will you use repetition? What imagery will you use? Choose poetic devices to use: simile, metaphor, personification, or others that will help convey your thoughts and feelings.

Begin by focusing on your thoughts and feelings and your topic. Then consider how best to convey them. Use the questions to guide you.

Take turns reading your poem to your partner. Then, when you are comfortable, share it with the class.

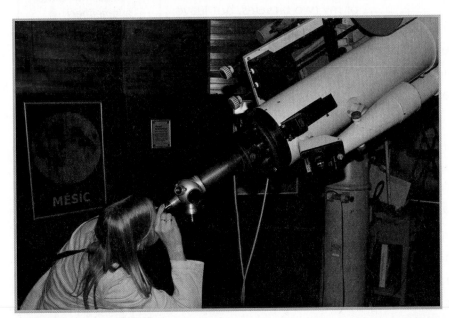

▲ A telescope makes stars appear closer.

Listening Skill

Listen for supporting details and reasons. Ask yourself, "Did the speaker explain why these ideas are important?"

Grammar

Expressions of Quantity: *both, either, neither*

Use *both, either,* or *neither* when you are talking about exactly two
items. Use a plural subject and verb with *both*. Use a singular subject
and verb with *either* and *neither*.

Both (of the)	= the two of them	**Both (of the) students are** there.
Either	= one of them	**Either (one or the other) student is** there.
Neither	= not either of them	**Neither student is** there.

When you name each individual person, place, or thing, use *and* with
both, or with *either,* and *nor* with *neither*.

Both . . . and	**Both** Anna **and** Luis **are** students.
Either . . . or	**Either** Anna **or** Luis **is** a new student.
Neither . . . nor	**Neither** Anna **nor** Luis **is** a sixth-grade student.

Grammar Skill

Either of the and *neither
of the* take a plural noun
but a singular verb.
Example: *Neither of the
students is* going to
college.

Practice A
176

Complete each sentence with *both, either* or *neither*.

1. _____Neither_____ my sister nor my brother has a car.

2. You can borrow _____ of my two bicycles, but leave
   one for me!

3. _____ the book and the movie were excellent.

4. _____ student knew the answer to the question.

5. _____ orange or yellow is a good color choice.

Grammar Check

✓ Which simple present
form of the verb be do
you use with *either*
and *neither*?

Practice B

Complete each sentence with the correct simple present form of the
verb in parentheses.

1. Either Meg or Tom (have) _____has_____ your phone.

2. Neither Paul nor Karen (be) _____ studying French.

3. Both restaurants (have) _____ delicious food.

4. Both Team A and Team B (hope) _____ to win.

5. Neither my brother nor my sister (go) _____ to
   my school.

Apply

In your notebook, write
a true sentence about
yourself or others with
each of the structures
below. Then read your
sentences to a partner.
Example: Neither . . .
nor . . . Neither my
mother nor my father is
at home right now.
1. Both . . . and . . .
2. Neither . . . nor . . .
3. Either . . . or . . .

Parallel Structure

Parallel structure means using a similar pattern of words in a sentence or series of sentences so that your writing flows and makes sense.

Try not to mix grammatical forms and keep all items in a list in the same form.

Parallel: At night, you can see **the Moon, the stars, and some planets**.   **Not parallel:** At night, you can see black, the Moon, and stars.
Parallel: The girls were **strong, good-looking,** and **well liked**.   **Not parallel:** The girls were strong, had good looks, and friendly.
Parallel: They would turn over their kayak and sit, **leaning** back against it, **admiring** the Moon's beauty.   **Not parallel:** They would turn over their kayak and sit, to lean back against it, and would be admiring the Moon's beauty.

Parallel: I wish he would show himself again and **I wish he would come** down here.   **Not parallel:** I wish he would show himself again and he will come down here.
Parallel: Both of the cousins **were held** by the Moon and **were lifted** up into the air.   **Not parallel:** Both of the cousins were held by the Moon and lifting them into the air.

> **Grammar Check**
>
> ✓ Why is it important to use **parallel structure** in compound and complex sentences?

Practice A
177

Put a check (✓) next to the sentences that have parallel structure. Put an X next to the sentences that do not.

1. __X__ She loves to cook, read, and shopping.
2. _____ It is easier to tell the truth than lied to people you love.
3. _____ This plan is creative, but having a risk.
4. _____ He is very tall, friendly, and athletic.

Practice B

Rewrite the sentences in Practice A that do not have parallel structure. Write them in your notebook.

1. She loves to cook, read, and shop.

> **Apply**
>
> Write sentences about yourself and the things you like and don't like to do. Make sure you use parallel structure. Then tell a partner about yourself.
>
> **Example:** I really like listening to music, reading books, and playing sports.

Punctuation: Semicolons

A semicolon (;) can be used instead of a period or a coordinating conjunction to connect two independent clauses (complete sentences) that are closely related. When a semicolon is used, the coordinating conjunction is usually dropped. Often, a semicolon is used before a clause that begins with a conjunctive adverb or transition. Remember to use a comma after the adverb or transition.

> In 1853, van Gogh was born; in his twenties, he became a painter.
> He believed night was rich with colors; **therefore**, he didn't use black in *Starry Night*.
> He suffered from mental illness; **as a result**, he was confined to hospitals.

Items in lists are usually separated with commas. However, if the items themselves contain commas, then semicolons can be used.

> He painted the stars yellow, pink, and green; the sky blue and violet; and the trees green.

Grammar Skill

Use a lowercase letter, not a capital letter, after a semicolon.

Grammar Check

 When would you use a **semicolon**? Give one example.

Practice A

 178

Add semicolons to form sentences below. The first one is done for you.

1. Some people write on a computer; others prefer a pen and paper.
2. Frank heard a car however, it wasn't visible.
3. She loves school she never misses class.
4. He didn't study the night before as a result, he failed the test.
5. I felt sick therefore, I stayed home.

Practice B

Work with a partner. Rewrite the sentences below in your notebooks, adding semicolons. The first one is done for you.

1. My sister likes chicken. My brother likes fish.
   <u>My sister likes chicken; my brother likes fish.</u>
2. The storm was terrible. As a result, school was canceled.
3. There were olives, nuts, and cheese. The main course was fish.
4. He wants to buy a skateboard. Therefore, he needs to save up for it.
5. The plane arrived late. Consequently, they missed their connection.

Apply

Work with a partner. Look at the first two paragraphs of the reading on page 340. Find sentences that you can combine or reword, using semicolons. Write them in your notebook, using semicolons correctly.

Punctuation: Colons

A colon (:) must come after an independent clause (complete sentence), never in the middle. A colon is often used before a list.

> independent clause
>
> He painted with many colors: yellow, pink, green, blue, and violet.
> NOT He painted with: many colors yellow, pink, green, blue, and violet.

A colon is also used when an appositive, or explanation, is introduced. The appositive may be a word, phrase, or clause. If it is an independent clause, it begins with a capital letter.

> Van Gogh wanted to paint the sky in a different way: He painted without using black.

Practice A
179

Work with a partner. Put a check (√) next to the sentences that contain correct punctuation. Put an X next to the incorrect sentences.

1. ___X___ These are my favorite subjects biology, math, and English.
2. _____ In the bag were the following: a pen, a notebook, and a cellphone.
3. _____ There are two students left, Mary and Jack.
4. _____ We need three kinds of drinks, juice, mineral water, and tea.
5. _____ Van Gogh suffered from mental illness: He was confined to mental hospitals.
6. _____ Spain is a very clean country, there is no trash on the beaches.

Practice B

Add proper punctuation and capitalization to the incorrect sentences in Practice A, and write them in your notebook.

1. These are my favorite subjects: biology, math, and English.

Writing

Write an Introductory Paragraph

At the end of this unit, you will write a research report about a topic of your choice that relates to the night sky. To help you do this, you are learning how to write different kinds of paragraphs to use in a report.

One type of paragraph is an introductory paragraph to use at the beginning of your report. An effective introductory paragraph introduces your research topic with an interesting question or fact.

Writing Prompt

Think about the night sky and what you want to find out more about. Do some research and read about your topic. Next, narrow your topic. After that, write a question to help you focus your research. Use your question to guide you as you find out more. Then write an introductory paragraph. Be sure to check punctuation and agreement of pronouns and antecedents.

1. **Prewrite** Begin by choosing a topic related to outer space.

   W B
   180

   • Use a graphic organizer to list a broad topic.

   • Next, list a narrower topic.

   • Then write a question to guide your research.

   • Write your ideas in a graphic organizer, such as an inverted pyramid.

Here's an organizer created by a student named Ari. He is writing an introductory paragraph for a research report about the life of a star.

Very broad topic
outer space and the things it contains

Narrower topic
stars

Question to direct research
What are the stages of a star's life?

(2) Draft Use your pyramid to help you write a first draft.

- Keep focused on your question. You can use it in your paragraph.
- Answer your question briefly, leaving details for the rest of your report.
- Remember that this paragraph just introduces your topic.
- Be sure to check punctuation and parallel structure.

(3) Revise Read over your draft. Look for places where the writing is unclear or needs improvement. Complete (√) the Writing Checklist to help you identify problems. Then revise your draft, using the editing and proofreading marks listed on page 401.

(4) Edit and Proofread Check your work for errors in grammar, usage, mechanics, and spelling. Trade papers with a partner to obtain feedback. Use the Peer Review Checklist on Workbook page 180. Edit your final draft in response to feedback from your partner and your teacher.

(5) Publish Prepare a clean copy of your final draft. Share your introductory paragraph with the class. Save your work. You'll need to refer to it in the Writing Workshop at the end of the unit.

Here is Ari's introductory paragraph for a research report about the life of a star. Notice how he begins his paragraph with an interesting question.

Ari Janoff

The Life of a Star

This question has always interested me: What are the stages of a star's life cycle? Because the stars look the same night after night, you might not know that they change at all. In fact, a Greek philosopher named Aristotle believed that stars were made of a special, unchanging material that was found only in space. However, within the last hundred years, astronomers have learned that, like people, stars do experience a limited life cycle: All stars are born in the same way, they may shine for millions or billions of years, and then they die. The size of a star determines how long it will live; size also determines the stages it will experience. These stages are described in detail within the paragraphs that follow.

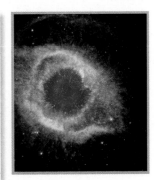

Prepare to Read

What You Will Learn

Reading
- Vocabulary building: *Context, dictionary skills, word study*
- Reading strategy: *Take notes*
- Text type: *Informational text (science)*

Grammar
- More transitions
- Present and past progressive
- Parentheses, brackets, ellipses
- Quoting sources

Writing
- Include quotations and citations

? THE BIG QUESTION

How does the sky influence us? Look at the picture below. Does the thought of traveling to space interest you? If you were given the opportunity to accompany astronauts on a space mission, would you accept? Discuss with a partner.

List what you know about exploration of the Moon, including Moon landings and the idea of a permanent base there. Next, list what you want to know. Then, after you finish reading, list what you learned.

What do you KNOW?	What do you WANT to know?	What did you LEARN?

Build Background

What do you know about manned and unmanned space flights to the Moon? Are you familiar with the idea of establishing a permanent Moon base? In this section, you will read two persuasive articles. The first is called "**The Moon.**" It presents an argument in favor of astronauts returning to the Moon. The second article, "**No Need to Establish a Moon Base,**" argues against both manned space flights and the construction of a permanent Moon base. As you read, notice how both authors present clear opinions and support their views with facts.

An astronaut on a space walk near the International Space Station ▶

Vocabulary

Listening and Speaking: Key Words

Key Words
base
crater
lunar
mine
universe
voyage

Read and listen to these sentences. Use the context to figure out the meaning of the highlighted words. Use a dictionary to check your definitions. Then write each word and its meaning in your notebook.

1. Some people want space scientists to build a base on the Moon. From there, astronauts could travel to Mars.

2. The meteorite left a crater on the Moon's surface.

3. We used a telescope to see craters on the lunar surface.

4. One day, scientists hope to mine the Moon's surface for water and oxygen.

5. Our Moon is one of many in the vast universe.

6. The voyage resulted in the successful landing of a man on the Moon.

Practice 📖 181

Choose a key word from the box above to complete each sentence. Then take turns reading the sentences aloud with a partner.

1. The spaceship's _____ from Earth to the Moon took three days.

2. The spaceship landed on the _____ surface.

3. While on the Moon, the astronauts stayed at the _____, where their food was stored.

4. The astronauts walked near a deep _____.

5. They plan to _____ the lunar surface for additional materials.

6. Scientists want to know what is necessary to live on the Moon. This information could help humans explore the rest of the _____.

The lunar surface is covered with craters. ▼

Listening and Speaking: Academic Words

Study the **purple** words and their meanings. You will find these words useful when talking and writing about persuasive informational texts. Write each word and its meaning in your notebook. After you read "The Moon" and "No Need to Establish a Moon Base," try to use these words to respond to the texts.

Academic Words

investigate
issues
promote
research

investigate = try to find out the truth about something	➡	Scientists **investigate** the Moon and planets to learn more about the universe.
issues = subjects or problems that people discuss	➡	The government considers many **issues** when funding the space program.
promote = help something develop and be successful	➡	After considering the issues, the government decided to **promote** the construction of a permanent moon base.
research = serious study of a subject that is intended to discover new facts about it	➡	Astronauts conduct **research** both on Earth and in space.

Practice
182

Work with a partner to answer these questions. Try to include the **purple** word in your answer. Write the sentences in your notebook.

1. What do you think are some of the things that scientists and astronauts want to **investigate** on the Moon?

2. What do you think are some of the important **issues** with manned versus unmanned space flights?

3. Do you think that manned space flight is a better way to **promote** space exploration than unmanned? Why or why not?

4. How do you think that **research** on the Moon could help us learn more about Earth?

◀ Robotic rovers investigate and conduct research on the surface of Mars.

Word Study: Acronyms

Acronyms and initials are used frequently in many forms of communication. An acronym is formed by adding the first letters or syllables of several words together. For example, the acronym NASA is made from the first letters of these words: *National Aeronautics and Space Administration*. Read additional examples of acronyms in the chart below.

Acronym	Words That Form Acronyms
NATO	**N**orth **A**tlantic **T**reaty **O**rganization
laser	**l**ight **a**mplification by **s**timulated **e**mission of **r**adiation
asap	**a**s **s**oon **a**s **p**ossible

Practice
183

Work with a partner. Use a dictionary to find the definition of each acronym in the box below. Write the acronym and the words that form it in your notebook.

CD-ROM	radar	RAM	scuba	UFO	UNICEF

Reading Strategy | Take Notes

Taking notes keeps you focused. Taking notes also helps you organize and remember new information. Then, when you are finished reading and taking notes, you can use your notes to answer questions about a text. To take notes, follow these steps:

- In your notebook, write the title of the text and your reason for reading it. For this text, it is to find out information about the pros and cons of astronauts returning to the Moon.

- Next, make four columns: one for main ideas and one for details about the article in favor of astronauts returning to the Moon and then another for main ideas and one for details about the article opposed to astronauts returning to the Moon. In this way, you can compare the main ideas and details of each article.

- As you read, write key words in the appropriate main ideas column and details in the other. Remember to be brief.

As you read each article, stop after you read each paragraph and take notes about it on your chart. After you read the two articles, use your notes to help you answer questions about the articles.

184

Set a purpose for reading As you read, think about whether or not astronauts should return to the Moon. Is there a need to establish a Moon base? Compare the two sides of this issue.

The Moon

"That's one small step for man, one giant leap for **mankind**." Those famous words were spoken on July 20, 1969, by Neil Armstrong, just after he became the astronaut to take the very first step onto the Moon's surface.

An estimated half-billion viewers watched in **awe** on their television sets. Never before had so many people tuned in to watch a single **broadcast**. Indeed, the audiences knew that they were watching history in the making.

Armstrong and his fellow *Apollo 11* astronaut, Buzz Aldrin, spent approximately 2.5 hours walking on the Moon's surface and collected about 23 kilograms of lunar rock and soil for scientific study. The astronauts left behind a **plaque** that said:

> *Here men from the planet Earth first set foot upon the Moon. July 1969, A.D. We came in peace for all mankind.*

After that historical trip, ten other humans took a voyage to the Moon. However, since 1972, no human has walked on the Moon's surface. According to the National Aeronautics and Space Administration (NASA) in the United States, that may soon change. NASA plans to send astronauts back to the Moon. This time, though, instead of

▲ Astronaut Buzz Aldrin stands on the Moon's surface during the first U.S. lunar landing in 1969.

a 2.5-hour moonwalk, the astronauts will stay for longer periods of time. The lunar campaign will begin with a series of robotic missions to collect data needed for the human missions.

Looking to the Moon

So why bother studying the Moon? The process teaches us about our own planet. Scientists believe that the Moon can reveal a lot of information about Earth's history. Why? The Moon was once a part of Earth. According to a well-accepted scientific theory, four billion years ago, a small planet called Theia **collided** with Earth and sent chunks of our planet flying into space. Gravity bound the Earth chunks together and the Moon was formed.

---

mankind, all humans, considered as a group
awe, a feeling of great respect for someone or something
broadcast, program on radio or television
plaque, a piece of flat metal or stone with writing on it

---

collided, crashed violently into something

What the Apollo Missions Taught Us

Between 1963 and 1972, NASA's main focus was to land humans on the Moon and bring them back to Earth safely. NASA achieved this on six separate missions during which astronauts gathered a wealth of scientific data. What scientists learned includes the following:

- Earth and the Moon are very similar in composition.
- There is no evidence of life on the Moon.
- The age of Moon rocks ranges between 3.2 and 4.6 billion years old.
- Volcanoes have erupted on the Moon.
- The Moon's craters provide a key to understanding the **geologic evolution** of the planets.

What Can Be Gained from Future Lunar Missions?

In addition to uncovering more important information about the Moon, Earth, and

geologic evolution, the history of a planet based on its rock layers

other **celestial** bodies, NASA scientists will set up telescopes on the Moon to obtain a clear **vantage point** from which to study the universe.

Eventually, scientists hope to have humans living and working on the Moon for long periods of time. They also hope to launch missions from the Moon into deep space, including missions to Mars. But to live on the Moon for extended periods, humans must meet the necessities of human life. For example, they must have breathable air and **potable water**. Rather than carry these necessities from the Earth to the Moon, NASA plans to mine water, hydrogen, and oxygen from lunar soil. This process, known as "in-situ resource utilization" or ISRU, could make future exploration into deep space a reality.

celestial, relating to the sky
vantage point, a place that affords a good view
potable water, water suitable for drinking

▼ The Resource Prospector mission will launch to the Moon carrying ISRU instruments that it will use to search for water, hydrogen, and oxygen.

Before You Go On

1. In what ways do scientists think research about the Moon could be beneficial to people on Earth?

2. When was the last time human beings walked on the Moon?

On Your Own

Do you think having colonies of astronauts on the Moon is a good idea for future space exploration? Explain.

No Need to Establish a Moon Base

Matt Kachur

When Americans landed on the Moon in 1969, it was considered to be a triumph. Today, there is talk of sending astronauts back to the Moon and constructing a permanent base there. However, both actions are unnecessary, dangerous, and expensive.

In truth, the need for manned space flights has decreased as the use of robots has increased. In fact, today's robots can perform most of the tasks previously assigned to humans and can do so in a more **precise** way. Recent achievements in space—such as discovering more than 1,000 planets outside our solar system and finding **evidence** of water on Mars—have come from unmanned space telescopes or robots.

Furthermore, unmanned space missions **pose** a smaller threat to human life than manned space missions. It's easy to forget how

precise, exact
evidence, proof
pose, present

▼ An unmanned robot

▲ The Hubble Space Telescope

dangerous manned space flights can be. Since 1967, they have
been responsible for the deaths of more than twenty people.

In addition to the cost in human life, manned space missions
are expensive. One space shuttle launch alone can cost $465
million. Much of that money is used to create systems that
keep humans alive in space. This, added to the cost of building
a Moon base, would require hundreds of billions of dollars.
In order to meet this need, the U.S. government would have to
cut important social programs or raise taxes.

It is for these reasons that it makes sense to **abandon** the idea
of a return to the Moon and the construction of a permanent base.
Instead, humans should **invest** our time, money, and energy into
additional robotic projects.

▲ The launch of the
space shuttle *Discovery*

abandon, leave behind
invest, spend

Before You Go On

1. Why has the need
   for manned space
   flights decreased?

2. What have robots
   achieved in space?

On Your Own

Do you think
robots should replace
humans in space?
Explain.

Comprehension
185

Recall

1. Who were the first astronauts to walk on the Moon?

2. During what years did the United States conduct missions to the Moon?

Comprehend

3. Why should NASA build a Moon base?

4. Name three reasons why NASA should not build a Moon base.

Analyze

5. Although he opposes a Moon base, do you think the author of "No Need to Establish a Moon Base" thinks space exploration and research are important? Explain by analyzing information in the text.

6. How could the Moon's location be helpful to astronauts who are going to Mars?

Connect

7. Do you think it is important for humans to investigate space? Explain.

8. What benefits do you think further space exploration could bring?

In Your Own Words

Work with a partner. Write the issues presented in "The Moon" and "No Need to Establish a Moon Base" in the correct column. Try to use as many new vocabulary words as possible. Then summarize one of the articles for your partner.

"The Moon"	"No Need to Establish a Moon Base"

> **Speaking Skill**
>
> Summarizing is an important communication skill. Remember to first focus on the main ideas you are trying to communicate. Details can come later.

> **Learning Strategy**
>
> If you can't remember a specific word you want to use, try to define it, use other words to describe it, or use a synonym.

Discussion

Discuss with a partner or in a small group.

1. Based on what you read, would you recommend human colonies on the Moon? Why or why not?

2. What do you think is the greatest challenge and the greatest benefit of exploring more about the Moon? Explain.

 How does the sky influence us? Do you think people around the world should support and **promote** space exploration? What do you think of the space programs you know about? Explain.

Listening Skill

Think about what each speaker says and whether you agree or disagree. Try to focus on what the speaker is saying as you do this. Take notes about important points. Wait until the speaker finishes. Then, use your notes to briefly summarize what the speaker said and tell whether you agree or disagree and why.

Read for Fluency

When we read aloud to communicate meaning, we group words into phrases, pause or slow down to make important points, and emphasize important words. Pause after a comma and pause a little longer after a period. Pay attention to rising and falling intonation at the end of sentences.

Work with a partner. Choose a paragraph from the reading. Discuss which words seem important for communicating meaning. Practice pronouncing difficult words. Take turns reading the paragraph aloud and giving each other feedback.

Extension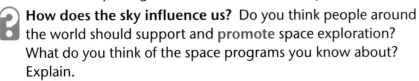
185

You read about robots in space. Work with a partner. Use the internet or go to the library to research one particular space robot. Try to find the following information: the name of the robot, a picture of the robot, and a description of the robot's job(s) in space. Use as many new academic words as possible. Then present this information to your class.

Learning Strategy

To better acquire and understand new academic language, use and reuse these words in meaningful ways in your writing.

Use the T-chart below to organize your research.

Robots in Space

Name	Description

Grammar

More Transitions

Transitions help your reader make logical connections between sentences, paragraphs, and sections of your writing. Transitions direct your reader's attention to a specific idea.

To Add or Emphasize Information: furthermore, moreover, that is, indeed, in fact, in addition	Robots can perform tasks previously assigned to humans; **in addition**, they can do so more precisely.
To Contrast: rather, alternatively, instead	The authors of the two articles do not agree. **Instead**, they have different viewpoints.
To Show Cause & Effect: accordingly, hence, as a result	Manned space flights are quite dangerous. **As a result**, some astronauts have died.
To Clarify: that is, to illustrate, for example	He argues against manned space flights. **For example**, he says robots can do the same work as humans.
To Summarize: finally, in conclusion, eventually, in summary	The authors have different visions of space exploration. **In summary**, important choices will need to be made.

Grammar Skill

The transitions presented here are interchangeable within their categories. For example, you can use *accordingly* or *hence* in place of *as a result*.

Grammar Check

✓ How do you decide what **transition** you need to connect thoughts?

Practice A 186

Add punctuation (periods, commas, semicolons) to the sentences. Underline the transition.

1. He is always reading. For example, he was reading on the bus.
2. He forgot his homework As a result he arrived late for school
3. She did extremely well in fact she won
4. There were no humans on the ship that is it was unmanned

Practice B

Work with a partner. Circle the transition that best completes each sentence. The first one is done for you.

1. The team doesn't have enough players. (Rather / (As a result)), they can't play.
2. Max studies hard. (Indeed / Finally), he gets good grades.
3. Brett plays baseball; (in fact / in addition), he plays soccer.
4. Sid loves animals. (In conclusion /Accordingly), he owns many.

Apply

Work with a partner. Copy the sentence starters into your notebook. Finish them with your own ideas.

1. I enjoy . . . . As a result, . . .
2. I love . . . . In fact, . . .
3. I hate . . . . Instead, . . .
4. I never . . . . Hence, . . .

Present and Past Progressive

The present progressive shows an action in progress now. It can also show some future actions. Form the present progressive with *is, am,* or *are* and a present participle.

> NASA **is gearing up** to send astronauts back to the Moon.
> Tonight, **I'm watching** a program about space exploration.

Form the past progressive by using the correct form of the *be* verb + present participle. Use the past progressive to show an action that continued over a period of time in the past. To show a continuous action in the past that is interrupted, use the simple past. You can also use an adverb, such as *while* with the past progressive and *when* with the simple past. Look at the examples:

> For the first time ever, people **were walking** on the Moon!
> **While** we **were looking** through the telescope, clouds **blocked** our view.
> We **were looking** through the telescope **when** clouds **blocked** our view.

Grammar Skill

The present participle is formed by adding -*ing* to the base form of the verb: *help* + -*ing* → *helping*. If the base form ends in -*e*, drop the *e*: *giving*.

Grammar Check

✓ When using the **past progressive**, what form is the verb that interrupts the action?

Apply

Write four sentences that relate to the articles about establishing a moon base. Make sure you use a continuous action in the past and an action that interrupted it. **Example:** The astronaut was walking on the Moon . . . when NASA released his famous words.

Practice A
187

Complete each sentence with the correct form of the verb in parentheses.

1. I _____was watching_____ (watch) TV last night at 9.
2. She _____ (leave) on a trip next week.
3. I _____ (not study) last night when
   you _____ (call).
4. While they _____ (work) in the
   garden, it _____ (start) to rain.

Practice B

Complete each sentence with the correct form of the verb in parentheses.

1. _____Is_____ she _____arriving_____ (arrive) this week or
   next week?
2. What _____ you _____ (do) when the
   lights went out?
3. _____ he _____ (come) to the party next
   Friday night?

Parentheses, Brackets, and Ellipses

Parentheses ( ) are used to show extra information or to set off an abbreviation.

> The astronauts (**Buzz Aldrin and Neil Armstrong**) became world famous.
> The National Aeronautics and Space Administration (**NASA**) is gearing up to send astronauts back to the Moon—eventually, to stay!

Brackets [ ] are used to show changes made to original text.

> **Original:** It could also serve as a launching pad for destinations farther than people have ever traveled.
> **Changed:** [**Sending astronauts back to the Moon**] could also serve as a launching pad for destinations farther than people have ever traveled.

Ellipses (. . .) replace a word or phrase in a statement.

> Recent achievements in space . . . have come from unmanned space telescopes.

Practice A
188

Rewrite these sentences in your notebook. Use parentheses, brackets, or ellipses.

1. The International Space Station ISS can be seen from Earth. (parentheses) *The International Space Station (ISS) can be seen from Earth.*
2. Scientists can live for months in space on the ISS. → Scientists can live for months on the ISS. (ellipses)
3. It is the most dangerous time. → The rocket launch is the most dangerous time. (brackets)

Practice B

Work with a partner and complete in your notebooks. Use parentheses, brackets, or ellipses for the boldfaced information.

1. Scientists believe **that 4 billion years ago**, a small planet **the size of Mars** smashed into Earth. (ellipses) *Scientists believe . . . a small planet . . . smashed into Earth.*
2. The Moon has no oxygen, **a gas that humans must breathe**. (parentheses)
3. Eventually, they plan to mine some supplies **from the Moon's surface**. (brackets)
4. It was **considered to be** a triumph for NASA. (ellipses)

Grammar Skill

Use a period after a parenthesis that comes at the end of a sentence.

Use a space before and after ellipses.

Grammar Check

✓ When do you use **parentheses**? When do you use **brackets**? When do you use **ellipses**?

Apply

Work with a partner. Find other examples in the reading "The Moon" on pages 354–355 where you can use parentheses, brackets, and ellipses. Write the sentences in your notebook.

Quoting Sources

In a research paper, you can use direct or reported speech to quote a source. If you use just a phrase from a quotation, the phrase is set off with quotation marks and begins with a lowercase letter.

> **Direct Speech:** Neil Armstrong said as he stepped on the Moon's surface, "That's one small step for man, one giant leap for mankind."
>
> **Reported Speech:** Armstrong said that stepping on the Moon's surface was a small step for man, and a giant leap for mankind.
>
> **Phrase from Reported Speech:** Armstrong stated that stepping on the Moon was a "giant leap" for humankind.

When you want to quote several sentences from a source, set them off in block quotations. Block quotations are indented, do not have quotation marks, and are usually introduced with a colon.

> Matt Kachur contends:
> In truth, the need for manned space flights has decreased as the use of robots has increased. In fact, today's robots can perform most of the tasks previously assigned to humans and can do so in a more precise way.

Grammar Skill

When you use block quotations or quotation marks around a quote, the quote must be word for word from the original text.

Practice A

189

Work with a partner. Follow the instructions below to quote from "The Moon" on page 354. Write the sentences in your notebook.

1. Quote paragraph three, sentence seven directly.
   <u>According to the writer, "This time, though, instead of a 2.5-hour moonwalk, the astronauts will stay for longer periods of time."</u>
2. Quote paragraph one, sentence one directly.
3. Report what paragraph three, sentence one says.
4. Block quote paragraph one, sentence two.

Grammar Check

✓ When **quoting sources** directly, when do you use quotation marks?

Practice B

Work with a partner. Discuss space and space exploration. In your notebook, write down examples of direct and reported speech, based on what your partner says.

Example: Ralph said, "I would love to visit the International Space Station." Ralph said that he would love to visit the ISS.

Apply

Look at one of the selections in this unit. In your notebook, write down a direct quotation, a reported quotation, and a block quotation.

Writing

Include Quotations and Citations

You learned that a research report contains paragraphs with main ideas supported by facts, details, and paraphrases. An effective research report will also include quotations from people who are experienced and knowledgeable about the research topic. Remember that whenever you copy another person's writing or speech word for word, you must put the text in quotation marks. After the quotation, you must provide an in-text citation. See the Writing Handbook on the Pearson English Portal for how to cite various sources.

Writing Prompt

Write a paragraph about future travel in space or another space-related topic. Include quotations and citations. Be sure to use parentheses, brackets, and ellipses correctly.

① **Prewrite** Begin by choosing a topic for your paragraph.

W B
190

- Use the library or the internet to find information about your topic.

- Identify a main idea for your paragraph.

- Decide which information from your sources you can use to support your main idea.

- Include quotations and citations and make a "Works Consulted List."

- Use a graphic organizer like the one below to list your quotations and sources.

Here's a source chart created by a student named Andrew for a paragraph about space tourism.

Quotation	Source
"Private companies in Russia, Europe, and the United States are competing to become future leaders of space tourism."	"All about Space Tourism. "Space. com 25 October 2007. http://www.space.com/space-tourism/

② **Draft** Use your source chart to help you write a first draft.
- Support your main idea with facts and details.
- Paraphrase information from sources.
- Create a "Works Consulted List."
- Be sure to use parentheses, brackets, and ellipses correctly.

③ **Revise** Read over your draft. Look for places where the writing is unclear or needs improvement. Complete (√) the Writing Checklist to help you identify problems. Then revise your draft, using the editing and proofreading marks listed on page 401.

④ **Edit and Proofread** Check your work for errors in grammar, usage, mechanics, and spelling. Trade papers with a partner to obtain feedback. Use the Peer Review Checklist on Workbook page 190. Edit your final draft in response to feedback from your partner and your teacher.

⑤ **Publish** Prepare a clean copy of your final draft. Share your paragraph with the class. Save your work. You'll need to refer to it in the Writing Workshop at the end of the unit.

Here is Andrew's paragraph. Notice that he includes an in-text citation and a "Works Consulted List."

Andrew Denkus

Space Tourism

In 2001, the first space tourist, Dennis Tito, flew into space aboard a Russian spacecraft. Since that successful experience, several others have also paid enormous amounts of money, more than $20 million per trip, for the chance to spend time on the International Space Station. Experts predict that this new industry, space tourism, is sure to grow in the future. In fact, "private companies in Russia, Europe, and the United States are competing to become future leaders of space tourism" ("All about Space Tourism"). Company leaders believe that as space tourism becomes more affordable, it will also become more common. They envision the creation of new vehicles, similar to airplanes, that would be used to transport people into space. They even foresee luxury hotels orbiting Earth!

Works Consulted List

"All about Space Tourism." 2007. Space.com 25 October 2007 <http://www.space.com/space-tourism/>.

Link the Readings

Critical Thinking

Look back at the readings in this unit. Think about what they have in common. They all relate to the unit theme: How does the sky influence us? Yet they do not all have the same purpose. The purpose of one reading might be to inform, while the purpose of another might be to entertain or persuade. In addition, the content of each reading relates to the sky differently. Now complete the chart below.

Title of Reading	Purpose	Big Question Link
"The Girl Who Married the Moon"		tells about the Moon's phases in a unique way
"Stars" "Escape at Bedtime" "Starry Nights"		
"The Moon" "No Need to Establish a Moon Base"	to persuade	

Discussion

Discuss with a partner or in a small group.

- Which unit selection did you enjoy the most? Which one did you learn the most from? Why?

- **How does the sky influence us?** How does each unit selection, in its own way, show that the sky influences our lives? In your view, which one shows this best? Why?

Media Literacy & Projects

Work with a partner or in a small group. Choose one of these projects.

(1) Create a skit based on "The Girl Who Married the Moon." Perform the myth as a play for the class. Practice your character's lines. Use simple costumes and music, too.

(2) Use the internet to create a profile of an astronaut or astronomer. Use the NASA website to get started: https://www.nasa.gov/. Search for "famous astronauts." Download or copy a picture of the person, or draw one. Display your picture for the class.

(3) Visit a planetarium, a science museum, or some other place that gives information about space. Gather information and take notes. Report on your experience and on what you learned to the class.

(4) Divide the class into two groups. Have a debate about manned space flights and a permanent Moon base. One group will argue in favor and one group will argue against. Be sure to support your position with facts and reasons.

Further Reading

Choose from these reading suggestions. Practice reading silently for longer periods with increased comprehension.

The War of the Worlds, H. G. Wells
In this classic story, a metal object falls from the sky over the south of England, and strange creatures come out of it.

Stars, Seymour Simon
In photo-essay format, *Stars* takes us on a tour of the galaxies. The book describes ordinary stars such as our sun, as well as stars called red giants and white dwarfs.

They Dance in the Sky: Native American Star Myths, Ray A. Williamson and Jean Guard Monroe
This collection of stories includes star myths from Native American tribes. Wolves, bears, eagles, and other animals inhabit the stories and the night sky. The stars themselves tell tales of children who have danced away from home and of the great wounded sky bear, whose blood turns the autumn leaves red.

The Little Prince, Antoine de Saint-Exupéry
In this fable, a pilot crashes in the desert and meets a mysterious little boy, the Little Prince. The boy is a space traveler. The story helps the reader to focus on what is really important in life.

Oral Report

You will give an oral report on a topic related to the sky.

1 Think About It

Think about the poems, informational texts, and the myth you read in this unit. The authors of these texts looked at the sky from different perspectives. Which readings did you find most interesting? Why? Discuss your thoughts in small groups.

With your group, develop a list of topics related to the sky. For example:

- Space travel
- Constellations
- Moon
- Planets
- Clouds

2 Gather and Organize Information

Choose a topic from your group's list. Decide how you want to approach your topic: for example, from a scientific, literary, artistic, or mythological perspective. Complete the first two columns of a K-W-L chart with what you already know about your topic and what you want to find out about it.

Research Go to the library or search the internet to find information about your topic. Record what you learned in the third column of your K-W-L chart. Choose the main points you want to include in your oral report, and make sure you have facts, details, and examples to support them.

Order Your Notes Copy your main points and supporting information onto note cards. Then arrange your cards in a logical order. Be prepared to share your sources with the audience.

Use Visuals Make or find photos, drawings, and/or other visuals that will help the audience understand your main points.

③ Practice and Present

Practice giving your oral report to friends or family members. Make sure your listeners can hear and understand you. Ask if your ideas are clear and easy to follow. Revise or rearrange your note cards if necessary. Keep practicing until you can speak confidently, looking at your audience and glancing occasionally at your note cards. Remember to show your visuals at the appropriate times.

Deliver Your Oral Report Before you begin, make sure your note cards and visuals are in order. Remember that an oral report is a formal presentation. Speak at a good pace, not too quickly or too slowly, and pronounce each word carefully. At the end of your report, ask your listeners if they have any questions.

④ Evaluate the Presentation

You will improve your skills as a speaker and a listener by evaluating each presentation you give and hear. Complete (✓) this checklist to help you evaluate your oral report and the ones presented by your classmates.

- ☐ Was the topic of the oral report clear?
- ☐ Did the speaker present the main points in a logical order?
- ☐ Were the main points supported by facts, examples, and details?
- ☐ Did the speaker use formal or informal language? Was it appropriate?
- ☐ Could the oral report be improved?

Speaking Skill

Think of a way to introduce your topic and get your audience's attention at the same time. Consider using a quote, a question, or a humorous, but brief incident related to your topic.

Listening Skills

As you listen, identify the speaker's topic. Listen for the general meaning, main ideas, and details.

Take notes about the main points. Write down any questions you have to ask at the end of the presentation.

Listen for the speaker's sources and write them down. Ask for clarification if you need it.

After each report, discuss its main points with a partner to confirm your understanding.

Strengthen Your Social Language

In your classes, you will need to be able to communicate with your teacher and classmates. Go to Digital Resources and do the activity for this unit. This activity will help you to learn and use routine language necessary for classroom communication.

Writing Workshop

Research Report

Write a Research Report

To write a research report, investigate your topic thoroughly and explain your findings. Use information from different sources and cite them. Begin by presenting the main focus of your research in an introductory paragraph. Support your main point, using details, examples, and explanations in three body paragraphs. End with a concluding paragraph to sum up your findings. Restate your main point.

Writing Prompt

Choose a topic related to the sky that interests you. Consider doing research about the stars and planets, constellations, astronauts and space travel, art or literature about the sky, or myths that explain occurrences in the sky. Then, write a five-paragraph research report about it. Use a variety of reliable sources, such as encyclopedias, newspapers, or university or government websites. Use transitions to connect ideas. Be sure to use quotations and citations correctly.

(1) **Prewrite** Review the paragraphs you wrote in this unit in preparation for writing your research report. Brainstorm possible topics and write them in your notebook.

W B
191

- Choose the one topic that most interests you the most.

- Ask yourself: What specific question about my topic will help me narrow it? What resources will help me find the answer to my question?

- Use these resources to take notes on note cards.

- Consult sources such as books, magazines, encyclopedias, and websites. Use these resources to take notes on note cards.

- Organize your note cards and make an outline.

Here is an outline created by a student named Haley.

> I. Introduce the United States Space Program
>   A. Headed by NASA
>   B. Understanding of space shaped by endeavors
> II. Projects Mercury and Gemini
>   A. To see if humans could live in space
>   B. To make longer distance space travel possible
> III. Project Apollo
>   A. To land humans on the Moon
>   B. Alan Shepard first person to travel into space
> IV. Space Shuttles
>   A. Useful in launch of Hubble Telescope
>   B. Also put satellites in space for cell phones and TV
> V. Conclude with U.S. Space Exploration
>   A. Understanding of space has been expanded
>   B. New information gained as technology advances

(2) **Draft** Use your outline and the model on pages 375–376 to help you write a first draft.

- Begin with a paragraph that states your main point.

- Read your sources, think about them, and use your own words to write the report.

- Develop your main point in three body paragraphs: each with a main idea and supporting details.

- Use quotations and citations correctly.

- End with a concluding paragraph that sums up your main point.

- List your sources at the end of your report. Check them for accuracy. Use the sources in the chart on page 372 as models. Notice the style, punctuation, and order of the sources.

Book
Stanchak, John. <u>Civil War</u>. New York: Dorling Kindersley, 2000.

Magazine article
Kirn, Walter. "Lewis and Clark: The Journey That Changed America Forever." <u>Time</u> 8 July 2002: 36–41.

Internet website
Smith, Gene. "The Structure of the Milky Way." <u>Gene Smith's Astronomy Tutorial</u>. 28 April 1999. Center for Astrophysics & Space Sciences, University of California, San Diego. 20 July 2009 <http://casswww.ucsd.edu/public/tutorial/MW.html>.

Encyclopedia article
Siple, Paul A. "Antarctica." <u>World Book Encyclopedia</u>. 1991 ed.

(**3**) **Revise** Read your draft to check how well you've addressed your purpose (to inform) and your audience. Consider these questions: Is my report well organized? Is the content and the tone appropriate for my audience? Does the report provide a good overview of my topic? Keep these questions in mind as you revise your draft. Complete (√) the Writing Checklist to help you identify other revisions you may need to make. Use the editing and proofreading marks on page 401 to mark changes.

Six Traits of Writing Checklist

☐ **Ideas:** Does my first paragraph introduce my topic and main point about it?

☐ **Organization:** Do I support main ideas with facts, details, and examples?

☐ **Voice:** Is my tone serious and suited to the topic?

☐ **Word Choice:** Do I use specific words that make the information clear?

☐ **Sentence Fluency:** Do my sentences vary in length and type?

☐ **Conventions:** Does my writing follow the rules of grammar, usage, and mechanics?

Here are the revisions Haley plans to make to her first draft.

The Space Program of the United States

The National Aeronautics and space Administration (NASA) is the
U.S. govermental branch responsible for space exploration. There have
been many important endeavors that have helped shape the U.S. space
program Knowledge about the Moon, planets, such as Mars and the rest of our
galaxy continues to add to our research about living in space.

Revised to include an example.

Project Mercury was the first space program in the United States.
The goal of Project Mercury was to learn whether or not humans
could endure space flight. In May 1961, Alan Shepard became the first
U.S. astronaut to travel into space. In February 1962,
John Glenn became the first U.S. astronaut to orbit planet Earth.

The Gemini Project, which followed Project Mercury, was implemented
to discover ways of enabling longer distance space travel.

Then In 1961, President John F. Kennedy announced the goal of "landing
a man on the Moon and returning him safely to the Earth" ("Man on
the Moon"). This became the aim of NASA's next mission, Project Apollo.
On July 20, 1969 Apollo 11 succeeded in its mission. Neil Armstrong,
the commander of the three-man crew, was the first person to walk
on the Moon. As he stepped onto the Moon, Armstrong famously said,
"That's one small step for man, one giant leap for mankind"("The Apollo
11 Mission").

Revised to improve paragraph organization.

Revised to include a transition word to improve word choice, and to punctuate quote correctly.

Reusable launch ships, also known as space shuttles, are now used for space exploration. Space shuttle missions have been very helpful in the launch and maintenance of the Hubble Telescope. it takes pictures that reach far out into space to increase our understanding about living in space. Space shuttles are also important because they put satellites in place that are used for cell phones and television. In addition, since space shuttles are able to orbit close to Earth. They have been able to aid in the repairing and replenishment of the International Space Station.

In all of these missions, communication has been strengthened, and our understanding of space has been expanded. great strides in exploring space have been made through the space program of the United States. Throughout the twenty first century, the United States will strive to learn more about space as technology advances.

Revised to improve sequence of ideas and to use a more complex sentence pattern.

Revised to correct an error in mechanics.

Works Consulted List

"Man on the Moon: Kennedy Speech Ignited the Dream." CNN.com/space. 25 May 2001. Cable News Network. 08 October 2009 16 December 2018 <http://www.cnn.com/2001/TECH/space/05/25/kennedy.moon/>.

National Aeronautics and Space Administration. 17 December 2018 <https://www.nasa.gov/mission_pages/apollo/missions/apollo11.html>.

Parsons, Jane. The Way the Universe Works. New York: Dorling Kindersley, 2002.

(4) **Edit and Proofread** Check your work for errors in grammar, usage, mechanics, and spelling. Then trade essays with a partner and complete the Peer Review Checklist to give each other feedback. Edit your final draft in response to feedback from your partner and your teacher.

191

Peer Review Checklist

- ☐ Was the topic clearly introduced in the first paragraph?
- ☐ Was the information supported with details and facts?
- ☐ Did the writer show a thorough understanding of the topic?
- ☐ Did the writer use transitions to show a logical sequence of ideas?
- ☐ Did the concluding paragraph sum up the main ideas in an interesting way?
- ☐ Could changes be made to improve the research report?

Here are the additional changes Haley plans to make to her final draft as a result of her peer review.

Haley Coy

The Space Program of the United States

The National Aeronautics and space Administration (NASA) is the U.S. governmental branch responsible for space exploration. There have been many important endeavors that have helped shape the U.S. space program. Knowledge about the Moon, planets such as Mars, and the rest of our galaxy continues to add to our research about living in space.

Project Mercury was the first space program in the United States. The goal of Project Mercury was to learn whether or not humans could endure space flight. In May 1961, Alan Shepard became the first U.S. astronaut to travel into space. In February 1962, John Glenn became the first U.S. astronaut to orbit planet Earth.

The Gemini Project, which followed Project Mercury, was implemented to discover ways of enabling longer distance space travel. Then, in 1961, President John F. Kennedy announced the goal of "landing a

Revised to correct an error in mechanics.

man on the Moon and returning him safely to the Earth" ("Man on the Moon"). This became the aim of NASA's next mission, Project Apollo. On July 20, 1969, Apollo 11 succeeded in its mission. Neil Armstrong, the commander of the three-man crew, was the first person to walk on the Moon. As he stepped onto the Moon. Armstrong famously said, "That's one small step for man, one giant leap for mankind" ("The Apollo 11 Mission").

Revised to correct an error in mechanics.

Reusable launch ships, also known as space shuttles, are now used for space exploration. Space shuttle missions have been very helpful in the launch and maintenance of the Hubble Telescope. it takes pictures that reach far out into space to increase our understanding about living in space. Space shuttles are also important because they put satellites in place that are used for cell phones and television. In addition, since space shuttles are able to orbit close to Earth, they have been able to aid in the repairing and replenishment of the International Space Station.

Revised to correct an error in mechanics.

In all of these missions, communication has been strengthened, and our understanding of space has been expanded. Great strides in exploring space have been made through the space program of the United States. Throughout the twenty first century, the United States will strive to learn more about space as technology advances.

Revised to correct an error in mechanics.

⑤ **Publish** Prepare a clean copy of your final draft. Share your research report with the class.

192

Test Preparation

Practice

Read the following test sample. Study the tips in the boxes. Work with a partner to circle the correct answers.

Chinese New Year

1   Everyone is invited to celebrate the Year of the Tiger in Chinatown on February 19 and 20. The two-day event is fun for the whole family.

2   Friday, the festival starts with a fashion show. Local musicians will play traditional Chinese tunes in front of the Hong Kong Market. Dancers will take the stage at 5:00 PM. Children are invited to make tiger masks in honor of the Year of the Tiger.

3   On Saturday, visitors will enjoy the traditional dragon dance. Again, bands will entertain visitors throughout the day. Chefs from several restaurants in Chinatown will offer free samples of food. The evening will end with a huge fireworks display.

1 According to the selection, what is the first event?
  A   Musicians on stage
  B   The dragon dance
  C   A fashion show
  D   Children making masks

2 Where would you most likely find this passage?
  A   In a local newspaper
  B   On a highway billboard
  C   In a restaurant menu
  D   On a map of Chinatown

3 When will the dancers perform?
  A   Saturday at 12:00 noon
  B   During the dragon dance
  C   After the fireworks display
  D   Friday at 5:00 PM

Taking Tests
You will often take tests that help show what you know. Study the tips below to help you improve your test-taking skills.

Tip
Your first choice is usually right unless you find you have misread the question.

Tip
When a test asks for specific information, skim the selection for key words. For question 3, skim for the word *dancers* to find what time they perform.

193–196

Capturing Cosmic Beauty

Many of us live in urban areas where there are a lot of lights on at night, so we do not get a good look at the stars. But if you sit in a dark field where there are no city lights, you can see the sky the way our ancestors saw it: a great area filled with countless stars. Artists often try to capture the beauty and mystery of the sky in their artwork.

Alma Thomas, *The Eclipse* (1970)

The moon moved in front of the sun during an eclipse that Alma Thomas once saw. She captures this eclipse with a dark, solid blue circle that sits off-center in her painting. Small painted blocks of cooler colors, such as green and light blue, spread out from the center. By the time she got to the edge of the canvas, Thomas was working in warmer oranges and yellows, which run right off the borders. Despite its cool center, the entire painting gives off a joyful celebration of color and light.

"A world without color would seem dead," Thomas once said. "Color is life. Light is the mother of color. Light reveals to us the spirit and living soul of the world."

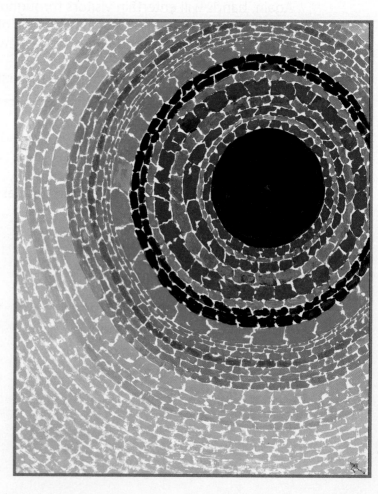

Alma Thomas, *The Eclipse,*
1970, acrylic, 62 x 49¾ in.,
Smithsonian American Art Museum ▶

◀ Charles Burchfield,
Orion in December, **1959**,
**watercolor and pencil, 39⅞ x 32⅞ in.,
Smithsonian American Art Museum**

Charles Burchfield, *Orion in December* (1959)

One December night, artist Charles Burchfield could not sleep. He looked out of his bedroom window and watched the clouds sweep across the sky. Then suddenly he saw three stars in a row. He knew at once that it was Orion, a famous constellation. Orion was named after a Greek mythical figure who was a hunter. The three brightest stars represent his belt, and the three smaller stars that drop down from the belt represent his sword.

In *Orion in December,* Burchfield uses few colors to capture not only the coldness of that evening but also the beauty and sense of calm he felt. The stars in Orion rest in the center of the painting and form an upside-down V of dots above the point of a treetop. Burchfield outlined the trees with strong black lines, which gives them a ghostly appearance. He also outlined each star with a strong black circle, but added a white glow around those circles to give them a soft light.

Artists usually appreciate light and shadow that we never really notice. They are drawn to the dramatic play of light in the sky as the sun and moon rise and set each day.

Discuss What You Learned

1. Both artists capture light in different ways. What is similar about the two paintings, and what is different?

2. Do you agree with Alma Thomas that "color is life [and] light is the mother of color"? Explain your answer.

 BIG QUESTION
Why do you think the sky is such a popular topic for so many artists?

197–198

The Parts of Speech

In English there are eight **parts of speech**: nouns, pronouns, adjectives, verbs, adverbs, prepositions, conjunctions, and interjections.

Nouns

Nouns name people, places, or things. There are two kinds of nouns: **common nouns** and **proper nouns.**

A **common noun** is a general person, place, or thing.

person	thing	place
The **student** brings a **notebook** to **class**.		

A **proper noun** is a specific person, place, or thing. Proper nouns start with a capital letter.

person	place	thing
Joseph went to **Paris** and saw the **Eiffel Tower**.		

A noun that is made up of two words is called a **compound noun**. A compound noun can be one word or two words. Some compound nouns have hyphens.

One word: **newspaper, bathroom**
Two words: **vice president, pet shop**
Hyphens: **sister-in-law, grown-up**

Articles identify nouns. *A, an,* and *the* are articles.

A and *an* are called **indefinite articles**. Use the article *a* or *an* to talk about one general person, place, or thing.

Use *an* before a word that begins with a vowel sound. Use *a* before a word that begins with a consonant sound.

I have **an** idea.
May I borrow **a** pen?

The is called a **definite article**. Use *the* to talk about one or more specific people, places, or things.

Please bring me **the** box from your room.
The books are in my backpack.

Pronouns

Pronouns are words that take the place of nouns or proper nouns. In this example, the pronoun *she* replaces, or refers to, the proper noun *Angela*.

proper noun   pronoun
Angela is not home. **She** is babysitting.

Pronouns can be subjects or objects. They can be singular or plural.

	Subject Pronouns	Object Pronouns
Singular	I, you, he, she, it	me, you, him, her, it
Plural	we, you, they	us, you, them

A **subject pronoun** replaces a noun or proper noun that is the subject of a sentence. A **subject** is who or what a sentence is about. In these sentences, *He* replaces *Daniel*.

subject   subject pronoun (singular)
Daniel is a student. **He** goes to school every day.

An **object pronoun** replaces a noun or proper noun that is the object of a verb. A verb tells the action in a sentence. An **object** receives the action of a verb.

In these sentences, *him* replaces *Ed*, which is the object of the verb *gave*.

object   object pronoun (singular)
Lauren gave **Ed** the notes. Lauren gave **him** the notes.

An object pronoun can also replace a noun or proper noun that is the **object of a preposition**. Prepositions are words such as *for, to,* and *with*. In these sentences, *them* replaces *José* and *Yolanda*, which is the object of the preposition *with*.

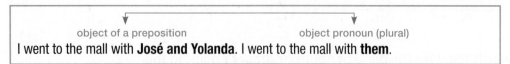

| object of a preposition | object pronoun (plural) |

I went to the mall with **José and Yolanda**. I went to the mall with **them**.

Pronouns can also be possessive. A **possessive pronoun** replaces a noun or proper noun. It shows who owns something.

	Possessive Pronouns
Singular	mine, yours, his, hers, its
Plural	ours, yours, theirs

In these sentences, *hers* replaces the words *Kyoko's coat*. It shows that Kyoko owns the coat.

It is **Kyoko's coat**. It is **hers**.

When an auxiliary verb (such as the verb *be*) follows a subject pronoun, it is usually contracted, especially in spoken English. In contractions, an apostrophe (') replaces the deleted letter.

Full Form	Contractions
I **am**	I'm
He She **is** It	He's She's It's
You We **are** They	You're We're They're

The **reciprocal pronouns** *each other* and *one another* are used in situations in which an action is carried out by two (or more) people at the same time. Use the reciprocal pronoun *one another* when referring to three or more people. Note that reciprocal pronouns can take the possessive form.

Danny and David met **each other** when they were in eighth grade.
When we were babies, my sisters and I looked similar to **one another**.
Scientists believe that lions can recognize **one another's** roars.

Adjectives

Adjectives describe nouns. An adjective usually comes before the noun.

tall grass **big** truck **two** kittens

An adjective can also come *after* the noun it describes.

The bag is **heavy**. The books are **new**.

Do not add -*s* to adjectives that describe plural nouns.

the **red** houses the **funny** jokes the **smart** teachers

Adjectives can also be possessive. A **possessive adjective** shows ownership.

	Possessive Adjectives
Singular	my, your, his, her, its
Plural	our, your, their

In these sentences, *their* shows who owns the car.

It's **Sam and Paul's** car. It's **their** car.

Verbs

Verbs express an action or a state of being.

subject verb   subject verb
Jackie **walks** to school. The school **is** near her house.

An **action verb** tells what someone or something does or did.

Actions You Can See			Actions You Cannot See		
dance	sit	talk	know	remember	think
play	swim	write	name	sense	understand

A **linking verb** shows no action. It links the subject of a sentence with information that describes the subject.

	Linking Verbs
Forms of *be*	am, is, are, was, were
Verbs related to the five senses	look, smell, sound, taste, feel
Verbs that reflect a state of being	appear, become, grow, remain, seem, turn

In this sentence, the adjective *tired* tells something about the subject, *cat*.

Our cat **seems** tired.

In this sentence, the noun *friend* tells something about the subject, *brother*.

Your brother **is** my friend.

A **helping verb** comes before the main verb. It adds to the main verb's meaning. Helping verbs can be forms of the verbs *be*, *do*, or *have*.

	Helping Verbs
Forms of *be*	am, is, are, was, were
Forms of *do*	do, does, did
Forms of *have*	have, has, had
Other helping verbs	can, must, could, have (to), should, may, will, would

In this sentence, *am* is the helping verb; *walking* is the action verb.

helping action
verb verb
I **am walking** to my science class.

In questions, the subject comes between a helping verb and a main verb.

subject
Did Liang **give** you the CD?

Mood in verbs relates to the attitude of the speaker or writer. The **indicative** mood expresses factual statements. The **imperative** mood expresses commands, instructions, or requests. The **subjunctive** mood expresses something that is doubtful or not factual. This includes sentences that express things such as wishes, commands, emotion, possibility, necessity, or something that is contrary to fact.

Indicative mood	I **am reading** a book right now.
Imperative mood	**Read** Chapter 12 for Monday.
Subjunctive mood	She didn't understand the book. If she **were** older, she would have understood it better.

Adverbs

Adverbs describe the action of verbs. They tell *how* an action happens. Adverbs answer the question *Where? When? How? How much?* or *How often?*

Many adverbs end in *-ly*.

easily	slowly	carefully

Some adverbs do not end in *-ly*.

seldom	fast	very

In this sentence, the adverb *everywhere* modifies the verb *looked*. It answers the question *Where?*

verb   adverb
Nicole looked **everywhere** for her cell phone.

In this sentence, the adverb *quickly* modifies the verb *walked*. It answers the question *How?*

verb   adverb
They walked home **quickly**.

Adverbs also modify adjectives. In this sentence, the adverb *very* modifies the adjective *dangerous*. It answers the question *How much*?

> adverb adjective noun
> This is a **very** dangerous road.

Adverbs can also modify other adverbs. In this sentence, the adverb *fast* modifies the verb *runs*. The adverb *quite* modifies the adverb *fast*.

> verb adverb adverb
> John runs **quite** fast.

Prepositions

Prepositions can show time, place, and direction.

Time	Place	Direction
after	above	across
before	below	down
during	in	into
since	near	to
until	under	up

In this sentence, the preposition *above* shows place.

> preposition
> A bird flew **above** my head.

In this sentence, the preposition *across* shows direction.

> preposition
> The children walked **across** the street.

A **prepositional phrase** starts with a preposition and ends with a noun or pronoun.

In this sentence, the preposition is *near* and the noun is *school*.

> prepositional phrase
> The library is **near the new school**.

Conjunctions

A **conjunction** joins words, groups of words, and whole sentences.

Conjunctions			
and	for	or	yet
but	nor	so	

In this sentence, the conjunction *and* joins two proper nouns; the conjunction *or* joins two prepositional phrases.

noun   noun   prepositional   prepositional
                                └──phrase──┘   └─phrase─┘
Jonah **and** Teresa want to go to the movies **or** to the mall.

In this sentence, the conjunction *and* joins two independent clauses.

└── independent clause ──┐   └─independent clause ─┐
Amanda baked the cookies, **and** Eric made the lemonade.

Interjections

Interjections are words or phrases that express emotion.

Interjections that express strong emotion are followed by an exclamation point. Interjections that express mild emotion are followed by a comma.

Hey! Watch out for that ball!
Hey, I'm sorry that your team lost.

A Note about Case

Case refers to a word's grammatical role or function within a sentence. In English, nouns and pronouns have three cases: **nominative**, **objective**, and **possessive**. The nominative refers to the subject of the sentence; the objective refers to something that is the object of a verb or preposition; and the possessive refers to a noun that possesses or owns another noun. The nominative and objective cases of nouns are identical, but the possessive case takes a different form.

Case	Noun	Pronoun
Nominative	<u>Adam</u> has a new puppy.	<u>He</u> has a new puppy.
Objective	They gave <u>Adam</u> a puppy.	They gave <u>him</u> a puppy.
Possessive	<u>Adam's</u> puppy is cute.	<u>His</u> puppy is cute.

Clauses

Clauses are groups of words with a subject and a verb. Some clauses form complete sentences; they tell a complete thought. Others do not.

Clauses that form complete sentences are called **independent clauses**.

> subject   verb
> Our **teacher smiled**.

Clauses that don't form complete sentences are called **dependent clauses**.

> subject   verb
> when the **class gave** her the present.

Clauses can be combined to form a sentence.

> ┌independent clause┐ ┌─── dependent clause ───┐
> Our **teacher smiled** when the class gave her the present.

Sentences

Sentences have a subject and a verb, and tell a complete thought. A sentence always begins with a capital letter. It always ends with a period, question mark, or exclamation point.

> subject action verb
>   ↓   ↓
> The **cheetah runs** very fast.
>
> helping
> verb   subject   action verb
> ↓   ↓   ↓
> **Do you play** soccer?
>
> subject linking verb
> ↓   ↓
> **I am** so late!

Simple, Compound, and Complex Sentences

Some sentences are called simple sentences. Others are called compound sentences. A **simple sentence** has one independent clause.

> ┌────────independent clause────────┐
> He sent the package to his grandmother.

Compound sentences are made up of two or more simple sentences, or independent clauses. They are joined together by a **conjunction**.

> ┌— independent clause —┐   ┌ independent clause ┐
> The band has a lead singer, **but** they need a drummer.

Complex sentences have an independent clause and one or more dependent clauses. In a complex sentence, the main idea is in the independent clause.

> ┌ dependent clause ┐ ┌— dependent clause —┐ ┌— independent clause —┐
> Although it's raining, and in spite of the cold, we still plan to go for a run.

Compound-complex sentences have more than one independent clause and at least one dependent clause.

> ┌— dependent clause —┐ ┌— independent clause —┐   ┌— independent clause —┐
> After the movie ended, we all said it was good, but secretly, we didn't like it.

Sentence Types

There are four types of sentences. All four have different purposes: **declarative** sentences are statements, **interrogative** sentences are questions, **imperative** sentences are commands, and **exclamatory** sentences express strong feelings.

Sentence Type	Example	Ending Punctuation
Declarative	We're going to the beach.	a period
Interrogative	Will you come with us?	a question mark
Imperative	Put on your jacket.	a period or exclamation point
Exclamatory	This is delicious!	an exclamation point

Mechanics

End Marks

End marks come at the end of sentences. There are three kinds of end marks: periods, question marks, and exclamation points.

Use a **period** to end a statement (declarative sentence).

> The spacecraft *Magellan* took pictures of Jupiter.

Use a **period** to end a command or request (imperative sentence) that isn't strong enough to need an exclamation point.

> Please change the channel.

Use a **question mark** to end a sentence that asks a question (interrogative sentence).

> Where does Mrs. Suarez live?

Use an **exclamation point** to end a sentence that expresses strong feeling (exclamatory sentence).

> That was a great party!
> Look at that huge house!

Use an **exclamation point** to end an imperative sentence that gives an urgent command.

> Get away from the edge of the pool!

Periods are also used after initials and many abbreviations.

Use a **period** after a person's initial or abbreviated title.

Ms. Susan Vargas	Mrs. Fiske	J. D. Salinger
Gov. Lise Crawford	Mr. Vargas	Dr. Sapirstein

Use a **period** after the abbreviation of streets, roads, and so on.

Avenue	Ave.	Road	Rd.
Highway	Hwy.	Street	St.

Use a **period** after the abbreviation of many units of measurement. Abbreviations for metric measurements do *not* use periods.

inch	in.	centimeter	cm
foot	ft.	meter	m
pound	lb.	kilogram	kg
gallon	gal.	liter	l

Commas

Commas separate, or set off, parts of a sentence, or phrase.

Use a comma to separate two independent clauses linked by a conjunction. In this sentence, the comma goes before the conjunction *but*.

> ┌─ independent clause ─┐   ┌─ independent clause ─┐
> We went to the museum, **but** it is not open on Mondays.

Use commas to separate the parts in a series. A series is a group of three or more words, phrases, or very brief clauses.

	Commas in Series
To separate words	Lucio's bike is red, white, and silver.
To separate phrases	Today, he rode all over the lawn, down the sidewalk, and up the hill.
To separate clauses	Lucio washed the bike, his dad washed the car, and his mom washed the dog.

Use a comma to set off an introductory word, phrase, or clause.

	Commas with Introductory Words, Phrases, or Clauses
To set off a word	Yes, Stacy likes to go swimming.
To set off a phrase	In a month, she may join the swim team again.
To set off a clause	If she joins the swim team, I'll miss her at softball practice.

Use commas to set off an interrupting word, nonrestrictive phrase, or nonrestrictive clause. (Note: A nonrestrictive phrase or clause can be left out of a sentence without changing the sentence's meaning.)

	Commas with Interrupting Words, Phrases, or Clauses
To set off a word	We left, finally, to get some fresh air.
To set off a phrase	Carol's dog, a brown pug, shakes when he gets scared.
To set off a clause	The assignment, I'm sorry to say, was too hard for me.

Use a comma to set off a contrasting expression.

I like tea, not coffee.
The exam is this Friday, not next Friday.

Use a comma to set off a speaker's quoted words in a sentence.

Jeanne asked, "Where is that book I just had?"
"I just saw it," said Billy, "on the kitchen counter."

In a direct address, one speaker talks directly to another. Use commas to set off the name of the person being addressed.

Thank you, Dee, for helping to put away the dishes.
Phil, why are you late again?

Use a comma between the day and the year.

My cousin was born on September 9, 2003.

Use a comma between a city and a state and between a city and a nation.

My father grew up in Bakersfield, California.
We are traveling to Acapulco, Mexico.

Semicolons and Colons

Semicolons can connect two independent clauses. Use them when the clauses are closely related in meaning or structure.

> The team won again; it was their ninth victory.

Colons introduce a list of items or important information.

Use a colon after an independent clause to introduce a list of items.

> The following animals live in Costa Rica: monkeys, lemurs, toucans, and jaguars.

Use a colon to introduce important information. If the information is in an independent clause, use a capital letter to begin the first word after the colon.

> There is one main rule: Do not talk to anyone during the test.

Dashes

Dashes are used to make a break in a sentence. They can be used as a replacement for commas, semicolons, colons, and parentheses. They appear more often in informal writing than formal writing.

Dashes are used to express added emphasis.

> There's only one person who can lead our team to victory—Steve.

Dashes are used to indicate an interruption.

> We were walking in the quiet park when—suddenly—we heard a loud noise over by the lake.

Dashes help to set off an abrupt change of thought.

> Could you please get me a—oh, never mind. I'll get it myself.

Quotation Marks

Quotation marks set off direct quotations, dialogue, and some titles. A **direct quotation** is the exact words that somebody said, wrote, or thought.

Commas and periods *always* go inside quotation marks. If a question mark or exclamation point is part of the quotation, it is also placed *inside* the quotation marks.

> "Can you please get ready?" Mom asked.
> My sister shouted, "Look out for that bee!"

If a question mark or exclamation point is *not* part of the quotation, it goes *outside* the quotation marks. In these cases there is no punctuation before the end quotation marks.

> Did you say, "I can't do this"?

Conversation between two or more people is called **dialogue**. Use quotation marks to set off spoken words in dialogue.

> "What a great ride!" Pam said. "Let's go on it again."
> Julio shook his head and said, "No way. I'm feeling sick."

Writers will sometimes use quotation marks around a word or phrase to change its meaning from literal to ironic or sarcastic. Read this example of sarcasm:

> Our teacher gave us a "simple" homework assignment to do over the weekend.
> It's going to take me all weekend to finish it!

From context, we can infer that the writer was told an assignment was going to be simple, but he or she doesn't believe that it will be.

Now read this example of quotation marks used to indicate irony:

> The army fired shots at houses in the "safe haven" of the war zone.

Here the writer seems to be implying that even though an area is called a safe haven, it really isn't a safe place to be.

Use quotation marks around the titles of short works of writing or other art forms. The following kinds of titles take quotation marks:

Chapters	"The Railroad in the West"
Short stories	"The Perfect Cat"
Articles	"California in the 1920s"
Songs	"This Land Is Your Land"
Single TV episodes	"Charlie's New Idea"
Short poems	"The Bat"

Titles of all other written work and artwork are underlined or set in italic type. These include books, magazines, newspapers, plays, movies, TV series, and paintings.

Apostrophes

Apostrophes can be used with singular and plural nouns to show ownership or possession. To form the possessive, follow these rules:

For singular nouns, add an apostrophe and an *s*.

Maria's eyes	hamster's cage	the sun's warmth

For singular nouns that end in *s*, add an apostrophe and an *s*.

her boss's office	Carlos's piano	the grass's length

For plural nouns that do not end in *s*, add an apostrophe and an *s*.

women's clothes	men's shoes	children's books

For plural nouns that end in *s*, add an apostrophe.

teachers' lounge	dogs' leashes	kids' playground

Apostrophes are also used in **contractions**. A contraction is a shortened form of two words that have been combined. The apostrophe shows where a letter or letters have been taken away.

I will
I'll be home in one hour.
do not
We **don't** have any milk.

Capitalization

There are five main reasons to use capital letters: to begin a sentence and in a direct quotation; to write the word I; to write a proper noun (the name of a specific person, place, or thing); to write a person's title; and to write the title of a work (artwork, written work, magazine, newspaper, musical composition, organization).

Use a capital letter to begin the first word in a sentence.

> Cows eat grass. They also eat hay.

Use a capital letter for the first word of a direct quotation.

> Carlos said, "We need more lettuce for the sandwiches."

Use a capital letter for the word *I*.

> How will I ever learn all these things? I guess I will learn them little by little.

Use a capital letter for a proper noun. Capitalize the important words in names.

Robert E. Lee	Morocco	Tuesday	Tropic of Cancer

Capital Letters in Place Names	
Streets	Interstate 95, Center Street, Atwood Avenue
Cities and towns	Rome, Chicago, Fresno
States	California, North Dakota, Maryland
Regions	Pacific Northwest, Great Plains, Eastern Europe
Nations	China, Dominican Republic, Italy
Continents	North America, Africa, Asia
Mountains	Mount Shasta, Andes Mountains, Rocky Mountains
Deserts	Mojave Desert, Sahara Desert, Gobi Desert
Islands	Fiji Islands, Capri, Virgin Islands
Rivers	Amazon River, Nile River, Mississippi River
Lakes	Lake Superior, Great Bear Lake, Lake Tahoe
Bays	San Francisco Bay, Hudson Bay, Galveston Bay
Seas	Mediterranean Sea, Sea of Japan
Oceans	Pacific Ocean, Atlantic Ocean, Indian Ocean

Capital Letters for Specific Things	
Historical periods, events	Renaissance, Battle of Bull Run
Historical texts	Constitution, Bill of Rights
Days and months	Monday, October
Holidays	Thanksgiving, Labor Day
Organizations, schools	Greenpeace, Central High School
Government bodies	Congress, State Department
Political parties	Republican Party, Democratic Party
Ethnic groups	Chinese, Latinos
Languages, nationalities	Spanish, Canadian
Buildings	Empire State Building, City Hall
Monuments	Lincoln Memorial, Washington Monument
Religions	Hinduism, Christianity, Judaism, Islam
Special events	Boston Marathon, Ohio State Fair

Use a capital letter for a person's title if the title comes before the name. In the second sentence below, a capital letter is not needed because the title does not come before a name.

I heard **S**enator Smith's speech about jobs. The **s**enator may come to our school.

Use a capital letter for the first and last word and all other important words in titles of books, newspapers, magazines, short stories, plays, movies, songs, paintings, and sculptures.

Lucy wants to read The Lord of the Rings.
The newspaper my father reads is The New York Times.
Did you like the painting called Work in the Fields?
This poem is called "The Birch Tree."

Practice

The Parts of Speech

1. Choose the eight parts of speech from the list below and write them in your notebook. Then write an example sentence for each one, underlining the relevant part of speech.

nouns	adjectives	prepositions	pronouns
verbs	sentences	interjections	objects
subjects	adverbs	conjunctions	interrogatives

2. In your notebook, rewrite each sentence using the reciprocal pronoun *each other* or *one another*.
   a. Sandy gets along well with Laura, and Laura gets along well with Sandy.
   b. Elephants communicate with other elephants by using many different kinds of calls.
   c. At our school, students have to share the science lab with other students.
   d. The band has to listen to the orchestra's concerts, and the orchestra has to listen to the band's concerts.

3. In your notebook, rewrite the following paragraphs using contractions.

> Hi Alejandra,
> I have not seen you at school for a few days. Have you been sick? I hope you are OK. You are not missing much in social studies, but we are going to have a big exam in math next week, so I hope you will be back in school soon. There is a lot for you to catch up on!
> Take care,
> Melissa

> Hi Melissa,
> You are right—I have been sick for a couple of days. I am feeling much better today, so I will definitely be in school tomorrow. Let us get together this weekend to study math, OK? Maybe you can help me catch up! ☺
> See you soon,
> Alejandra

4. Copy the sentences into your notebook. After each one, say whether the underlined verb is in the indicative, imperative, or subjunctive mood.
   a. If I <u>were</u> you, I'd try to switch classes.
   b. <u>Call</u> me when you get home, OK?
   c. I usually <u>read</u> for half an hour before I go to sleep.
   d. I wish we <u>played</u> on the same team.

5. Copy the sentences into your notebook. After each one, say whether the underlined noun or pronoun is in the nominative, objective, or possessive case.
    a. Please give this book to <u>him</u>.
    b. <u>She</u> has beautiful eyes, doesn't she?
    c. Is this notebook <u>yours</u>?
    d. The <u>doctor's</u> office is on the second floor.

Clauses
6. Copy the sentences into your notebook. After each one, say whether the underlined clause is a dependent clause or an independent clause.
    a. <u>Whenever I go to bed late</u>, I feel tired the next day.
    b. If you win this race, <u>our team will be in first place</u>.
    c. I lost my gloves <u>before I got on the bus</u>.
    d. Since you don't have a ride, <u>you can come with us</u>.

Sentences
7. Copy the sentences into your notebook. After each one, say whether the sentence is compound, complex, or compound-complex. Underline the dependent clauses once, and the independent clauses twice.
    a. Before you can start, you have to read the instructions.
    b. When we first moved here, I didn't know anyone, but now I have a lot of friends.
    c. I'm still hungry even though I just ate a sandwich.
    d. While the rest of the class watched, my classmate and I gave our presentation, and the teacher videotaped us.
8. Copy the sentences into your notebook. After each one, say whether the sentence is declarative, interrogative, imperative, or exclamatory.
    a. Wow—what a nice-looking car!
    b. What time is it now?
    c. Matthew and Yolanda are leaving soon.
    d. Just leave your books in your locker.

Mechanics
9. Copy the sentences into your notebook. Add commas where appropriate.
    a. His kindergarten teacher Mrs. Richardson came to his graduation.
    b. They prefer rock not pop music.
    c. The paper she gave me if I can find it has all the information you need.
    d. My mom's car a four-door sedan doesn't have room for all of us.

10. Copy the sentences into your notebook. Add dashes where appropriate. Be sure to adjust capitalization, as needed.

   a. If I could travel anywhere, I know where I would go. Spain.

   b. His goal in life is clear. He wants to become a musician.

   c. My best friend, Andrés Diaz, is the funniest person in the world.

   d. I wish I could find my . . . oh, never mind. Here it is.

11. Read the sentences. Notice how the quotation marks are used to indicate irony or sarcasm. Then choose a sentence that has the same meaning as the sentence with the quotation marks.

   a. Boy, that was an "easy" test. I'll be lucky if I get a C on it!

      1. The test was simple.

      2. The test was hard.

      3. The test was enjoyable.

   b. My "friend" Lisa never invites me to any of her parties.

      1. Lisa is not really my friend because she doesn't invite me to her parties.

      2. Lisa is my close friend even though she doesn't invite me to her parties.

      3. Lisa is the most popular girl in school.

12. Copy the following article into your notebook. Add the correct capitalization and punctuation where needed.

---

the biggest and the best

do you like shopping if so you should consider taking a trip to alberta canada thats the home of the biggest shopping center in the world the west edmonton mall this amazing entertainment center has more than 800 stores and services including an aquatic park a golf course and an ice rink

how would you like a little chocolate in july of 2006 nestlé singapore announced it had made the worlds largest chocolate bar the 2.668 ton bar surpasses the previous record of 2.28 tons according to the guinness book of records

you dont have to fly to the moon to experience weightlessness just go to six flags great adventure in new jersey usa where you can ride kingda ka the tallest and fastest roller coaster in the world this remarkable ride goes from 0 to 128 mph in 3.5 seconds and sends you 456 feet up into the sky hold onto your hats everyone

---

Editing and Proofreading Marks

To:	Use This Mark	Example:
add something	$\wedge$	We ate rice, bean$_\wedge^s$ and corn.
delete something	^{g}	We ate rice, beans, and corns.
close space	$\smile$	We $\smile$ ate rice, beans, and corn.
start a new paragraph	¶	¶ We ate rice, beans, and corn.
add a comma	$\wedge$	We ate rice, beans$_\wedge$ and corn.
add a period	$\odot$	We ate rice, beans, and corn$\odot$
switch letters or words	$\sim$	We ate rice, baens, and corn.
change to a capital letter	$\underline{\underline{a}}$	we ate rice, beans, and corn.
change to a lowercase letter	$\cancel{A}$	WE ate rice, beans, and corn.
let the marked text stand	(stet)	We ate rice, beans, and corn. (stet)

Glossary

accompanied went somewhere with someone

accurate without errors or faults

achieved succeeded in doing something, especially by working hard

advances developments or improvements

advantages a positive trait, location, or state assisting a person or thing

aid help or support given to someone

alter to make or cause a change

analyze examine or think about something carefully in order to understand it

approach a way of doing something or dealing with a problem

aspect one part of something that has many parts

assisted helped someone

assumed thought that something was true without having proof

attached emotionally connected to

attitudes thoughts or feelings about something or someone

authoritative respected and trusted as being true, or making people respect or obey you

available able to be used or seen

barriers things, such as rules or problems, that prevent you from doing something

base the main place where the work of a company or expedition is done

benefit something that helps you or gives you an advantage

challenge something difficult that you need skill or ability to do

character motivation a reason that explains a character's thoughts, feelings, actions, or speech

characters the people or animals that take part in the action of a story

code a way to use words, letters, or numbers to record information

communicate express your thoughts or feelings so other people understand them

community all the people living in one place

conditions a state of being or existing

conflict a struggle between opposing forces

confront to address a problematic situation in a straightforward way

compatible able to exist together without problems

consent permission to do something

continuous without end

correspond communicate by letter

crater a round hole in the ground made by something that has fallen on it or exploded on it

created made or invented

cultivate to develop something positive

crucial critical or extremely important

data information collected for tests, or to conclude things

depth a measurement used starting at the top layer of something

determine to come to a conclusion based on data

Glossary

determination having a firm purpose

developed something that was made better than it used to be

device a thing that you use for a particular purpose

devices how words are used in literature to achieve an effect

display a setup in a store or other location to show things easily

dialogue a conversation between characters

disadvantage a trait, location, or state that prevents a person or thing from easily suceeding

distributes gives something to different people or places

drama a story written to be performed by actors

emergency an urgent, unexpected, and unsafe incident

elements important parts of a whole system that work together to tell a story or create a feeling

encounter an occasion when you meet someone without planning to

enemy a person or country that is not friendly to you or wants to harm or fight you

examined observed carefully

exhibit a public show of objects such as paintings, photographs, etc.

experience a time something has happened to you

flashback an event that happened earlier than the story

focus pay special attention to a particular person or thing instead of others

foreshadowing the author's use of clues to hint at what might happen later in a story

fortunately something good happening due to chance

function the purpose of something

goal something you want to do in the future

guidance advice or recommendation

idea a plan or thought

illegal not allowed by law

image a picture that you can see on a camera, on a television, in a mirror, etc.

imagery the use of words or phrases to describe ideas or actions in literary works

immigrants people who enter another country in order to live there

impact effect that an event or situation has on someone or something

incentive something that encourages or motivates

incredible hard to believe; amazing

identical without any differences; completely alike

indicate say or do something that shows what you want or intend to do

individuals people; not a whole group

influence someone or something that has an effect on other people or things

injured hurt

insight something you suddenly realize that is very important or meaningful

Glossary

inspector an official whose jobs it is to visit places and see if there is anything wrong with them

instructed taught or showed someone how to do something

invention something completely new that is made for the first time

investigate try to find out the truth about something

involved included in a project or situation

irony a situation that is unusual or amusing because something strange happens, or the opposite of what is expected happens

issues subjects or problems that people discuss

job a particular duty or responsibility

legend a widely told story about the past that may or may not be true

lunar relating to the moon

mine dig into the ground for coal, iron, gold, etc.

mission the purpose or the most important aim of an organization

myth an old fictional story that explains natural events such as wind or rain

neighborhood a small area of a town and the people who live there

occupants people who live in a building, room, etc.

occurs happens

oral tradition stories passed along by word of mouth from one generation to the next

patent a special document that says you have the right to make or sell a new invention or product and that no one else is allowed to do so

persistence determination to do something even though it is difficult or other people oppose it

personification the representation of an animal, thing, or a quality as a person

phase one stage of a process of change

point of view the perspective from which a story is written

political relating to the government or politics of a country

positive good or useful

preserved kept something from being harmed or damaged

proceed move forward or continue

produce to create something

promote help something develop and be successful

reacted behaved in a particular way because of what someone has said or done

reaction the way you behave in response to someone or something

regulations official rules or orders

reluctant feeling uncomfortable about doing something

remarkable amazing or worthy of attention

rescue to help someone or something get away from a bad or unsafe situation

research serious study of a subject that is intended to discover new facts about it

Glossary

residents people who live in a place

resources a supply of materials used to complete a task

response something that is said, written, or done as a reaction or reply to something else

rhyme when a word ends in the same sound as another

rhyme scheme the regular pattern of words that end with the same sounds

setting the time and place of a story's action

shipped to deliver something

significant noticeable or important

similarities the qualities of being similar or the same

simile an expression using *like* or *as* that describes something by comparing it with something else

speaker the imaginary voice a poet uses when writing a poem

stage directions notes in a drama that tell the actors what they should do and how they should do it

stanza a group of lines in poetry that are usually similar in length and pattern and are separated by spaces

survive continue to live after an accident, illness, or natural disaster

symbol a picture, letter, or sign that means or stands for something else

symbolize represent a quality or a feeling

technology all the knowledge and equipment used in science

tenement a large building divided into apartments, especially one that is located in a poor area

theme the central message, concern, or purpose in a literary work

theory an accepted idea that explains why certain things happen

tradition a belief or custom that has existed for a long time

traits a special feature of a person, place, or thing, making it unique

universe all of space, including all the stars and planets

violence behavior that hurts someone in a physical way

voyage a long trip, especially by ship or in a space vehicle

Index of Skills

Index of Skills

Use a concept map for new
vocabulary, 23
Use a vocabulary log, 207, 317
Use new academic language,
29, 75, 153, 359
Use words you already know,
35, 205, 265, 335
Writing dialogue, 139

Listening and Speaking
Dramatic reading, 228, 276, 342
Gathering and organizing
information, 52, 114, 178,
236, 302, 368
Reader's theater, 44, 88, 106,
138, 170, 214, 294, 326
Workshops
how-to demonstration,
178–179
oral report, 368–369
personal narrative, 114–115
radio commercial, 302–303
team presentation, 52–53
TV news show, 236–237

Literary Analysis
Genre
legend, 162–169
letter, 338–339
myth, 318–325
novel excerpt, 130–137,
208–213
personal narrative, 84–86
play, 268–275
poetry, 87, 224–227, 340–341
science text, 8–13, 24–27,
68–73, 104–105, 354–357

short story, 38–43, 98–103,
286–293
social studies text, 148–151,
194–197, 252–257
Literary response and
evaluation
analyzing text, 45
comparing your experiences
to text, 89
roleplay, 107
researching history, 277
researching legends, 171
writing dialogue, 139, 215
writing from another point of
view, 295
writing job descriptions, 327
writing poetry, 229
writing thank-you letters, 45,
343
Literary terms
character motivation, 159
characters, 81
conflict, 95
dialogue, 283
drama, 265
flashback, 205
foreshadowing, 127
imagery, 35
irony, 127
legend, 159
myth, 315
oral tradition, 159
personification, 315
point of view, 81, 95
rhyme, 335
rhyme scheme, 335
setting, 35, 205
simile, 35

speaker, 221
stage directions, 265
stanza, 335
symbol, 221
theme, 283

Media and Technology
Internet use, 29, 52, 113, 153,
171, 177, 178, 235, 301, 302,
332, 359, 364, 367, 368
Library use, 29, 52, 171, 178,
235, 302, 332, 359, 364,
368
Newspapers and news
magazines, 153, 236, 262,
370

Reading
Comprehension, 14, 28, 44–45,
74, 88–89, 106–107, 138,
152, 170–171, 198, 214–215,
228, 258, 276, 294–295,
326, 342, 358
Critical thinking, 50, 112, 176,
234, 300, 366
Fluency, 15, 29, 75, 153, 199,
259, 359
Further readings, 51, 113, 177,
235, 301, 367
Strategies
analyze text structure, 223,
337
compare and contrast, 147
identify main idea and details,
251
identify problems and
solutions, 83
identify with a character, 161

Index of Skills

make inferences, 285
predict, 97
preview, 7
read aloud, 267
read for enjoyment, 317
recognize cause and effect, 67
recognize cultural context, 129
recognize sequence, 23
summarize, 207
take notes, 353
use visuals, 193
visualize, 37
Text structure
informational text, 8–13, 24–27, 68–73, 104–105, 148–151, 194–197, 252–257, 354–357
legend, 162–169
letter, 338–339
myth, 318–325
novel excerpt, 130–137, 208–213
personal narrative, 84–86
play, 268–275
poetry, 87, 224–227, 340–341
short story, 38–43, 98–103, 286–293

Research and Study Skills
Internet use, 29, 52, 113, 153, 171, 177, 178, 235, 301, 302, 332, 359, 364, 367, 368

Library use, 29, 52, 171, 178, 235, 302, 332, 359, 364, 368
Newspapers and news magazines, 153, 236, 262, 370

Vocabulary
Academic words
accompanied, 66
achieved, 6
advances, 6
aid, 66
alter, 284
analyze, 336
approach, 82
aspect, 250
assisted, 266
assumed, 146
attached, 222
attitudes, 6
authoritative, 160
available, 96
benefit, 192
challenge, 66
code, 66
communicate, 82
community, 192
compatible, 316
consent, 160
correspond, 266
created, 22
crucial, 284
determination, 206

devices, 336
display, 96
distributes, 128
elements, 336
encounter, 160
examined, 222
focus, 146
function, 22
goal, 36
guidance, 206
illegal, 6
image, 336
immigrants, 192
impact, 250
incentive, 192
indicate, 206
individuals, 146
injured, 96
insight, 36
instructed, 316
investigate, 352
involved, 36
issues, 352
job, 316
occupants, 266
occurs, 206
persistence, 250
phase, 316
positive, 128
proceed, 284
promote, 352
reacted, 36
reaction, 160

Index of Skills

Index of Skills

Index of Authors, Titles, Art, and Artists

Acknowledgments

Credits

Credits

Credits

Smithsonian American Art Museum
List of Artworks

UNIT 1 Invention and Change
Page 60
Hans Hofmann
Fermented Soil
1965
oil on canvas
48 x 60 in.
Smithsonian American Art Museum, Gift of S. C. Johnson & Son, Inc.

Page 61
Samuel Colman
Storm King on the Hudson
1866
oil on canvas
32⅛ x 59⅞ in.
Smithsonian American Art Museum, Gift of John Gellatly

UNIT 2 The Challenge of Illness
Page 122
Alice Eugenia Ligon
Embroidered Garment
about 1949
embroidered muslin and cotton crochet
43¾ x 38½ in.
Smithsonian American Art Museum, Gift of Herbert Waide Hemphill Jr.

Page 123
J. Bond Francisco
The Sick Child
1893
oil on canvas
32 x 48 in.
Smithsonian American Art Museum, Museum purchase

UNIT 3 Embracing Family, Friends, and Neighbors
Page 186
Franz Kline
Merce C
1961
oil on canvas
93 x 74⅝ in.
Smithsonian American Art Museum, Gift of S. C. Johnson & Son, Inc.

Page 187
Charles "Chaz" Bojórquez
Placa/Rollcall
1980
acrylic on canvas
68¼ x 83⅛ in.
Smithsonian American Art Museum, Gift of the artist
© Smithsonian American Art Museum

UNIT 4 Acknowledging the Past, Reaching for the Future
Page 244
Carmen Lomas Garza
"Camas Para Sueños (Beds for Dreams)"
©1985 Carmen Lomas Garza
Gouache painting 28⅛ x 20½ inches
Collection of the Smithsonian American Art Museum

Page 245
Hung Liu
The Ocean Is the Dragon's World
1995
oil on canvas, painted wood panel, and metal bird cage
96 x 82½ in.
Smithsonian American Art Museum, Museum purchase in part through the
Lichtenberg Family Foundation © Smithsonian American Art Museum

UNIT 5 Everyday Obstacles, Everyday Courage
Page 310
Residents of Bourbon County, Kentucky
Fan Quilt, Mt. Carmel
1893
cotton, wool, silk, velvet, lace, paint, chromolithographic paper, and canvas
85 x 72¼ in.
Smithsonian American Art Museum, Gift of Herbert Waide Hemphill Jr.

Artworks (continued)

Page 311
Daniel Chester French
Spirit of Life
1914
bronze
51 x 28 x 30 in.
Smithsonian American Art Museum, Museum purchase through
the Luisita L. and Franz H. Denghausen Endowment

Michael Olszewski
Speaking to Hear
1989
silk with acid dyes
parts A and B: both 22½ x 21¼ in.
Smithsonian American Art Museum, Gift of KPMG Peat Marwick
© 2007 Smithsonian American Art Museum

UNIT 6 Capturing Cosmic Beauty
Page 378
Alma Thomas
The Eclipse
1970
acrylic on canvas
62 x 49¾ in.
Smithsonian American Art Museum, Gift of the artist

Page 379
Charles Burchfield
Orion in December
1959
watercolor and pencil on paper
39⅞ x 32⅞ in.
Smithsonian American Art Museum, Gift of S. C. Johnson & Son, Inc.